HANDS-ON
SOCIAL
MARKETING

For my father, Michael Kline,
in whose footsteps I follow but whose shoes I could never fill.

Nedra Kline Weinreich

HANDS-ON SOCIAL MARKETING

A

Step-

by-

Step

Guide

SAGE Publications
International Educational and Professional Publisher
Thousand Oaks   London   New Delhi

For information:

 SAGE Publications, Inc.
2455 Teller Road
Thousand Oaks, California 91320
E-mail: order@sagepub.com

SAGE Publications Ltd.
6 Bonhill Street
London EC2A 4PU
United Kingdom

SAGE Publications India Pvt. Ltd.
M-32 Market
Greater Kailash I
New Delhi 110048 India

Printed in the United States of America

Library of Congress Cataloging-in-Publication Data

Weinreich, Nedra Kline.
    Hands-on social marketing : A step-by-step guide / by Nedra
Kline Weinreich.
        p. cm.
    Includes bibliographical references and index.
    ISBN 0-7619-0866-8 (cloth: acid-free paper)
    ISBN 0-7619-0867-6 (paper: acid-free paper)
    1. Social marketing. I. Title.
    HF5414 .W44 1999
    658.8—dc21   99-6007

02 03 04 8 7 6 5 4

Acquiring Editor:	Harry Briggs
Production Editor:	Astrid Virding
Editorial Assistant:	Nevair Kabakian
Typesetter/Designer:	Danielle Dillahunt
Indexer:	Teri Greenberg

CONTENTS

PREFACE

Have you ever read an article or emerged from a workshop, excited about using social marketing techniques in your own program, only to come back to the office and say "Now what do I do?" And how often do people say "We need to take a social marketing approach" without really understanding what that means? If you have this book in your hands, then you probably have at least a general idea of what social marketing is. If you keep reading, you will gain the skills to put social marketing to work for you.

Several excellent books on the art and science of social marketing provide conceptual knowledge about what social marketing is and the rationale for how and why to use it. For many, however, the jump from theory to practice is a precipitous leap of faith into uncharted territory rather than a step-by-step process of strategic planning and development. This book provides practical advice not offered by the more theoretical texts, gently guiding you in the development of a social marketing program from the beginning all the way through to evaluation and points beyond.

Hands-On Social Marketing was written for both practitioners and students who want to learn how to apply the concepts of social marketing in the "real world." Organizations at the community level might not have at their fingertips the benefit of extensive resources and expert assistance that often are found in state and national social marketing programs. Each chapter takes into account the challenges faced by organizations with small budgets and little experience with developing and implementing this type of program. Despite this orientation, the information in this book is equally applicable to those working at the state, national, and international levels.

The beauty of social marketing is that it provides a clearly defined process for program development. This book explains that process and provides detailed advice on how to successfully accomplish each stage. Moreover, the book is designed to be user-friendly and functional—a tool as much as a teacher. By using the many accompanying worksheets in your planning, you will have a ready-made "consultant" asking you all the right questions as you go along. For best results, read the whole book through *before* starting to plan your program. If you would like additional readings on particular aspects of the social marketing process, Appendix A provides a list of social marketing resources, both in print and online.

The main message I hope you get from this book is that you *can* do social marketing yourself. You do not need to hire a high-priced advertising agency or spend large sums of money to put these ideas into practice. This book emphasizes low-cost research methods and tells how to stretch a small budget without sacrificing quality. The biggest investment you will need to make is mental not material; it is simply to develop the understanding needed to begin thinking from a social marketing perspective.

I would like to thank Harry Briggs, my editor at Sage Publications, as well as Karen Bernstein, Kelli McCormack Brown, and another anonymous reviewer whose comments and constructive suggestions assisted me in refining the manuscript to make it a more useful tool. A special thanks goes to my husband, Gil, my in-house editor, cheerleader, taskmaster, and caregiver at all the appropriate times, as well as my son, Ariel, whose impending birthdate provided a powerful incentive to complete the labor and delivery of this book.

WHAT IS
SOCIAL MARKETING?

Section Overview

Before jumping into creating your social marketing program, you must under-stand the fundamentals of social marketing and how best to use it. Section I consists of the following chapters:

- Chapter 1: Social Marketing Basics
- Chapter 2: Not Just Business as Usual
- Chapter 3: The Social Marketing Mix
- Chapter 4: The Social Marketing Process

SOCIAL MARKETING BASICS

Social marketing—one of the newest ideas in public health and human services practice, right?

Actually, social marketing is not so new; the idea has been around for more than a quarter of a century. But only recently have "street-level" practitioners discovered that social marketing is something they can do themselves, without the assistance of an advertising agency or a sky-high budget. As social marketing concepts filter down to community-based organizations from successful national and international projects, professionals are increasingly becoming familiar with the term. But, like most buzzwords, the term often is misused.

All too often, the well-intentioned nonprofit director who uses marketing techniques to raise funds for the director's organization or the health educator who creates a television commercial without even talking to the people the educator is trying to reach believes that he or she is practicing social marketing. Use of the term to mean many different things has led to confusion about what social marketing is.

DEFINING SOCIAL MARKETING

Very simply, social marketing is the use of commercial marketing techniques to promote the adoption of a behavior that will improve the health or well-being of the target audience or of society as a whole. These are the same methods that a company such as Coca-Cola uses to sell its soft drinks—a focus on its consumers, market research, and a systematic process for developing a marketing program. The key characteristic that

---

WHO USES SOCIAL MARKETING?

This is just a sample of the many types of organizations that use social marketing in their education and prevention efforts:

- Centers for Disease Control and Prevention
- National Cancer Institute
- National Heart, Lung, and Blood Institute
- U.S. Environmental Protection Agency
- U.S. Department of Agriculture
- U.S. Agency for International Development
- Foreign health ministries
- State health departments
- Local health departments
- Community-based organizations
- National nonprofit organizations
- Universities
- Social service agencies
- Private foundations
- Community coalitions

**WHAT ISSUES HAVE
BEEN ADDRESSED WITH
SOCIAL MARKETING?**

- HIV/AIDS
- Breast Cancer
- Family Planning
- Immunization
- High Blood Pressure
- Cholesterol
- Radon
- Nutrition
- Panic Disorder
- Asthma
- Breast-feeding
- Drug Abuse
- Smoking
- Oral Rehydration Therapy
- Volunteerism
- Child Abuse
- Osteoporosis
- Physical Activity
- School Enrollment
- Bicycle Helmets
- Depression

distinguishes social marketing from commercial marketing is its purpose; that is, the benefits accrue to the individual or society rather than to the marketer's organization.

The field of social marketing is somewhat like Dr. Frankenstein's monster in the following ways:

- *It is made up of bits and pieces of many different disciplines.* These include health education, marketing/advertising, anthropology, and social psychology.

- *It has taken on a life of its own.* Over the past few decades, it has become recognized as a distinct discipline.

- *It often is misunderstood.* Many people incorrectly use the term to mean any type of marketing or advertising done by a health- or socially oriented organization, no matter who the product benefits or how the program was developed.

But unlike Dr. Frankenstein, we can harness the strength of social marketing, using the best of all its component parts while carefully controlling its direction.

STRENGTHS AND LIMITATIONS

As with any tool, social marketing cannot be expected to solve every type of health and social problem. Social marketing is at its best when used to effect and sustain healthful or socially beneficial behavior change, increase program use, or build customer satisfaction with existing services.

A social marketing program might not be as effective for certain issues such as complex problems with many contributing or confounding factors, problems not under individual control (e.g., genetic flaws), and addictive disorders. You also would be ill advised to undertake a social marketing approach if you are unwilling or unable to commit the resources needed to do it well. In some cases, an organization might be better off using its funds to add staff or capacity to its current services rather than to develop a social marketing project.

NOT JUST BUSINESS AS USUAL

The social marketing approach differs greatly from how health and human service organizations typically go about developing programs or materials. Often, professionals in these organizations think they know what people's problems are, what services they require, and what they need to know. These professionals believe that if they could only get all the information out to the general public, then the people they are trying to help would see that they are at risk and change their behavior. Unfortunately, this common approach often is ineffective.

TARGETING YOUR AUDIENCE

The first lesson of social marketing is that there is no such thing as targeting the general public. To be most effective, specify the audience for your program as precisely as possible. Think about all the different groups you want to involve in your social marketing program. They might include the following:

- Your clients or the people you want to reach
- People who influence your primary audience such as parents, spouses, teachers, physicians, and peers
- Policymakers
- Media professionals
- Your supervisors or board of directors
- Your employees, co-workers, and volunteers

These all are quite distinct groups, each of which requires different types of communications and strategies for the social marketing program to work.

Even within each of the preceding categories, there are many different types of people. For example, a program to prevent sexually transmitted diseases among teenagers might take different approaches for males and females, for younger and older adolescents, for those who do not believe they are at risk and those who do but need help convincing their partners to use condoms, or for those who get regular Pap smears and those who do not. Some teens read at a 12th-grade level, and others require pictures to understand the messages. Clearly, the same approach will not work for all of these subgroups.

The objectives of your program will guide you in identifying the appropriate audience, and research will help you tailor your approach to that audience. The social marketing method of segmentation advocates dividing your audience into different subgroups and developing strategies specifically for one or more of these groups.

RESEARCHING YOUR AUDIENCE

Too often, the typical approach to program development is that program administrators base messages and strategies on what they think the target audience needs to know. They develop multifaceted programs with expensive audiovisual presentations, four-color brochures, and newspaper advertisements. Staff think that the program is great, but they cannot understand why no one shows up for their services.

What is wrong with this picture? Did they ever ask the people they are trying to reach what types of programs or services they need? Maybe if they asked, they would find out that people in the target audience would like to have come but could not for any of the following reasons:

- They could not afford babysitters
- They would rather be connected with a job service or drug rehab center than take health education classes
- The program was scheduled during the day, while everyone was working
- They do not read the newspaper and so missed the advertisement

Social marketers know that to create effective programs, they must talk (and listen) to the people in their target audience to find out what they want and need as well as what would have the greatest effect on changing their behavior. Research forms the cornerstone of social marketing and makes program development a bottom-up process—with guidance coming from the target audience—rather than the usual top-down approach.

FOLLOWING A
SYSTEMATIC PROCESS

The following situation might sound familiar.

The Springfield Blister Council just realized that National Blister Prevention Week is coming up in a couple of months. Every year, the Council scrambles to put together a campaign and to get the word out through the media. Brochures are cobbled together from other materials, posters are designed from an idea the intern came up with, and press releases are sent to the main newspaper and television stations. Somehow, the campaign does not seem to have much effect, particularly among the people at highest risk for blisters. Council staff have resolved that this year they will start earlier and send press releases to a greater number of media outlets.

Not surprisingly, if this is all the Blister Council staff are changing, then the campaign is unlikely to be any more effective than it has in the past. No matter how far in advance the staff begin work, haphazard planning results in a disjointed campaign. Without information on how best to reach the people most likely to get blisters, which messages are most effective in motivating behavior change, and results of evaluations of past campaigns, the council might not be doing much more than making its members feel good.

Social marketing provides a systematic process to follow that ensures that campaign materials are based on research rather than on one person's idea of what looks good. Ideally, a campaign like this one would be part of the organization's long-term social marketing strategy rather than a one-shot blip on the blister prevention radar screen. By developing a comprehensive strategy based on research, the Blister Council staff would already know the key messages they need to convey to the target audience and which media would be most effective in reaching it as they prepare for National Blister Prevention Week.

DEVELOPING A SOCIAL
MARKETING MIND-SET

Social marketing involves more than just blindly following a step-by-step process. Successful practitioners adopt a social marketing mind-set that affects their perception of every aspect of their programs, similar to the "customer-centered mind-set" described by Andreasen.[1] In other words, they see the world through social marketing-colored lenses.

Just as Copernicus radically altered how people thought about the world by showing that the earth revolves around the sun, social marketing has moved clients into the center of the universe for the professionals serving them. An effective social marketing program focuses on the consumer; all of its elements are based on the wants and needs of its target audience rather than on what the organization happens to be "selling."

For example, a program to prevent alcohol and drug use among junior high school students decided to conduct social marketing research to learn how to be more effective. By talking to the students themselves about their needs, the researchers found that the students already knew all of the information presented in the usual anti-drug assemblies and viewed them only as a chance to be out of the classroom. They also learned that many teens drink and use drugs because they feel that there is nothing else to do in their community. Instead of assemblies, the program decided to provide fun drug- and alcohol-free events on the weekends as an alternative to drug use.

Once you adopt a social marketing mindset, you might look at your organization in a different way. Rather than providing services or designing materials the way in which the program director likes them best, social marketers ask their clients what they need to adopt a particular behavior. In all decisions, they look at the issue from the consumers' point of view, asking themselves "How can we best serve our clients?" instead of "How can we make life easier for ourselves?" And as in commercial marketing, they keep their eyes on the bottom line—not sales but rather behavior change.

Social marketing concepts are extremely versatile. You can use these techniques for many different purposes:

- To develop a public awareness or education campaign
- To create promotional or educational materials
- To improve the services your organization provides
- To create new programs

Whatever your final objective, the guiding principles remain the same.

In a famous tale, the Jewish sage Hillel was asked by a non-Jew to define the essence of his religion while standing on one foot. Hillel responded, "What is hateful unto you do not do unto your neighbor. The rest is commentary; now go and study."[2] Likewise, the essence of social marketing (one-footed or otherwise) is that you must target and research your audience to create a consumer-centered program. The rest is commentary; now keep reading the book.

chapter three

THE SOCIAL MARKETING MIX

To develop a comprehensive strategy, social marketing borrows an idea from traditional marketing practice called the "marketing mix." In the planning process, research with the target audience assists in making programmatic decisions about the following:

- Product
- Price
- Place
- Promotion

These often are called the "four P's" of marketing. They have been adapted to fit social marketing practice and are used somewhat differently from how they are used in commercial marketing.

Social marketing also adds some P's of its own:

- Publics
- Partnership
- Policy
- Pursestrings

Considering each of these strategic elements as you develop the social marketing mix increases the likelihood of a successful program.

PRODUCT

If motivating people to change their health or social behavior were as easy as convincing them to switch brands of toothpaste, then there would be no need for the subfield of social marketing. But trying to affect complex and often emotion-based decisions is rather different from selling a tangible product. The social marketing "product" is the behavior or offering you want the target audience to adopt. The product may fall anywhere along a continuum ranging from physical products (e.g., smoke detectors), to services (e.g., medical examinations), to practices (e.g., breast-feeding, eating a heart-healthy diet), to more intangible ideas (e.g., environmental protection).

To have a viable product, people must first feel that they have a genuine problem and that the product offered is a good solution to that problem. If your target audience members do not see themselves as being at risk or in an improvable situation, then they are unlikely to take measures to protect or better themselves. You might need to build awareness or provide the necessary skills before going about promoting behavior change.

You also might find that you need to refine the product you are offering to make it more effective in reducing the problem, easier to use, or more attractive to the target audience. A family planning clinic with inconvenient hours, rude staff, and a waiting room with big windows that allow passersby to see who is inside probably needs to focus on fixing its product before looking at other elements of the marketing mix.

Your product must be designed to appeal to the target audience and be presented in a way that highlights its attractive features. Show how your product is different and better by creating a niche for it (i.e., promoting it for specific types of people or to solve a particular problem) or by identifying the benefits that make it more appealing than the competition. This is called "positioning" your product. Answer the consumer's question, "What's in it for me?"

Identify the attributes and benefits that can help position the product in the minds of the target audience. An attribute is an objective fact describing the product, whereas a benefit tells you the value that the consumer gets from the attribute. For example, a car might have a convertible top as an attribute, but the benefit for some consumers is that they can have the wind whistling through their hair as they drive, making them feel young and free. The car might have leather seats, with the resulting benefits that its owners can feel wrapped in luxury and that other people can see they are persons of means.

To identify benefits, ask your audience members "So what?" to determine why an attribute might be valuable to them. You can create a "ladder" that links various attributes to their associated benefits. For example, in the hypothetical benefits ladder in Table 3.1, some attributes of physical exercise are that it increases the heart rate and helps to burn fat and increase metabolism. The immediate benefit of these attributes, as identified by the target audience, is that they result in weight loss. The benefits associated by the target audience with losing weight are improved appearance and self-image. Laddering these benefits even further yields the information that looking good and feeling good about one's own body makes a person sexier. By probing what your target audience members truly deem important (at the end of the benefits ladder), you can uncover more effective ways of appealing to them.

TABLE 3.1 Benefit Ladder: What Are the Attributes and Benefits of Physical Exercise (the product) That We Can Use to Appeal to the Target Audience?

Attribute →	Benefit →	Benefit →	Benefit
Increases heart rate	Lose weight	Look better	Be sexier
Helps to burn fat and increase metabolism		Feel better about yourself	
Increases high-density lipoproteins	Lowers cholesterol level	Live a longer and healthier life	Watch your grandchildren and great-grandchildren grow up
	Lowers risk of heart disease		
Decreases blood pressure	Lowers risk of stroke		
	Lowers risk of heart disease		
Produces endorphins	Reduce your stress levels	Feel more energetic	Feel more in control of your life
			Get more done in your day
Builds muscle strength	Become stronger	Be more independent in your daily activities	Have more freedom
Can be done with other people	Spend time with your family and friends	It is an opportunity to socialize	Have fun
Can be done alone	Spend time for yourself	Get away from it all	You deserve to have private time
Many people do it	Join the trend toward exercise	You will fit in	People will approve of you

Position the product by showing its key benefits relative to the competition. In social marketing, the competition can be other behaviors or simply nonadoption of the target behavior. For example, if the behavior you are promoting is breast-feeding, then the competition would be feeding the baby formula from a bottle. If you are trying to encourage people to eat more fresh fruits and vegetables, then the competition would depend on the positioning you chose. As a snack food, the competition might be potato chips or cookies; promoting fruit as a dessert, the competition could be ice cream or low-fat diet desserts; and for vegetables as a side dish to a meal, the competition might be instant mashed potatoes, garlic bread, or no side dish at all.

To illustrate the idea of the social marketing mix, let us say that we work for a hypothetical heart disease prevention organization that has as its goal motivating middle-aged men and women to exercise more. Of course, in an actual program, we would specify very clearly who our target audience is and conduct research with its members to learn whether they see heart disease as a potential problem for themselves and see exercise as a possible solution.

What is the product? It might simply be engaging in some sort of regular exercise, but it should be more specific than that. Ideally, the target audience members should do cardiovascular exercise three or more times per week to reduce heart disease risk. If the people we are targeting currently are doing some form of exercise, then we might only need to channel that propensity for exercise into more beneficial activities or encourage additional sessions of exercise. For the target audience members who do not currently exercise at all, we might need to start more slowly by promoting simple ways in which they can incorporate additional physical activity into their lives such as taking walks or using the stairs rather than the elevator. We could have different products geared for different subgroups of the target audience.

Our research with the target audience members would uncover which of the benefits are most important and appealing to them. We also would discover the main sources of competition for our product, which might include television, after-work commitments such as volunteer work or chauffeuring children to their activities, fad diets, or going to the movies. Depending on how we positioned the product—as a health improvement method, weight loss device, or recreational activity—we would be able to identify and address the relevant competition.

PRICE

Price refers to what the target audience has to give up to adopt the behavior. The price could be monetary, but more often in social marketing it involves intangibles such as time, effort, and old habits. Emotional costs can be part of the price as well; in the use of condoms by young men, for example, the price might include feelings of embarrassment when buying the condoms, the possibility of rejection by partners who do not want to use condoms, or giving up the pleasure of unprotected sex. By determining through research what the target audience considers to be the price of performing the behavior, the marketing mix can be designed to minimize the costs so that they do not outweigh the perceived benefits. If the costs outweigh the benefits for an individual, then the product will not be as attractive, and the likelihood of adoption will be low. But if the benefits are perceived as greater than their costs, then chances of trial and adoption of the product are much greater.

Setting a monetary price, particularly for a physical product such as contraceptives, can be tricky. If the product is priced too low or is provided free of charge, then consumers might perceive it as being less valuable. If the price is too high, then some will not be able to afford it. Social marketers must balance these considerations and often end up charging at least a nominal fee to increase perceptions of value and affordability. If your program is able to provide services or products for free, you can determine how the target audience will respond through your research.

In our exercise example, what are some of the costs that the target audience might associate with starting to exercise regularly?

- Time
- Energy
- Pain or discomfort
- Money (e.g., health club dues, exercise clothes, equipment)
- Child care
- Sleep
- Missing a favorite television show

In addition to things that the target audience members will have to give up, what are some other barriers that might stand in the way of regular exercise?

- Lack of knowledge/skills
- Lack of motivation
- Nobody to exercise with or perhaps lack of privacy
- Unsafe neighborhood

How can we best position the product to minimize the perceived costs associated with exercising or to get around other barriers that stand in the way of the target audience?

- It does not take much time—only 30 minutes, three times a week.
- The more you exercise, the less it hurts and the more energy you will have.
- It is easy; all you have to do is walk.
- You do not need equipment or fancy clothes.
- You can do it alone, with your friends, or with your family—whichever you prefer.
- You can do it in your own home, even in front of the television set.
- This is how you do it. . .

By conducting research with our target audience, we can find out which are the biggest barriers to exercise and which positioning statements are most believable and convincing.

PLACE

In commercial marketing, "place" generally refers to the distribution channels; that is, where and how are the customers going to get the product? Because in most social marketing programs the product is a behavior rather than a physical item, the question then becomes, "Where is the behavior available to the target audience?" This helps to determine where to expose the target audience members to the program's messages or to put systems in place that facilitate adopting the behavior.

You need to make it very easy for your target audience members to perform the behavior or to encounter the messages you want them to think about; they will not go out of their way to find your campaign. Ideally, your messages should reach people in a place where they are making decisions related to the behavior (e.g., a bar or dance club for messages related to AIDS or birth control). Or, if you want to reach busy professionals with messages about nutritious snacking, then put your message where and when people are thinking about snacking—on the way home from work (drive-time radio or billboards) or at the grocery store.

Another element of place is ensuring that the product is accessible to those you want to reach and maintaining the quality of delivery of the message. If your campaign urges the target audience to see doctors for screenings or information, then two pieces must be in place. First, target audience members must have access to doctors. Second, the doctors should be prepared to do what the campaign says they will do. Otherwise, individuals might act on the campaign messages but without the desired outcome. By determining the activities and habits of the target audience, as well as its level of access to the delivery system, you can pinpoint the best place for your product.

Think about the mechanics of how the product will be delivered. Will you have a "sales force" of community members who will promote the product within their social networks? If so, how will they receive and provide the product? How will you integrate partner organizations or businesses into your distribution network? Are there other existing product delivery systems that you could "piggyback" on to get yours to the audience? Consider less conventional product distribution methods beyond just media-based approaches.

For a program promoting exercise, what are some of the places we could use to get the message out to the target audience?

- Television news programs
- Radio talk shows
- Newspaper sports sections
- Supermarket snack food aisles
- Doctors' office waiting rooms

- Their children's schools
- Shopping malls
- Worksite bulletin boards
- World Wide Web
- Toll-free telephone numbers
- Commuting routes
- Community members' homes
- Shoe or clothing stores
- Sports venues

PROMOTION

Because of its visibility, promotion is what many people think of when they hear about social marketing. Although it is just one part of an integrated strategy, it is a very important one. Promotion deals with how you get your message about the product out to the target audience. The focus is on motivating people to try and then to continue performing the behavior.

Promotion can involve many different methods of conveying the message including the following:

- Advertising (e.g., television or radio commercials, billboards, posters)
- Public relations (e.g., press releases, letters to the editor, appearances on talk shows)
- Promotions (e.g., coupons, contests, in-store displays)
- Media advocacy (e.g., press events designed to encourage policy change)
- Personal selling (e.g., one-on-one counseling, peer educators)
- Special events (e.g., health fairs, concerts)
- Entertainment (e.g., dramatic presentations, songs, television shows)

Research will tell you which are the most effective and efficient ways of reaching a particular target audience. Find out the following: What media does it watch? Where does it get its information? What spokespeople are most credible to the group?

Thinking about our example, what would be some possible methods of promoting exercise messages to our target audience?

- Television or radio commercials
- Water bottles
- Coupons from local vendors

- Competitions or other incentives (e.g., walking club, walk-a-thon)
- Brochures and posters
- Billboards
- Grocery bags
- Fast food restaurant placemats
- Discussions initiated by physicians
- Storyline in a television show involving exercise or portrayal of celebrity role models exercising
- Media event promoting the development of safe walking or biking paths in the community
- Appearance on a local talk show to discuss integrating exercise into one's life

---

Beyond the four P's of traditional marketing—product, price, place, and promotion—social marketing adds four more P's, as discussed in the following sections.

PUBLICS

As mentioned earlier, social marketers often have many different audiences that their program must address to be successful. "Publics" refers to both the external and internal groups involved in the program. The most important external public certainly is the target audience—those people whose behaviors and attitudes you want to affect. Beyond the primary audience, there might be several secondary audiences whose members influence the decisions of the target audience members (e.g., friends, family members, teachers, physicians). Another external public could be policymakers who have the ability to create an environment conducive to behavior change or maintenance. Also, those who act as "gatekeepers" in controlling the messages that your target audience receives from the program, such as media professionals and business owners, might need to be convinced that your issue is important and worthy of their attention.

In addition to the many external audiences you might face, addressing your internal publics from the beginning can be the most critical to the success of the program. Often, staff and supervisors must "buy in" to the concept and planned execution of a campaign before it is ever shown to a target audience member. If the head of your organization does not understand what social marketing is and why you need to do things differently from standard operating procedures, the program might never get off the ground. Or, if your campaign provides a phone number and the receptionist does not know how to respond to the callers, then all the hard work that brought the target audience to that point is lost. Educating your staff and supervisors about social marketing, as well as keeping everyone informed about the specifics of the campaign and their roles in it, is crucial.

What might be some of the publics to consider in designing the exercise program?

- Target audience (middle-aged men and women)
- Target audience's relatives (e.g., spouses, children, parents)
- Target audience's friends and co-workers
- Heads of local businesses
- Health care providers
- Public service directors at radio and television stations
- Local reporters in various media
- City council members or state/federal legislators
- Board members
- Staff of your organization at all levels

PARTNERSHIP

Social and health issues often are so complex that one organization cannot make a dent by itself. By teaming up with other groups in the community, your organization can extend its resources as well as its access to members of the target audience. Figure out which organizations have similar audiences or goals as yours—although not necessarily the same goals—and identify ways in which you can work together so that both can benefit.

What types of organizations might be beneficial for us to join forces with in our exercise program?

- Health clubs
- Clothing or shoe stores
- Restaurants
- Television or radio stations
- Local parent-teacher associations
- Local employers
- Service organizations (e.g., Kiwanis, Rotary Club)
- Grocery stores
- Drug stores
- Local/state health department
- Voluntary organizations (e.g., American Heart Association)

POLICY

Social marketing programs can do well in motivating individual behavior change, but that is difficult to sustain unless the environment surrounding the target audience supports that change for the long run. In many cases, policy change has been very effective in providing that type of support. For example, as it has become more difficult for smokers to light up in the workplace and other public places because of policies at various levels (from organizational to federal), many people have decided that smoking is not worth the hassle. Media advocacy techniques, which influence or put pressure on policymakers or an industry through the generation of media attention, and other legislative advocacy such as lobbying can be effective components of a social marketing program.

What types of policies or legislation might be useful in helping people exercise regularly?

- Development of safe walking or biking paths
- Flextime at work so that people can come in later or extend their lunch breaks to exercise
- Creation of bike lanes on city streets
- Employee incentives to walk or bike to work
- Installation of bike racks in the community

PURSE STRINGS

Finally, social marketing generally differs from commercial marketing in the sources of its funding. A company selling a product for its own profit generally will use money for its marketing efforts from start-up capital put down by its owners or from the revenue the company earns. Most organizations that develop social marketing programs operate through funds provided by sources such as foundations, governmental grants, and donations. This adds another dimension to the strategy development: namely, where will you get the money to create your program? You might already have funding at this point, or you might be considering seeking money for a specific project. This book may assist in developing a funding proposal by helping you think through the key elements of your proposed program and your budget needs. You also might consider selling a tangible product as part of your program to keep it self-sustaining.

What are some potential sources of funding for our exercise program?

- American Heart Association
- Federal or state grants
- Foundations dealing with health and wellness issues
- Corporate sponsor (e.g., Reebok, Nike)
- Sales of exercise products emblazoned with the program's logo

THE SOCIAL
MARKETING PROCESS

Although the prospect of creating a social marketing program might be daunting, following the common advice of breaking a large task into smaller ones will help. Social marketing provides a straightforward framework for program development that, if followed, ensures that each critical piece occurs at the proper time. The process involves research at every stage, with constant reevaluation to assess whether the program is on track. In practice, social marketing is not necessarily a clear series of linear steps but rather a process of feedback and adjustment that might require revisiting past stages to make changes based on new information. For the purposes of this book, however, we discuss these steps in sequence.

STAGES IN THE
SOCIAL MARKETING PROCESS

The social marketing process consists of five general stages, each of which involves several different types of activities:

1. Planning
2. Message and materials development
3. Pretesting
4. Implementation
5. Evaluation and feedback

The process can be visually depicted as the pyramid shown in Figure 4.1.

Step 1. The planning phase forms the foundation on which the rest of the process is built. To create an effective social marketing program, you must understand the problem you are addressing, the audiences you are targeting,

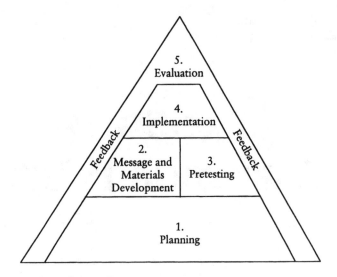

Figure 4.1 The Social Marketing Process

and the environment in which the program will operate. Research is used to analyze these factors and to develop a workable strategy for effecting behavior change.

Step 2. The message and materials development phase uses the information learned in the planning phase to design the messages to be conveyed as well as the materials that will carry the messages to the target audience.

Step 3. The pretesting phase involves using various methods to test messages and materials with the target audience members to determine what works best to accomplish the program's objectives. It is not uncommon to go back and forth several times between development and pretesting as you make necessary changes in the messages, materials, or overall strategy and explore whether the new approach works.

Step 4. In the implementation phase, the program is introduced to the target audience. Preparation is essential for success, and implementation must be monitored to ensure that every element proceeds as planned.

Step 5. Finally, the evaluation and feedback phase assesses the effects of the program as a whole as well as the individual elements of the strategy. Evaluation occurs throughout the process of program development, not just at the end, and feedback is used at each stage to improve the program.

Each of the following chapters explains the steps of the social marketing process in detail.

ETHICAL CONSIDERATIONS IN THE SOCIAL MARKETING PROCESS

Social marketing can be used to either good or ill effect. Beyond just good intentions, its purveyors have a societal duty to carry out their mission in an ethical manner. This means looking at each aspect of your program as you plan and implement it to consider whether it has the potential to do harm in any way. Behavior change is serious business, and it is preferable to do nothing rather than to implement a program that makes matters worse. For example, manipulating or deceiving people to bring about a positive health or social outcome never can be justified. Neither can coercion in any form, even if the actual behavior change is voluntary. Offering an impoverished woman a large sum of money in exchange for her becoming sterilized might force her to make a choice she really does not want to make.

Not all ethical issues are so cut-and-dried. A program that promises more than the product can deliver, or that omits information about the risks of adopting a particular behavior, also might be ethically suspect. In some instances, placing the entire responsibility for change on the individual rather than on the social institutions that created a problem in the first place (e.g., polluting factories causing respiratory problems in a community) might be not only ineffective but also an injustice to its victims.

Thinking a program through to its next logical step might help to avoid problems arising as an unintended consequence of your efforts. This will preclude situations such as the woman who has just learned of a potential tumor through a social marketing-based mammography screening program but is not told what to do as a result. Another example is the man who responds to a smoking cessation promotion, only to find that all of the classes are booked for the next four months and, therefore, loses the motivation brought about by the social marketing campaign. Look at your program from all sides, particularly at the point where it ends, to identify any potentially harmful effects or ethically questionable components.

> ### CASE STUDY: THE "DON'T KID YOURSELF" CAMPAIGN
>
> To illustrate the steps of the social marketing process, each chapter will end with a description of the corresponding stage in one real-life program— the "Don't Kid Yourself" campaign. This project was funded by the U.S. Public Health Service's Title X family planning grant program. In a six-state region: Colorado, Montana, North Dakota, South Dakota, Utah, and Wyoming. As one element of their initiative to reduce unintended pregnancies in the region, the grant administrators from each state decided in 1995 to pool their resources to develop a social marketing program.
>
> Organizers of the project formed a steering committee composed of representatives from each state and the Public Health Service regional office. Although most of the grantees were state health departments, the project was headed up administratively by the Planned Parenthood Association of Utah. The steering committee members first educated themselves by attending a major social marketing conference. Once they determined that they wanted to employ a social marketing campaign, they put together a request for proposal and sent it to social marketing firms and consultants to solicit bids for the project. After a long proposal review and interview process, they ultimately selected Weinreich Communications to lead the campaign.

SECTION I NOTES

1. Alan Andreasen, *Marketing Social Change* (San Francisco: Jossey-Bass, 1995), 41.

2. From the Talmud, as recounted in Joseph Telushkin, *Jewish Literacy* (New York: William Morrow, 1991), 121.

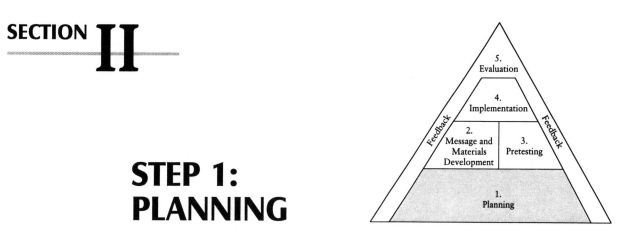

STEP 1: PLANNING

Section Overview

Like an architect's blueprints, the planning stage of social marketing lays the foundation for the rest of the program to build on. In Step 1, you will make decisions that shape the direction and focus of the program—decisions that are based on solid research. This section consists of the following chapters:

- Chapter 5: Formative Research in Social Marketing
- Chapter 6: Analysis
- Chapter 7: Segmenting the Target Audience
- Chapter 8: Strategy Development

chapter
five

FORMATIVE RESEARCH IN SOCIAL MARKETING

The role of formative research in social marketing is to guide the initial development of the program. It helps to answer questions such as the following:

- What is the problem you are addressing?
- What is the context in which the problem exists?
- Who will be your target audience?
- How does your target audience think and behave as related to the problem?
- What product can you offer that will appeal to your target audience?
- How can you best reach your target audience?
- Which messages and materials work best?
- What is the best social marketing mix?

Formative research occurs throughout the first three steps of the process: planning, message and materials development, and pretesting.

Before you start any research, know why you are collecting that information. Andreasen[1] suggests a process called "backward research," in which you first identify the key decision points of the program and then determine the information needed to make those decisions. From there, ascertain the best way in which to secure that information. Someone else might have already done the work for you by conducting research on that topic, or you might need to collect the data yourself. For example, to decide how best to reach your target audience with your message, you will need to find data on the types of media it pays attention to and where it gets its information on your issue, not just the standard knowledge, attitudes, and behaviors statistics. By thinking through the exact type of data needed, you can decide whether to use primary or secondary research and quantitative or qualitative approaches.

PRIMARY AND SECONDARY RESEARCH

Generally, the most efficient way in which to gather information is through secondary research—data from studies already conducted by other researchers or organizations. Secondary research includes sources such as journal articles, books, census data, marketing databases, and unpublished

---

SOURCES OF
SECONDARY DATA

Depending on the type of information you need, there are many sources for local, state, national, and international data. Here are some places to start:

Local and State Data

▓   Local or state health departments
▓   Community organizations
▓   Universities
▓   Census bureau (http://www.census.gov)
▓   State data Web sites (http://www.prb.org/prb/info/stateweb.htm)

National Data

▓   **National Center for Health Statistics** (http://www.cdc. gov/nchswww.
    html; phone: [301] 436-8500): Studies and surveillance data including the National Health Interview Survey, the National Health and Nutrition Examination Survey, and the National Survey of Family Growth
▓   **National Health Information Center** (http://nhic-nt.health. org; phone: [301] 565-4167 or [800] 336-4797): Referrals to appropriate federal clearinghouses and information centers as well as other organizations serving as resources for a particular topic
▓   **Centers for Disease Control and Prevention** (http://www.cdc.gov/scientific.
    htm): Online links to research data, including large-scale health surveys and the *Morbidity and Mortality Weekly Report*
▓   **Roper Center for Public Opinion Research** (http://www.ropercenter.uconn.edu; phone: [860] 486-4440): Database of thousands of public opinion poll questions from 1936 to the present (fee charged to access this information)
▓   National organizations (e.g., American Cancer Society, Alan Guttmacher Institute)
▓   Academic journals
▓   Private marketing research firms
▓   Foundations
▓   Professional associations

International Data

▓   **World Health Organization health-related statistics** (http://www.who.int/whosis/): A wide range of international survey and surveillance data
▓   **Pan American Health Organization** (http://www.paho.org): Country health profiles
▓   **Population Reference Bureau** (http://www.prb.org/prb/; phone: [202] 483-1100): Data on U.S. and international population trends
▓   **Demographic and health surveys** (http://www.macroint. com/dhs/): USAID survey data for various countries

A very useful free publication is available from the federal government: *A Compendium of Selected Public Health Data Sources* (Washington, DC: U.S. Department of Health and Human Services, Public Health Service, Agency for Health Care Policy and Research, 1996). Order Publication No. AHCPR97-0004 from the AHCPR Publications Clearinghouse, P.O. Box 8547, Silver Spring, MD 20907-8547, phone: (800) 358-9295; http://www.ahcpr.gov.

studies. The advantage is that your organization does not require on-staff expertise (beyond understanding and interpreting the research) or the additional expense of conducting its own research. It is rare, however, to find secondary research that answers all of your questions or addresses your specific target audience. You most likely will need to use a combination of secondary and primary research (i.e., data you collect yourself).

Primary research has the benefit of being tailored to the specific needs of your program. By using the process of backward research, you will know the questions to ask to get the information you need for strategic decision making. And you will be conducting research with precisely the people for whom the program is being developed.

Primary research is unavoidable in the pretesting stage; you must test your messages and materials with your own target audience. Such research also is necessary to assess the effects of the social marketing program once it has been implemented. As you will learn, primary research does not have to be difficult or expensive. You can conduct your own research, and your organization will be better off for it.

QUANTITATIVE AND QUALITATIVE RESEARCH

Another research concept that you need to know is the distinction between quantitative and qualitative research methods. When you think of the word "research," what comes to mind? Things like statistics, experiments, and precision? The type of research most of us are familiar with involves quantitative methods such as standardized surveys, random samples, and statistical analysis. The results of quantitative research help you to understand how many people believe or behave a certain way, which characteristics are related to each other, and the probability that any behavior change was related to exposure to your program. In the quantitative world, things are black and white; they are either statistically significant or not. The only answers you obtain are those for which you thought to ask questions.

EXAMPLES OF QUANTITATIVE AND QUALITATIVE RESEARCH

Quantitative Research

Surveys (e.g., mail, telephone, self-administered, computerized)
Systematic observation
"Counts"/record keeping
Experiments
Analysis of marketing, census, or epidemiological data

Qualitative Research

Focus groups
In-depth interviews
Ethnographic observation
Content analysis
Town meetings

On the other hand, qualitative research methods help you to understand the "why" of an issue, bringing you beneath the surface of an answer. Many of these methods, such as focus groups, in-depth interviews, and observational studies, come from anthropology as well as commercial marketing. Qualitative research helps you to understand the issue from the target audience members' points of view and enables you to find out the reasons why they think or do something the way they do. Responses are placed in context, and something as complex as human behavior is not reduced to a multiple-choice question.

Using both quantitative and qualitative research provides different perspectives on the same situation. There are times when one type of data is more appropriate than the other, but by integrating research methods throughout the program development process, your overall understanding of the issue will be much deeper.

ANALYSIS

Social marketers must know as much about the market they are entering as someone considering opening a new pizza delivery service in a particular community. Is there a demand for pizza delivery? Who are the potential customers? Who is the main competition? Why have previous companies failed or succeeded? What are the start-up costs? Before investing money and effort in starting the company, a good businessperson would investigate these issues thoroughly.

Similarly, social marketers must analyze several major issues when beginning to plan a social marketing program, including the following:

- The problem to be addressed

- The environment in which the program will be implemented

- Resources available for the program

By understanding the problem and environment, you will be better able to identify potential opportunities and stumbling blocks for the program. A realistic assessment of your available resources will help to narrow the scope of the program or may highlight the need for participation from other groups.

ANALYZING THE PROBLEM

If you are planning a social marketing program, then you probably are already familiar with the topic you will be addressing. If not, then you might need to learn more about the issue before proceeding. Either way, research will help determine the approach the program should take. Secondary research is the best place to start to find the information you need. Once you have more narrowly defined the target audience and scope of the project, you also should conduct your own primary research.

**CONDUCTING A
LITERATURE REVIEW**

A literature review reveals the research information that already exists
on your issue and helps you apply that
knowledge to your own program. The
process consists of the following
steps:

1. Start at the library, preferably at a
   university with a medical school
   and/or school of public health (if
   your issue is health related).

   - Have an idea of the type of
     information you need to learn
     about your issue such as bio-
     logical or psychosocial as-
     pects, epidemiology, and pre-
     vious interventions that have
     been attempted.

   - Search the relevant computer
     or CD-ROM databases such as
     Medline, Psychinfo, and Pop-
     line to obtain references and
     abstracts for the academic lit-
     erature. (Many of these data-
     bases are available on the In-
     ternet to search as well.) Look
     for each article in the journals
     carried by the library and make
     copies of the most relevant
     ones.

   - Search the library's own cata-
     log for books and periodicals
     related to your issue. Other re-
     sources such as the *Reader's
     Guide to Periodical Literature*
     can help you find information
     on your topic in the popular
     press.

   - Look at the references listed at
     the end of relevant articles to
     see whether there are others
     you should look up as well.

(continued)

The questions you can answer using secondary research
include the following:

- *What aspect of the problem will you address?* There are many
  ways in which to approach a problem. For example, a
  social marketing program addressing child abuse might
  try to convince abusive parents to stop hitting their children. It could make it easier for teachers or community
  members who suspect abuse to make reports to the
  authorities. It could teach abused children to ask trusted
  adults for help. It might promote preventive behaviors to
  parents who have not yet abused their children but are at
  high risk. Or, it could help adult victims of child abuse get
  needed treatment. Each of these angles is a way in which
  to address the issue of child abuse, and further research
  might steer you toward the more effective approaches. The
  angle you choose will help narrow the target audience
  options.

- *What is the epidemiology of the problem?* Epidemiology
  describes how a disease or problem is distributed in a
  population. Ideally, you should try to find data for your
  specific community or the geographic area of the program. How common is the problem (its prevalence)? How
  quickly are new cases occurring (its incidence)? Who is
  most at risk of acquiring the disease or social problem? Is
  the problem more severe among certain groups of people?
  For example, although the prevalence of HIV infection is
  relatively high among older gay White men, its incidence
  rate has slowed in comparison to other groups such as
  women and young minority men. Those who are at highest risk or who suffer the most serious consequences are
  good candidates to be your target audience.

- *What can be done to prevent the problem from occurring or
  spreading?* By understanding the causes of the disease or
  problem, you can identify the key preventive behaviors to
  promote. Skin cancer, for example, is associated with
  exposure to the ultraviolet rays of the sun. Preventive
  behaviors would include using sunscreen, wearing a wide-
  brimmed hat, covering exposed skin, and staying out of
  the sun during peak sunlight hours. Depending on your
  program's goals and the target audience you choose, you
  might decide to promote one specific preventive behavior
  or all such behaviors.

- *What are the consequences of the problem?* Visualization of
  the potential negative consequences of an action often is
  effective in averting an unhealthy behavior. As a result of
  efforts by Mothers Against Drunk Driving (MADD) to
  highlight the devastating effects of drunk driving through

its media campaigns, people who have been drinking might think twice before getting behind the wheel. Older smokers often quit when they realize that they might not be around to see their grandchildren grow up. As you design your program, you can test various consequences to see whether any of them "hit home" with the target audience.

■ *What knowledge, attitudes, and behaviors are related to the problem?* Determine whether members of the potential target audiences are even aware of the issue and consider themselves at risk. How many of them think that the disease or condition is serious or that they can do something to prevent it? How many are actually practicing preventive behaviors? Are there differences between certain groups such as men and women or younger and older teens? For example, if girls are more likely to engage in aerobic exercise and boys prefer weight training, then a school-based exercise curriculum might need to encourage boys to incorporate more cardiovascular activity into their routines.

■ *How successful have previous attempts been to address the problem?* If you are not aware of what has already been tried, you might indeed be condemned to repeat the past including making the same mistakes as others. Rather than reinventing the wheel, learn which interventions have been effective. Search the literature for other programs that have addressed the same issue, and contact the sponsoring organizations for more information. You can conduct expert interviews with people who have worked on similar projects around the country. Ask them what worked and what they would do differently next time. Many people are willing to give their advice, and you might find the time it takes well worth it.

ANALYZING THE ENVIRONMENT

Having learned as much about the problem as possible, particularly as it relates to your community or area, turn your attention now to the environment that will surround the social marketing program. Nothing occurs in a vacuum, and your program is no exception. Your campaign will be just one of many messages that people receive in the course of their days. Knowing what you are competing with will help you break through the clutter.

The environment can be either a help or a hindrance, presenting opportunities or barriers. To create sustained

---

**CONDUCTING A
LITERATURE REVIEW**
(continued)

2. Surf the Internet.

   ▓ Using search engines such as Yahoo!, AltaVista, and Excite, look for Web sites that address your issue. Many organizations and individuals offer their own information and data or provide lists of other Web sites that are related to the topic. You can find everything from general information to very specific data resources.

   ▓ Follow links within each Web site to find other sites that have more information or links until you have exhausted what is out there (or until you are exhausted yourself).

3. Contact organizations that work to address your topic (e.g., federal agencies, national nonprofits).

   ▓ Ask whether they offer publications with the information and data that you need (there might be a fee involved).

   ▓ Speak with individuals involved in projects similar to yours to learn more about their programs and to obtain their insights.

4. Integrate all the material you find into a useful reference.

   ▓ Group the information from each source by subject, and write it up into a coherent summary. Keep track of where each piece of information came from in case you need to refer back to its source (i.e., create references or footnotes).

   ▓ Clearly highlight key information and provide recommendations for developing your own program based on what you learned from the literature review.

EXPERT INTERVIEWS

You can quickly learn a lot about how to develop your program by speaking with people who have been there before. In all likelihood, you are not the first to address the problem or target audience, so why not benefit from the experience of others? Expert interviews are a way of learning the lessons of other programs, whether they were successful or not.

Locate appropriate people to interview by first checking the literature to find published descriptions of programs addressing your issue and then contacting those projects' directors. They might not have exactly the same angle or target audience, but there may be enough commonality that you can gain some valuable insights for your own program. Ask as many people as possible who work in the field whether they know of any current or past programs similar to yours. Your interviewees probably will be able to steer you to additional people to interview. Relevant federal clearinghouses also might be able to give you a list of government-funded projects related to your issue around the country.

Tell your participants as much as you can about your project so that they can speak to the particular issues you might need to consider. The following questions could be helpful to use in your interviews:

- Could you describe the project? The goal? Messages? Media? What did the campaign ask people to do?
- Who was your target audience? How did you go about choosing it? How narrowly did you segment its members?
- Did you conduct any research with the target audience to help in developing the campaign?
- What did you learn from the research that might be applicable to other campaigns?

(continued)

behavior change, the environment must be conducive to the actions you are promoting. After analyzing the situation, you might realize that the program should devote resources to creating a supportive context for your target audience's behavior change efforts. For example, a program promoting good eating habits to inner-city residents without stores that sell produce or other fresh foods could remove that obstacle by establishing a farmer's market or working with neighborhood stores to stock healthful foods.

Your environmental analysis should consider the following questions as they relate to your issue:

- *What social, economic, or demographic factors might be at work in the community?* Find out the trends that might be affecting the lives of your target audience members. Social issues such as poverty, crime, and homelessness have obvious and not-so-obvious effects on what people may be willing or able to do to improve their health. If a large factory has just closed in a small city, then people might need to find new jobs before they can make other changes in their lives. Other factors such as a predominant religion (e.g., Mormonism in Utah) or a large gay community (e.g., in San Francisco) might be relevant to how you develop your program.

- *What is the political climate in relation to the topic or target audiences you are addressing?* Although not true for many issues, some topics have become so politicized that social marketers must be aware of potential conflicts as they develop their programs. Topics such as AIDS prevention, contraception, tobacco, alcohol, and guns have active proponents and opponents who have very different ideas about the subject. Determine who your potential allies and adversaries may be and forge strategic alliances whenever possible. You also might find it more effective to deal delicately with controversial subjects that are at odds with community norms.

- *What current policies or pending legislation might affect your target audience's response to the social marketing program?* Often, one of the most effective things your program can do is to get your hands dirty in the sausage making of legislation. Policies at the organizational, local, state, and federal levels—whichever are appropriate—can go a long way toward promoting a healthful environment. For example, stricter laws regarding selling alcohol or cigarettes to minors would reduce access to these substances by young people. Or, if Medicaid or private insurance companies do not cover an important preventive procedure, you might need to work to change that policy before urging people to ask for it from their doctors.

■ *What other organizations currently are addressing the issue in your community?* Before you plan your own program, investigate whether other organizations are working toward similar goals so that you can avoid duplication of efforts. There might be programs at the local, state, or national level addressing the same issue or target audience in your own community. One option is to join forces with those organizations and either complement or expand their efforts. Otherwise, you can decide whether to reinforce existing campaigns, approach the issue from a different angle, or target a different audience.

■ *What messages will be competing with your program for attention?* On average, your target audience members may be exposed to between 560 and 1,800 promotional messages daily,[2] so you need to make sure that your messages get noticed. Competing messages may come from the constant buzz of commercial advertising, from opponents of your cause, or even from within your own field. You can conduct a media audit to assess the messages in the media about your issue. You might find rampant misinformation, suggesting that your program needs to educate media professionals. You also might find that the "competition" uses certain communication channels in a particularly effective manner. For example, if you are working to keep young people from smoking, then determining where the most cigarette billboards are located will be useful in focusing your efforts.

■ *What channels are available in the community to promote your message?* In every community, many different resources are available through which you can get your message out to the target audience. Assess your options so that you can keep them in mind during the planning process. These resources may include the following:

   ▪ Media outlets (e.g., newspapers, television and radio stations)
   ▪ Community events (e.g., annual parade)
   ▪ Popular activities (e.g., high school sports, attending the movies)
   ▪ High-visibility or high-traffic areas (e.g., main street, public restrooms)
   ▪ Local businesses frequented by the target audience

As you conduct research, keep your eyes and ears open for clues about ways in which to reach your target audience. Be creative and go beyond the standard media channels.

EXPERT INTERVIEWS
(continued)

▪ Did you evaluate the campaign? What did you use to measure success?

▪ Do you have any experience developing programs for our population? What types of messages or media do you think would be most effective for them?

▪ Is there anything you wish you had done differently with your campaign that might be useful for us to watch out for as we develop ours?

▪ Was there anything that you found worked particularly well?

AUDITING MEDIA MESSAGES

If you will be employing media strategies in your program, you should have an idea of the types of messages that are already out there. Your target audience might gain much of its knowledge and form its opinions on your issue based on what it sees and hears in the media. To be most effective as you prepare to develop your program, conduct a media audit to identify whether and how your issue is covered. You also might wish to monitor the activities of your opponents as well; for example, a smoking prevention campaign should be aware of the latest promotional strategies employed by the tobacco companies. Cover news programs, television shows, and advertising messages in your audit, if appropriate. You also may include movies, popular music, music videos, and other entertainment media such as magazines and tabloid newspapers.

The media audit can last for a set amount of time (e.g., two weeks, one month) or can be ongoing throughout the life of your program. The scope of the audit will depend on the number of media outlets in your community and the number of your staff members willing to assist in monitoring activities. You might wish to limit the audit to the major daily newspaper, top-rated local television newscasts, or most popular television shows if you cannot cover all the media in your community.

To assess the news coverage of your issue, skim each section of the newspaper every day and clip any stories that are related to your issue in some way. Similarly, watch the television newscast or listen to the radio news each day (you might find it easier to record these to review at a later time). If you are not able to spend the time doing this yourself, then you can contract with a media monitoring service, which will scan the media outlets you designate and provide you with the actual newspaper clippings or audiovisual program transcripts of all stories that contain references to your topic or organization. Some well-known national services are Luce Press Clippings (phone: [800] 528-8226), Burrelle's Information Services (phone: [800] 631-1160), and Bacon's Clipping Bureau (phone: [800] 621-0561). They also can analyze the content of the stories, providing you with a comprehensive report that shows which topics are covered by each outlet and the biases of reporters covering your issue. You can do a content analysis yourself, using a short checklist such as the following and tabulating the results.

NEWS MEDIA:

Date/time_____

Medium: ☐ Newspaper   ☐ Television   ☐ Radio

Name of outlet:_____

Name of reporter: _____

Wire service or syndicate (if applicable): _____

Type of story: ☐ Hard news   ☐ Feature   ☐ Column   ☐ Opinion   ☐ Other

Topic of story/headline: _____

Issues/items included (customize checklist for your issue):

Epidemiology ☐ Prevention   ☐ Treatment   ☐ Consequences

Opposition   ☐ New research   ☐ Policy   ☐ Our organization

Editorial slant: ☐ Positive   ☐ Negative   ☐ Neutral

****

(continued)

AUDITING MEDIA MESSAGES *(continued)*

ENTERTAINMENT MEDIA:

Date/time: _____

Medium: ☐ Television show   ☐ Music/music video   ☐ Movie
                 ☐ Publication   ☐ Other

Name of production/publication: _____

How issue arose: ☐ Portrayed desirable behavior

                             ☐ Portrayed competing behavior

                             ☐ Mentioned issue

                             ☐ Other _____

Describe the scene/context:

Overall depiction of issue: ☐ Positive   ☐ Negative   ☐ Neutral

Approximate number of relevant seconds/minutes or paragraphs:

****

ADVERTISING MESSAGES:

Date/time: _____

Medium: ☐ Newspaper   ☐ Television   ☐ Radio

Name of outlet: _____

Name of advertiser/product: _____

Probable target audience: _____

Benefits promoted: _____

Other messages included: _____

ANALYZING YOUR RESOURCES

Before you get too excited about everything you would like to tackle through your social marketing program, come back down to earth. Realistically assess your available resources before proceeding any further. Your strategy will look much different if you have $10,000 to work with instead of $100,000, and this is the point at which to think about your budget.

Your Internal Resources

A program needs more than money to succeed; it takes skilled personnel, adequate office facilities, access to the target audience, and (not least of all) time. Some questions to ask yourself before moving forward include the following:

SAMPLE PROGRAMS WITH VARIOUS RESOURCE LEVELS

This table gives you examples of what programs with various-sized budgets might expect to accomplish in terms of research and production. It does not take into account any *pro bono* (free) services that you might be able to obtain to stretch your budget. As the budget becomes larger, items are added to those included in the previous lists.

	Small Budget (less than $20,000)[a]	*Moderate Budget ($20,000-$100,000)[a]*	*Large Budget (more than $100,000)[a]*
Step 1: Planning	Literature review Informal target audience research	Additional secondary research Focus groups	Knowledge, attitudes, and behaviors survey
Step 2: Message and Materials Development	Public service announcements (produced by local radio/television station) Print materials	Radio spots Newspaper ads	Television spots Billboards
Step 3: Pretesting	Informal target audience research Self-administered questionnaires Readability testing	Focus groups Expert/gatekeeper review	Intercept interviews Theater testing Multiple rounds of pretesting, if necessary
Step 4: Implementation	Partnering Public relations activities Record keeping	Kickoff media event Paid media placement Issue monitoring	Additional media buys Web site Management effectiveness/ efficiency analysis
Step 5: Evaluation and Feedback	Secondary data Data from existing records	Systematic observations Qualitative methods	Knowledge, attitudes, and behaviors survey

a. Dollar figures are approximate and in 1998 terms. Hiring outside contractors will add to the cost.

- What is the total budget you can afford for the social marketing program?
- How much of the budget comes from grants or other outside funding, and how much will be paid by your organization?
- Does the organization have staff with the ability to plan and carry out each step of the social marketing process including research and production?
- If not, do you have funds to hire a consultant or advertising/public relations agency?
- Do you and your staff have the necessary time to devote to developing, implementing, and monitoring a social marketing program?
- Does your organization have adequate office facilities and equipment?
- Does your organization have access to the target audience members?

SHOULD YOU USE
AN OUTSIDE AGENCY?

Although you are an expert in the work that you do, you might not have the same level of expertise in every field it takes to create a social marketing program. If you feel confident that you already possess those skills, that is great. If you feel you need some outside assistance for all or part of the program development, that is okay too. The Resource Analysis Worksheet (Worksheet 3) will help you to assess the areas where your staff have sufficient expertise and where you might wish to receive additional training. Following are some questions to consider in making a decision about hiring a contractor to work with you on the campaign:

What type of agency or consultant should you use? Advertising, public relations, marketing—how do you choose which type of agency you need? They often have similar capabilities, but each has a different focus. A marketing firm generally looks at the big picture, starting with a strategy based on research and determining the most appropriate activities within the larger context of the marketing mix. Advertising agencies and public relations firms focus on the narrower disciplines within marketing, with ad agencies usually creating and producing advertisements and public relations firms using other promotional strategies to get their clients' messages out. Ideally, look for a company that specializes in social marketing or at least has some experience in the area.

With which aspects of the program do you need assistance? You might already have research expertise in your organization or a freelance graphic artist with whom you always work but need help with placing your ads in the media. Or, you might want to develop the script for a television spot yourself but require assistance with the technicalities of production. Carefully consider whether you want someone to create your program from start to finish or to take on selected activities such as research, creative services, production, media planning and distribution, partnership development, and/or public relations.

What type of budget do you have? Even if you have only a small budget, do not hesitate to contact agencies for assistance if you need it. They might be willing to provide services at a reduced rate or might even take on your organization as a *pro bono* (free) client. If not, prioritize the activities you need help with and do the lower priority items in-house; it will be a learning experience. Some types of firms, such as media planning services, are compensated by the media outlets with which they place your ads and technically work at no cost to you (although you can save money by doing it yourself [see Chapter 16]). You might wish to consider hiring a social marketing consultant or freelancers rather than a full-service firm to save money.

How will you find agencies to choose from? Select a firm to do social marketing for you the same way in which you would select any other type of outside consultant. Ask for recommendations from people and organizations you trust. Look for examples of advertising materials or programs that you particularly like, and find out who produced them. If you do not know of agencies in your community, then check the reference desk of your library for publications such as *The Standard Directory of Advertising Agencies, O'Dwyer's Directory of Public Relations Firms,* and the *GreenBook International Directory of Marketing Research Companies and Services.* Local chapters of organizations, such as the American Association of Advertising Agencies and the Public Relations Society of America, also might be able to provide lists of firms in your area. Contact the most promising candidates and set up meetings to discuss your needs, or send out a request for proposal to solicit bids to produce your campaign.

What criteria will you use to select the contractor? Determine what skills and expertise you feel are most important to your program and find an organization that matches those criteria. If the firm has not done social marketing before, does it have experience with any health or social issues or with your target audience? Is the work that it has done for other clients effective and of high quality? Do you feel that the staff with whom you will be working understand your needs and will listen to you? Do not expect an agency you are considering to create a sample campaign before you have signed a contract, but an agency should be willing to discuss its overall strategic approach to developing your program.

How will you work together? Remember that you are the expert on your issue. It is up to you to provide the agency or consultants with the information needed to create your program. Share any research you have conducted, as well as your preliminary social marketing strategy, to ensure that you have similar expectations from the beginning. Make clear what you do and do not like about the ideas the agency or consultants offer, and communicate regularly throughout the development process.

■ Do you currently have any partner agencies with the skills or access that your organization lacks? Are there any other organizations with whom you could team up?

■ Do you need to seek additional funding before proceeding?

■ Given your answers to the preceding questions, is it feasible for your organization to develop a social marketing program at this time?

If you find that your current resources are not adequate for the type of program you had envisioned, then you have two choices: Either narrow the parameters of the project or find more funding. This might mean sending out more grant proposals or expanding project resources through partnerships with other organizations.

Working With Partners

As mentioned in Chapter 3, partnership is one of the "P's" in the social marketing mix. Even if you have sufficient funds, consider inviting others to join the project to expand the reach of your program. Build connections with key people and organizations that have the potential to bring attention and credibility. By pooling resources and promoting the campaign through many organizations working toward the same goal, you can produce a synergistic effect greater than each could achieve on its own. Just as the power of a choir derives from its union of many voices, a powerful campaign requires groups throughout the community to come together in a coordinated effort.

Depending on their resources and interests, partners might wish to participate in many different ways. You can specify what they will do or allow them to decide the type of role they would prefer. Some possibilities include the following:

■ Distributing your program materials to their clients/customers/constituents

■ Referring members of the target audience to your program

■ Including your messages in their own materials

■ Adapting your materials to include their contact information

■ Offering use of their staff or volunteers to the program

■ Writing letters of support for your program

■ Providing a well-known spokesperson for the program

■ Being involved in media interviews and press conferences

■ Assisting in research and evaluation activities

■ Providing financial support or "in-kind" contributions (e.g., printing, media time, use of their conference facilities)

Despite the benefits of working with partners, whenever you bring in additional organizations, you expose the program to new and different types of challenges. Too many partners also can make the program an administrative nightmare. It is up to you to decide the balance you need between expanding the program and letting go of control over parts of the process. Communication is essential to preventing potential problems before they start.

Some typical issues you might encounter and possible solutions include the following:

- *You feel a loss of ownership of the project.* With many organizations participating, you might end up compromising on some aspects of the program or letting go of some control over the project's direction. Giving your "baby" over to others can be a difficult thing, especially when they take the credit for its success. Try to avoid power struggles, and keep focused on the reasons you brought in the partners in the first place.

- *Partners do not participate as agreed.* There is nothing more frustrating than thinking that your partners are carrying out their tasks when the organizations have not even begun taking the necessary actions. Find out why they have not started. Do they have the materials? Do they know what to do? Do they need additional assistance from you? Help them to live up to their commitments without doing the work for them.

- *Partners go "off strategy."* Your partners might take the plan and materials you give them and use them in a way that was not intended. It may be fine for them to adapt the materials and program to fit their situations, but make sure that the use still fits with your original strategy.

- *Partnership becomes time-consuming.* By its nature, working with other organizations takes time and effort. This includes helping them to understand the project, determining areas of mutual benefit, meeting to work out logistics, and engaging in ongoing communications. Try to build enough time into your plan to allow for the extra effort and to give your partners advance notice of upcoming needs as well.

- *Your partners are getting bored with the project.* Just as your staff eventually might tire of the campaign, your partners occasionally will require a dose of motivation. Set long- and short-term goals for them to strive to meet. Have contests to see who can make the most referrals or hand out the most brochures, with prizes awarded at the end. Share success stories with them so they can see that what they are doing is making a difference.

PICKING PARTNERS

Think carefully about who would be good partners before approaching other groups. Just because an organization has expressed interest in being involved in the campaign does not mean that it is the best partner for your program. Be strategic in building alliances. Some criteria for choosing a campaign partner are whether the organization has the following attributes:

- Provides access to members of the target audience
- Has credibility or influence with the target audience
- Has resources (e.g., staff, financial) and/or skills (e.g., media relations) that it is willing to make available to the campaign
- Has qualifications appropriate to the topic of the campaign
- Has a preexisting relationship with you or your organization
- Is enthusiastic about the social marketing program

Some types of organizations to consider as partners include the following:

- Health departments
- Social service agencies
- Voluntary organizations (e.g., American Cancer Society, American Heart Association)
- Nonprofit community organizations
- State or national organizations
- Professional associations
- Corporations or local businesses
- Educational institutions
- Religious institutions
- Media outlets
- Public safety agencies
- Hospitals and health care agencies
- Service organizations (e.g., Elks, Rotary Club)
- Youth organizations (e.g., Girl Scouts, 4-H Clubs)
- Foundations
- Insurance companies and health maintenance organizations
- Political officials

WORKSHEET 1: Problem Analysis Worksheet

1. What is the problem or issue your social marketing program will address?

_____

_____

2. What are the possible angles you could take in addressing the problem or issue?

_____

_____

_____

3. From your secondary research, what is the epidemiology of the problem in your population?

    a. Prevalence (how often it occurs): _____

    b. Incidence (rate of new cases):   ☐ Rising   ☐ Staying the same   ☐ Decreasing

    c. Characteristics of people most at risk of having the problem:

        _____

        _____

        _____

        _____

    d. Are there groups in which the consequences of the problem are most severe?

        _____

        _____

        _____

        _____

4. What are the main ways in which the problem can be prevented?

_____

_____

_____

_____

(continued)

WORKSHEET 1: Problem Analysis Worksheet *(continued)*

5. What are the most common or most serious consequences of the problem?

_____

_____

_____

6. What knowledge, attitudes, and behaviors are related to the problem? How widespread are they among your population?

Approximate Percentage of Population

a. Knowledge:

_____   _____

_____   _____

_____   _____

_____   _____

b. Attitudes:

_____   _____

_____   _____

_____   _____

_____   _____

c. Behaviors:

_____   _____

_____   _____

_____   _____

_____   _____

7. What approaches have been used to address the problem by other organizations?

_____

_____

_____

_____

_____

(continued)

WORKSHEET 1: Problem Analysis Worksheet *(continued)*

8. Who are potential experts for you to interview?

Name	*Organization*	*Phone Number*

_____

_____

_____

_____

_____

WORKSHEET 2: Environmental Analysis Worksheet

1. **What are the geographic boundaries in which your program will take place (e.g., neighborhood, city, state)?**

   _____

2. **What trends or other factors might affect the environment in which your program will take place?**

   a. Social:

   _____

   _____

   _____

   b. Economic:

   _____

   _____

   _____

   c. Demographic:

   _____

   _____

   _____

   d. Political:

   _____

   _____

   _____

3. **Which groups, community leaders, or other individuals do you foresee opposing your program?**

   _____

   _____

   _____

   _____

(continued)

WORKSHEET 2: Environmental Analysis Worksheet (continued)

4. **Which groups, community leaders, or other individuals should you actively seek support from as allies?**

_____

_____

_____

_____

5. **Are there any policies, laws, or pending legislation that might affect how your target audience responds to the social marketing program? If so, do you want to try to address these issues in your program?**

| | Policy Change/Lobbying Necessary? | |
Policy/Legislation	*Yes*	*No*

6. **What other organizations currently are addressing the issue in your community?**

Organization	*Services Provided*	*Populations Served*

7. **What are the main messages that will be competing with your program for attention?**

   a. General advertising related to topic:

_____

_____

   b. Messages by opponents to your cause:

_____

_____

   c. Messages by allies to your cause:

_____

_____

(continued)

WORKSHEET 2: Environmental Analysis Worksheet *(continued)*

8. **What channels are available in the community to promote your message? Check all that apply:**

   ☐ Television
   ☐ Radio
   ☐ Daily newspapers
   ☐ Weekly newspapers
   ☐ Billboards
   ☐ Transit advertising
   ☐ Community events
   ☐ Sports events
   ☐ Movie theaters
   ☐ Local businesses
   ☐ Health or social service agencies
   ☐ Professional groups
   ☐ Other _____
   ☐ Other _____
   ☐ Other _____

WORSHEET 3: Resource Analysis Worksheet

1. **What is your total budget available for the social marketing program?** $ _____

2. **Where is the funding coming from?**

   a. _____ $ _____

   b. _____ $ _____

   c. _____ $ _____

3. **In which of the following areas related to social marketing do you or other staff members have skills or expertise? (check all that apply)**
   - ☐ Literature review
   - ☐ Quantitative research (e.g., surveys)
   - ☐ Qualitative research (e.g., focus groups, interviewing)
   - ☐ Partnership development
   - ☐ Message development
   - ☐ Materials development
   - ☐ Graphic design/print production
   - ☐ Audiovisual production
   - ☐ Public relations
   - ☐ Media planning/buying
   - ☐ Evaluation
   - ☐ Program planning and management

4. **Do you need to hire an outside agency to assist with any of the above activities?**
   ☐ Yes   ☐ No

   If yes, list the activities in order of priority:

   _____

   _____

   _____

   _____

5. **How much time do you and other staff members have to devote to the social marketing program?**

Staff Member	Hours per Week	Total Hours
_____	_____	_____
_____	_____	_____
_____	_____	_____
_____	_____	_____

(continued)

WORKSHEET 3: Resource Analysis Worksheet *(continued)*

6. **Do you have any additional space or equipment needs for the social marketing program?**

_____

_____

_____

7. **What level of access does your organization have to target audience members?**
   - ☐ Low: We would have to work hard to find them
   - ☐ Moderate: We have some dealings with them
   - ☐ High: They are the primary population that we serve

8. **What are the organizations you should consider partnering with for the social marketing program? Do you already have relationships with any of them?**

   Organization   *Relationship Established?*

   _____   _____

   _____   _____

   _____   _____

   _____   _____

   _____   _____

(continued)

WORKSHEET 3: Resource Analysis Worksheet *(continued)*

9. Preliminary Social Marketing Program Budget

Use this as a rough estimate for now, and refine it as you develop your strategy:

a. Personnel

_____ $_____

_____ $_____

_____ $_____

b. Research:

    (1) Formative research $_____

    (2) Process evaluation $_____

    (3) Outcome/impact evaluation $_____

c. Materials production $_____

d. Media buys $_____

e. Media/community events $_____

f. Mailing/distribution $_____

g. Other expenses

_____ $_____

_____ $_____

_____ $_____

_____ $_____

                                Subtotal $_____

    h. Contingencies (add 10%) $_____

                                  Total $_____

10. Do you need to seek additional funding before proceeding with the program?
   ☐ Yes   ☐ No

11. Is a social marketing program feasible to develop and implement at this time?
   ☐ Yes   ☐ No

chapter
seven

SEGMENTING THE TARGET AUDIENCE

Through the secondary research you did in the analysis phase, you probably have some ideas about who your primary target audience(s) might be. Although your initial inclination might be to create an all-inclusive campaign, segmentation will help you to be more strategic in developing your program. Even if the issue is one that affects people across the population (e.g., dental health), narrowing down the audience allows you to tailor the message to specific needs of particular groups. "Targeting" the general public is like using scattershot ammunition to try to hit a bull's-eye; it is possible but not very efficient.

WHY SEGMENT?

Target audience segmentation is one of the central features of social marketing borrowed from commercial practice. Companies such as McDonald's know their consumers inside and out and create advertising aimed at particular segments of the population. For example, one campaign might be created for working mothers who are too busy to cook dinner but want to feed their children wholesome meals. Another might target fathers who interact with their children mainly on weekends and want to make that time special. And free toys linked to the latest Disney movie are designed to make young children clamor for a "Happy Meal." The same product—a meal at McDonald's—is being promoted, but different benefits are touted to each consumer segment.

Similarly, social marketers can use segmentation to identify the groups most reachable by a social marketing campaign and to position their product for each segment. Segmentation helps you to develop an audience-centered program by getting to know and understand the various subgroups

51

(continued)

that might be in your target audience. Creating a profile of
the people in each segment can focus your thinking and keep
you on track as you go through the planning process.

In addition to aiding in understanding the audience, segmentation can help you to spend resources more efficiently.
The segments you choose to address through your program
will depend on the characteristics of each segment and your
own resources. If certain subgroups of the target audience are
at higher risk for the problem you are addressing ("targets of
risk"), then you might consider concentrating the program on
those groups. In addition, you might identify some segments
as being easier to reach or ready to make a behavior change
("targets of opportunity"). Where these two factors meet is
likely to be the most efficient and effective use of your funds.

WHAT IS A SEGMENT?

The goal of segmentation is to identify distinct groups of
people who are like each other in key ways and, therefore, are
liable to respond to particular messages similarly. Think of a
segment as a horizontal slice of a pyramid that represents the
whole population. Slices taken from near the base of the
pyramid will let you reach more people, but your program will
not be as "personalized" as if you took a slice from near the
top. The balancing act lies in choosing between segments that
are not very different from the population as a whole versus
being so specific that only a small number of people fall into
the segment.

Segments may be based on many factors[3] such as the
following:

- *Geographic:* size of city/county, residential density, climate
- *Demographic:* age, gender, income, occupation, education,
  number of children, race/ethnicity, immigrant generation,
  language, literacy
- *Physical/medical:* medical history, family history, health status,
  illnesses or disorders, risk factors
- *Psychographic:* lifestyle, personality characteristics, values,
  conceptions of social norms
- *Attitudinal:* attitudes, opinions, beliefs, judgments about product, benefits sought or barriers avoided, stage of behavior
  change
- *Behavioral:* product user status, frequency of behavior, occasion for use, other health-related activities, media habits

In social marketing, it often is more useful to go beyond simple demographics such as gender and race—although these also might be quite important—to attitudes and behaviors. People who smoke might be more similar to each other (for the purposes of a social marketing program) in their attitudes than in their demographics. A possible segmentation scheme for a program to encourage current smokers to quit might use the following factors as segmentation variables:

■ *Smoking status:* current smoker/not current smoker

■ *Desire to quit:* yes/ambivalent/no

■ *Ever tried to quit:* yes/no

■ *Self-efficacy about quitting:* high/medium/low

■ *Attitude about smoking's effects:* worried/fatalistic/invincible

■ *Age:* teenager/young adult/middle-aged adult/older adult

One possible segment for this program would be older adult smokers who want to quit, have tried to do so unsuccessfully and do not think they can do it and are worried about the effects of smoking. Another segment would be teenage smokers who are not certain about quitting, have not yet tried to quit, believe they have the ability to do so, and have a fatalistic attitude. Additional research also might reveal whether there are other important segmentation criteria such as reasons for smoking, barriers to quitting, and demographic characteristics.

In this example, there are hundreds of possible combinations of attributes for each segment. If the population you are addressing is fairly homogeneous to begin with, then extensive segmentation might not be necessary. But if you are dealing with a diverse population, or if your program has a national or state scope, segmentation can help make sense of the complexity.

TARGETING THE SEGMENTS

To determine the most important segmentation criteria, consider which are the most important factors that determine whether a target audience member adopts the relevant behavior. Think about the geographic, demographic, physical/medical, psychographic, attitudinal, and behavioral characteristics that might define subgroups of the target audience that would respond differently to your program.

Identify the targets of risk, that is, the segments that would be more likely to have the problem because of their behaviors, attitudes, or other factors. Targeting the people in these segments would have

---

**STAGES OF
BEHAVIOR CHANGE**
(continued)

In your research, you can assess which stage someone is in through the use of a question in the following format[b]:

Is a method that prevents pregnancy used every time you have intercourse?

a. No, and I do not intend to start using one every time within the next 6 months. *(Precontemplation)*

b. No, but I intend to start using one every time within the next 6 months. *(Contemplation)*

c. No, but I intend to start using one every time within the next 30 days. *(Preparation)*

d. Yes, I have been using one every time but for less than 6 months. *(Action)*

e. Yes, I have been using one every time for more than 6 months. *(Maintenance)*

a. James Prochaska and C. C. DiClemente, "Stages and Process of Self-Change of Smoking: Toward an Integrative Model of Change," *Journal of Consulting and Clinical Psychology* 51 (1983): 390-95.
b. Diane Grimley, Gabrielle Riley, Jeffrey Bellis, and James Prochaska, "Assessing the Stages of Change and Decision-Making for Contraceptive Use for the Prevention of Pregnancy, Sexually Transmitted Diseases, and Acquired Immunodeficiency Syndrome," *Health Education Quarterly* 20 (1993): 455-70.

the biggest payoff if they were to adopt the desired behavior. These might be groups that have the highest prevalence of the problem, that know the least about prevention, or whose members' lifestyles make it more likely that they will be affected by the problem.

In addition to thinking about risk factors, consider the targets of opportunity—that is, the segments that are easier to reach or change. It is only natural, especially in health and social programs, to want to change everyone at once or even to start with the hardest to reach groups first. But the advantage of targeting the people who are ready to change or are more easily reachable is that you will see results right away, and those people can then help you reach out to others. These segments might be at the preparation stage of behavior change, just needing your program to give them that extra nudge to take action. Or, they could be the people already using your services who have positive attitudes about making healthful changes in their lives.

Rank the segmentation criteria that you think are most important. If you target all of these factors, how many people will you actually be addressing in each segment? Is it a large enough number to make it worth your while? If not, consider going back up the list until the size of the segments justifies the allocation of resources. Although the targeting will be less specific, you should create only as many segments as you can handle efficiently. If you feel that your segments are too large but you do not have enough information to identify further criteria, then the next step is to conduct primary research with each segment to see whether it is fairly homogeneous or whether there are additional subgroups you can detect.

Allocating Resources

When you have determined the segmentation categories, you must decide how you will approach resource allocation within the program. Choose from among three basic strategies:

- Allocating equal amounts of resources to all segments
- Allocating different amounts of resources to each segment
- Allocating all resources to only one or a small number of key segments

Generally, programs of moderate size can realistically address from one to three segments. Those with less resources should focus on one segment at a time for best results.

Andreasen[4] offers a set of nine criteria to consider in creating segments and allocating resources. Approaches to each segment may differ because of the distinctive needs of some groups, differing responsiveness of segments, or the degree of efficiency in using separate strategies for each segment.

The nine factors are the following:

- *Segment size.* Are there enough people in a segment to comprise a useful market?

THE HEALTHSTYLES SEGMENTATION SYSTEM

Commercial marketers often use databases of information on consumers' buying habits, demographics, psychographics, and leisure activities to identify the most appropriate audience segments to target. One public relations firm, Porter/Novelli, combined such a database with additional data collected from the same respondents regarding their health-related beliefs, attitudes, and behaviors to create the American Healthstyles Audience Segmentation Project.[a]

Rather than just looking at an audience's lifestyles, the *Healthstyles* system provides insight into the psychological and social factors that affect the presence or absence of certain health behaviors. Porter/Novelli gathered information on five "indicator behaviors" that are more likely than others to reflect an audience's orientation to health: smoking, exercise, nutrition, weight control, and alcohol use. Analyses of the resulting database identified seven *Healthstyles* audience segments, which are briefly described here:

- *Decent Dolittles* (24% of the adult population). They are one of the less health-oriented groups. Although less likely to smoke or drink, they also are less likely to exercise, eat nutritiously, and work to stay at their ideal weights. Decent Dolittles know that they should be performing these behaviors to improve their health, but they do not feel that they have the ability. Their friends and family tend to avoid these behaviors as well. They describe themselves as "religious," "conservative," and "clean."

- *Active Attractives* (13%). They place a high emphasis on looking good and partying. Active Attractives are relatively youthful and moderately health oriented. They tend not to smoke and limit their fat intake more than do other groups. They are highly motivated, intending to exercise and keep their weight down, but they do not always succeed at this. Alcohol consumption is an important part of their lifestyle, and Active Attractives often are sensation seekers, constantly looking for adventure. They describe themselves as "romantic," "dynamic," "youthful," and "vain."

- *Hard-Living Hedonists* (6%). They are not very interested in health and tend to smoke and drink alcohol more heavily and frequently than do other groups. They also enjoy eating high-fat foods and do not care about limiting their fat intake. Despite this, they tend not to be overweight and are moderately physically active. Although they are the group least satisfied with their lives, they have no desire to make any health-related changes. Hard-Living Hedonists also are more likely to use stimulants and illicit drugs than are other segments. They describe themselves as "daring," "moody," "rugged," "independent," and "exciting."

- *Tense but Trying* (10%). They are similar to the more health-oriented segments except that they tend to smoke cigarettes. They are average in the amount of exercise they get and in their efforts to control their fat intake and weight. They have a moderate desire to exercise more, eat better, and control their weight more effectively as well. The Tense but Trying tend to be more anxious than other groups, with the highest rate of ulcers and use of sedatives and a higher number of visits to mental health counselors. They describe themselves as "tense," "high-strung," "sensitive," and "serious."

- *Noninterested Nihilists* (7%). They are the least health oriented and do not feel that people should take steps to improve their health. Accordingly, they smoke heavily, actively dislike exercise, eat high-fat diets, and make no effort to control their weight. Despite this, they tend to drink alcohol only moderately. Of all the groups, Noninterested Nihilists have the highest level of physical impairment, the most sick days in bed, and the most medical care visits related to an illness. They describe themselves as being "depressed," "moody," and "homebodies."

- *Physical Fantastics* (24%). They are the most health-oriented group, leading a consistently health-promoting lifestyle. They are above average in not smoking or drinking, exercising routinely, eating nutritiously, and making efforts to control their weight. They tend to be in their middle or latter adult years and have a relatively large number of chronic health conditions. Physical Fantastics follow their physicians' advice to modify their diets and routinely discuss health-related topics with others.

- *Passively Healthy* (15%). They are in excellent health, although they are somewhat indifferent to living healthfully. They do not smoke or drink heavily and are one of the most active segments. Although they eat a high amount of dietary fat, they are the trimmest of all the groups. The Passively Healthy do not place much value on good health and physical fitness and are not motivated to make any changes in their behaviors.

a. Edward Maibach, Andrew Maxfield, Kelly Ladin, and Michael Slater, "Translating Health Psychology into Effective Health Communication: The American Healthstyles Audience Segmentation Project," *Journal of Health Psychology* 1 (1996): 261-77.

- *Problem incidence.* Are there higher rates of the problem or risky behaviors in some segments?

- *Problem severity.* Are the consequences of the problem (e.g., deaths) more severe in some segments?

- *Defenselessness.* Are the members of the segment able to take care of the problem themselves, or do they need outside help?

- *Reachability.* Are some segments harder to reach because they are more difficult to find or require more costly methods?

- *General responsiveness.* Are some segments more ready, willing, and able to respond to the social marketing program than are others?

- *Incremental costs.* How much more will it cost in money and effort to reach additional segments? Is it worth it?

- *Responsiveness to marketing mix.* Will some segments respond differently to particular marketing mix elements and require different strategies?

- *Organizational capability.* Does your organization have the expertise to create and deliver differentiated strategies?

Segmenting Secondary Audiences

Once you have identified the likeliest primary target audience segments, consider whether there are any secondary target audiences that you might need to enlist as part of your social marketing program. Think about them in relation to the questions you have already asked yourself about the primary audience segments, for they should be segmented as well. Addressing them in addition to the primary target audience will involve extra costs—in research, development of a secondary marketing mix, and materials—but could be the best way in which to reach the primary audience.

Additional questions to ask yourself about secondary target audience segments include the following:

- What groups have the most influence over the behavior of the primary audience?

- How do they exert that influence?

- What benefits would the secondary audience receive from serving as a program intermediary?

- What might be the barriers to involving them in the program?

- What are the secondary audiences' own knowledge, attitudes, and behaviors related to the problem?

As with the primary target audience, the next step after identifying the likely segments within the secondary audience is to conduct your own research directly with the people in each key segment. This serves to refine the preliminary segmentation and to expand your knowledge about the people in these very specific groups.

RESEARCHING THE SEGMENTS

Now that you know exactly which segments you are targeting, build on the information you have already gathered from secondary research. To determine the best way in which to reach the people in each segment, go directly to the experts—members of the segments themselves. Words that come straight from the horse's mouth often are more useful in helping you to develop appropriate messages than are preprocessed secondary data. The key at this stage is to learn as much as possible about the world and worldview of each target audience segment.

The questions to ask through primary research are similar to those in the secondary research collection process, but with additional depth and detail. Your aim is to get a clear and complete picture of how best to reach each segment of your target audience. The research questions fall into the following generic categories, which you must customize for your program:

- Knowledge
  - Are the target audience members aware of the problem?
  - Do they know the key facts about the problem?
  - Do they have any misconceptions about the problem?
  - Do they know how to prevent or control the problem?
  - Where do they get their information about the problem?

- Attitudes and beliefs
  - Do target audience members believe they are at risk?
  - How important do they feel the problem is, compared to other issues they face in their lives?
  - What other issues are associated with the problem in their minds?
  - How do they feel about the behavior you will ask them to perform?
  - What are the benefits and barriers they see to performing the behavior?
  - Do they think that they can perform the new behavior?
  - Do they think that the people in their social network will provide positive support for the behavior? What are the perceived social norms related to the behavior?
  - Who or what has the most influence on the attitudes and beliefs of the target audience? Who do they look up to?

- Behaviors
  - What are the current behaviors of the target audience related to the problem?
  - At what stage of behavior change are they (precontemplation, contemplation, preparation, action, or maintenance)?
  - Have they tried the new behavior? If so, why have they not adopted it?
  - In what circumstances do they perform the behavior currently?
  - What would make it easier to perform the new behavior?
  - Do they need new skills to help them perform the behavior?

- Communication channels
  - Which media channels does the target audience pay the most attention to (e.g., television, radio, newspaper)?

- Which types of vehicles in each channel are preferred by the target audience (e.g., television shows, radio stations, newspaper sections)?
- At what times and places does the target audience view or listen to these media?
- What does the target audience do in its leisure time?
- What organizations do the target audience members belong to?
- What words do they use when talking about the problem?
- Who do they see as a credible spokesperson about the problem?

Social marketers use a variety of research techniques to gather this information and learn more how each target audience segment thinks about and deals with the problem. Ideally, both qualitative and quantitative methods should be used together for a more complete picture. These research techniques include the following:

Qualitative Methods

■ *Focus groups* bring together small groups of individuals with similar characteristics for a focused discussion about a particular topic. A moderator leads the discussion and probes how people think and their reasons for doing things. By conducting several focus groups with each segment, you might be able to identify the most effective messages or approaches to use. Step-by-step guidance in how to conduct focus groups yourself is provided in Chapter 13, which deals with how to pretest materials.

■ *In-depth interviews* with one person at a time let you explore more sensitive issues that people might be uncomfortable speaking about in front of a group. The objective and types of questions are the same as in focus groups, but the intimate nature of this method leads to more detail than you might get in a group setting. Analysis of the interviews looks at both individual responses and the aggregation of all the interview data.

■ *Case studies (ethnography)* focus on one person's or one organization's experience and the context in which it occurs. This is a way of gaining an in-depth understanding of the situation and its meaning for those involved while highlighting important lessons for program development.

■ *Observational studies* involve watching members of the target audience engage in an activity relevant to the program to determine whether they perform the desired behavior correctly or at all. They might know that they are being observed if asked to demonstrate how they do something, or they might not be aware if the researcher watches unobtrusively. Observations must be planned and recorded systematically, with a specific purpose.

Quantitative Methods

■ *Knowledge, attitudes, and behaviors (KAB) surveys* tell you how many people in the population are thinking or doing something. Although this can be an expensive and time-consuming undertaking, this type of survey can be very useful for identifying and understanding the audience's demographics, psychographics, and behaviors. A KAB survey conducted in the planning stage is most effective as baseline data, particularly if the same survey is repeated once the campaign has been implemented (see Appendix B for a sample KAB survey).

- *Intercept surveys* find their respondents by going to locations frequented by the target audience such as shopping malls and supermarkets. Interviewers systematically screen passersby to find target audience members who are willing to respond to an interview. Questionnaires typically are short and closed-ended to encourage participation, although they can include open-ended questions. Intercept surveys also are commonly used to pretest program materials.

- *Marketing databases* typically are compiled by commercial firms and provide information about a target audience's lifestyle, psychographics, media habits, and consumer spending activities. This information can be expensive, however, and might not include data for lower income populations.

If you do not have access to the expertise needed for more formal research methods, then informal information gathering also can provide helpful insights. Go out and find members of your target audience. Talk to them, but more important, listen to them. You can bring people together over pizza to talk about their thoughts regarding the problem, what would motivate them to change their behavior, and what their lives are like. Go to the laundromat and talk to people while they wait for their clothes, survey students on a college campus between classes, or chat with a group of teenagers hanging out at the local mall. If you do nothing else, at least invest some time in speaking directly with target audience members.

Even if you have very little money for research, there are low- to no-cost ways of gathering valid research data about your target audience:

- Public health or marketing students at a local university could do the research as a class project or an internship.

- An advertising or public relations firm might be willing to provide research or other services on a *pro bono* (free) basis or at a greatly reduced price if it is convinced of the value of the project.

- You might be able to "piggyback" on research that your partners or other organizations are conducting by adding some questions or expanding the research population.

- Receive training and then train your staff or volunteers to moderate focus groups or conduct interviews so that you will not need to hire an outside firm.

- Recruit research participants from your organization's current clients or those of a partner organization. You can get a "snowball sample" by having those people provide names of other friends and acquaintances who meet the target audience criteria.

- Observational studies often provide useful information without requiring more than the cost of staff or volunteer time. If, for example, you want to know whether people compare food nutrition labels, observe people as they shop at the supermarket and take notes on what you see.

SOURCES OF MARKET SEGMENTATION DATA

Claritas Inc.
1525 Wilson Boulevard, Suite 1000
Arlington, VA 22209
(800) 284-4868
info@claritas.com
http://www.claritas.com

The PRIZM lifestyle segmentation system provides detailed data combining demographics with product, media, and lifestyle preference information, sorted by zip code. Claritas also offers specialized information on seniors 55 to 85 years of age or older and a combination of health care databases from Medicaid, hospital patient discharge records, individual physician records, and national hospital disease databases.

Mediamark Research Inc. (MRI)
708 Third Ave., 8th Floor
New York, NY 10017
(212) 599-0444 or (800) 310-3305
info@mediamark.com
http://www.mediamark.com

MRI offers comprehensive demographic, lifestyle, product use, and media data collected annually from more than 20,000 consumers throughout the continental United States. Special reports focus on teenagers, affluent Americans, and local data for 10 major media markets.

Porter/Novelli
1120 Connecticut Avenue, NW
Washington, DC 20036
(202) 973-5800
emaibach@porternovelli.com
http://www.porternovelli.com

The Healthstyles audience database includes information on health practices and attitudes for American adults combined with more general lifestyle information such as media use, attitudes, self-perceptions, activities, and shopping patterns.

Simmons Market Research Bureau Inc. (SMRB)
309 West 49th Street
New York, NY 10019
(212) 373-8900
simmonsres@aol.com

SMRB's Study of Media and Markets measures the product, service, and media use of 20,000 Americans and is released semiannually. SMRB also offers a similar study focused on the Hispanic community. Other products include the STARS Simmons TeenAge Research Study (ages 12-19 years), the Kids Study (ages 6-14 years), and the Gay and Lesbian Market Study.

SRI International
333 Ravenswood Avenue
Menlo Park, CA 94025
(650) 859-4771
vals@sri.com
http://future.sri.com/vals/valshome.html

VALS (Values and Lifestyles) categorizes U.S. adult consumers into distinct groups based on their psychology and key demographics. Using factors such as self-orientation and resources, VALS defines eight consumer segments by their attitudes, behavior, and decision-making patterns.

(continued)

SOURCES OF MARKET SEGMENTATION DATA
(continued)

Standard Rate and Data Service (SRDS)
1700 Higgins Road
Des Plaines, IL 60018
(800) 851-7737
http://www.srds.com

The *Lifestyle Market Analyst* is an annual 1,200-page publication providing consumer information at the local, regional, and national levels for more than 200 markets in the United States. It includes data on lifestyle interests and hobbies, consumer habits, and demographics. You can match the lifestyle profiles with the corresponding media information offered in SRDS's other publications such as *Consumer Magazine Advertising Source* and *Direct Marketing List Source.*

For other syndicated sources of secondary data, check your public library or the nearest business school library for *FINDEX: The Worldwide Directory of Market Research Reports, Studies, and Surveys* (Cambridge Scientific Abstracts, [301] 961-6700, findex@csa.com), which is a guide to published, commercially available market and business research.

Collecting useful information might take some resourcefulness and creativity, but the end product will be invaluable in helping you as you design the social marketing program.

The data you gather at this stage of the process can serve as a baseline from which to identify any changes occurring as a result of your program. Start thinking about your evaluation now so that you can build into your research the types of methods and questions that will identify meaningful transformations that took place in the target audience. For example, you might wish to conduct a KAB survey during the planning phase, both to provide information for formative research and to compare to the results of a postcampaign survey for evaluation purposes later. Section VI can help you put an evaluation plan in place from the beginning.

WORKSHEET 4: Segmentation Worksheet

Using the secondary research you have gathered, answer the following questions as best you can:

1. **What geographic characteristics define separate segments within your population?**

   _____

   _____

   _____

2. **What demographic characteristics that are most relevant to the problem define separate segments within your population?**

   _____

   _____

   _____

3. **What physical or medical characteristics define separate segments within your population?**

   _____

   _____

   _____

4. **What psychographic characteristics, such as lifestyle, personality, values, and social norms, define separate segments within your population?**

   _____

   _____

   _____

5. **What behaviors put people most at risk of the problem?**

   (a) _____

   (b) _____

   (c) _____

6. **What behaviors help to reduce the risk or prevent the problem from occurring?**

   (a) _____

   (b) _____

   (c) _____

7. **How can you best segment the target audience on the basis of the key behaviors listed in Item 5 and/or Item 6 above (e.g., users/nonusers, frequency of use, reason for use)?**

   (5a) _____

   (5b) _____

   (5c) _____

   (6a) _____

   (6b) _____

   (6c) _____

(continued)

WORKSHEET 4: Segmentation Worksheet *(continued)*

8. **What attitudes or beliefs related to the problem or relevant behaviors listed above define separate segments within your population?**

   _____

   _____

   _____

9. **Are there any segments you definitely will not target in your program because, for example, it is not feasible or there are already programs in place addressing those groups?**

   _____

   _____

   _____

10. **Look over the possible segmentation criteria you have noted above and write down the five that you think are most important, in order:**

    (1) _____

    (2) _____

    (3) _____

    (4) _____

    (5) _____

11. **Using the segmentation criteria in Item 10, define the characteristics of the segment most at risk of having the problem you are addressing in your program (targets of risk):**

    (1) _____

    (2) _____

    (3) _____

    (4) _____

    (5) _____

12. **Using the segmentation criteria in Item 10, define the characteristics of the segment most easily reachable or changeable through your program (targets of opportunity):**

    (1) _____

    (2) _____

    (3) _____

    (4) _____

    (5) _____

13. **How will you allocate resources to the segments you will address through your program?**

    ☐ Allocate equal resources to all segments

    ☐ Allocate different amounts of resources to each segment

    ☐ Allocate all resources to only ___ (number) segment(s)

(continued)

WORSHEET 4: Segmentation Worksheet *(continued)*

14. **Are there any secondary audiences who influence the target audience that you should consider addressing in your program? Identify the most important segments:**

_____

_____

_____

15. **List the final segments you have chosen to target in your program:**

_____

_____

_____

WORKSHEET 5: Audience Research Worksheet

1. What methods will you use to research your key target audience segments?

Qualitative Methods

☐ Focus groups
☐ In-depth interviews

☐ Observational studies

☐ Informal information gathering

☐ Other _____

Quantitative Methods

☐ Knowledge, attitudes, and behaviors survey

☐ Intercept survey

☐ Marketing databases

☐ Other data sources

☐ Other _____

2. Do you or your staff members have the necessary skills to conduct and analyze the research methods you have chosen?

☐ Yes. We have the expertise on staff.

☐ Possibly. We need some additional training.

☐ No. We need to hire outside assistance.

If more training or outside assistance is needed:

a. What is your available budget? $_____

b. What type(s) of research or training do you need assistance with?

_____

_____

_____

c. From which companies or consultants will you solicit bids?

_____

_____

_____

If research will be done in-house:

3. What is your available budget? $_____

4. Who will be responsible for coordinating the research activities?

_____

(continued)

WORKSHEET 5: Audience Research Worksheet *(continued)*

5. Who will assist in the research activities?

Name   *Role*

_____   _____

_____   _____

_____   _____

_____   _____

6. Where will you find target audience members to participate in your research?

_____

_____

_____

7. How will you contact potential research participants?

☐ In person

☐ Telephone

☐ Mail

☐ E-mail

☐ Advertisements

☐ Third party: _____

☐ Other _____

8. Research timeline:

Activity	Date to Be Completed
Put research team in place	_____
Design research plan	_____
Develop questionnaires or other research instruments	_____
Test and finalize research instruments	_____
Train people who will be conducting the research	_____
Recruit research participants	_____
Conduct research	_____
Input or organize data	_____
Analyze data	_____
Create final report	_____

STRATEGY DEVELOPMENT

Based on the results of the research you have conducted, you can start to build a program strategy. This strategy might need to be modified as you do more research, but it will serve as a reference point throughout the program development process. In the strategy, you will set goals and measurable objectives, consider the elements of the marketing mix as they relate to your program, and create a workplan for program development.

SETTING GOALS AND OBJECTIVES

With the data you have gathered about the problem and the target audience, you can now set reasonable goals and objectives for the social marketing program. Having measurable objectives from the outset is a way in which to assess the success of the program. Without having a destination in sight, you might steer in the wrong direction, never knowing you have lost your way. You must be careful, however, to be realistic when setting goals. It is not very likely that you will reduce heart disease by 30% after a six-month campaign, but maybe you can increase by 30% the number of people who are aware that eating high-cholesterol foods is related to heart attack risk.

The *goal* of the program refers to the overall change in the health or social problem your program will strive to reach, for example, "to decrease the incidence rate of HIV infection in the target population by 10%" or "to increase the number of people in the target audience who exercise three or more times per week by 25%." A program may have a single goal or several distinct goals.

Objectives describe the intermediate steps that must be taken to reach each goal. They are not the strategies you will use but rather the desired outcomes of the program that will lead to attainment of the goal. The objectives may relate to changes in knowledge, attitudes, skills, or behaviors of the primary

> **SAMPLE GOALS AND OBJECTIVES**
>
> Some examples of goals and objectives for a traffic safety program might be as follows:
>
> Goal 1: To decrease by 10% the number of traffic deaths of drivers from 16 to 24 years of age by the end of a two-year period
>
>   Objective 1: To increase by 20% the number of drivers from 16 to 24 years of age who report using seat belts every time they drive
>
>   Objective 2: To increase by 50% the number of drivers from 16 to 24 years of age who believe that seat belts are safe and effective in preventing traffic injuries
>
>   Objective 3: To increase by 50% the number of drivers from 16 to 24 years of age who are aware that a seat belt must be worn, even if an air bag is present in the car
>
> Goal 2: To decrease by 20% the number of traffic deaths of children 4 years of age or under by the end of a two-year period
>
>   Objective 1: To increase by 30% the number of children 4 years of age or under who are observed buckled into child safety seats when dropped off at community day care sites
>
>   Objective 2: To increase by 100% the number of participating vendors in the community offering discounts on child safety seats to low-income parents
>
>   Objective 3: To distribute 5,000 traffic safety coloring books and parents' safety tips to children in local preschools and nursery schools by the end of September

or secondary target audiences; changes in the environment; or project milestones (e.g., attaining a certain number of project partners).

Effective objectives are clear and specific, stating *who* will do or change *what* by *when* and by *how much*. They must be measurable, for how else will you know if you have accomplished your objectives? They also should be reasonable, considering how much change you can realistically expect to achieve as compared to the baseline data. There is nothing worse for morale than to come up short against unrealistic objectives, particularly when you do achieve a relatively high degree of change. Check the research literature or ask others about their experience for indications of how much change you can reasonably expect. If you cannot find that type of information, you also can decide to measure your success by comparing baseline data to the evaluation data to detect statistically significant differences related to your objectives rather than designating an arbitrary percentage.

PRELIMINARY SOCIAL MARKETING MIX

As discussed in Chapter 3, the social marketing mix helps you to think through a comprehensive strategy for your program. Brainstorming about each element of the marketing mix based on what you found in your research will prepare you for the next stage of the social marketing process—message and materials development.

Consider each "P" of the social marketing mix in relation to your target audience segments (if you are targeting more than one segment, then you may have a different mix for each). Remember that the marketing mix may change as you have additional brilliant flashes of insight or learn through pretesting that the target audience is less than enthusiastic about your initial approach. Think of the resulting strategy as a living document that provides guidance but can be changed in response to new information:

- Product
  - What is the behavior you are asking the target audience to do?
  - What are the benefits it would receive from adopting the behavior?
  - What is the "competition," and why would the target audience prefer it to the behavior you are "selling"?

- Price
  - What are the costs the target audience associates with the product?
  - What are other barriers that prevent the target audience from adopting the product?
  - How can you minimize the costs or remove the barriers?

- Place
  - What are the places where the target audience makes decisions about engaging in the desired behavior?
  - Where do target audience members spend much of their time?
  - To which social or recreational groups do target audience members belong?
  - What distribution systems will be most efficient for reaching target audience members?

- Promotion
  - Which communication channels do target audience members pay the most attention to and trust the most?
  - How can you best package the message to reach the most target audience members effectively and efficiently?
  - Who is the most credible and engaging spokesperson on this issue for the target audience?

- Publics
  - Who are the people outside your organization you need to address to be successful?
  - Who are the people inside your organization whose support you need to be successful?

- Partnership
  - Are there other organizations addressing a similar problem that you could team up with?
  - Are there other organizations that could bring needed resources or skills to the project as partners?
  - Are there any organizations that would be politically advantageous for you to ally yourself with?

- Policy
  - Are there any policies that would create an environment more conducive to the desired behavior?
  - Is there any pending legislation that would affect your program's goals, either positively or negatively?
  - Are policymakers knowledgeable about or interested in the problem you are addressing?

- Purse strings
  - Is the funding that you currently have for this project enough to tackle all of your objectives?
  - Are there additional sources that you can apply to for funding, if necessary?
  - Are there potential corporate partners that might participate in the project in exchange for positive publicity?

"DON'T KID YOURSELF" CAMPAIGN: PLANNING

Initial Planning

In the "Don't Kid Yourself" campaign to prevent unintended pregnancies, the contract specified a six-month development and pilot-testing phase before extending the campaign to the entire region, so there was no time to waste. The project began with a meeting of the steering committee, the contractor, and the subcontractor to refine goals and objectives as well as to define key parameters of the project. The committee specified the target audience as women from 18 to 24 years of age with household incomes of less than 200% of the poverty level. This group was chosen for several reasons. First, the Title X program is intended to benefit lower income women. Second, the 18- to 24-year age group is at the highest risk of experiencing unintended pregnancies and does so in the greatest numbers. Third, the committee felt that there were already many programs addressing adolescent pregnancy but that young adults had been underserved on this issue.

The committee selected two pilot sites for the purpose of developing and testing the campaign. After a process of elimination, Salt Lake City, Utah, and Butte, Montana, were chosen as being representative of the larger and smaller cities in the region. They also were relatively easy to access for travel purposes and had family planning clinics that were eager to participate in the campaign development.

Analysis

For the problem analysis, the contractors first conducted a literature review to learn more about the causes of unintended pregnancies and previous approaches used to address the issue. They also gained some valuable insights by interviewing professionals at a number of organizations that had addressed this issue through the mass media. In both cases, they did not find much information related to their target audience; most of the other programs had focused on teenagers or women in urban populations.

The environmental analysis revealed that people in this region tended to be politically conservative and that certain religious groups predominated in the two cities chosen as pilot sites: Mormons in Salt Lake City and Catholics in Butte. Many of the school systems in the region do not teach about contraception or pregnancy prevention as part of the sex education curriculum. In many of the smaller cities and less populated areas, the Title X-funded family planning clinics are the only organizations addressing the issue of unintended pregnancies in their communities. In addition, the two biggest cities in the region, Salt Lake City and Denver, Colorado, have relatively larger numbers of minority residents than do most of the other cities, which comprise very small minority populations.

In analyzing the resources available to the project, the contractors determined to do what they could to minimize the costs of research and development. This included using existing resources, such as staff and facilities, whenever possible and enlisting volunteers to assist with various tasks. The focus also would be on using less expensive media options and maximizing the gain from every dollar spent.

Segmenting and Researching the Target Audience

Beyond the characteristics specified at the project kickoff meeting, the contractors decided to narrow the target audience further. The additional segmentation criteria included whether the individual was sexually active and, if so, whether an effective contraceptive method was used every time she had sex. The project would focus its resources on one very specific segment of the population, defined as follows:

- Women
- 18 to 24 years of age
- Household income of less than 200% of poverty level
- Sexually active
- Do not use contraception every time they have sex

(continued)

"DON'T KID YOURSELF" CAMPAIGN: PLANNING *(continued)*

To research this target audience, the contractors conducted focus groups in Salt Lake City and Butte with three different categories of women: those who used contraception consistently, those who did not use contraception consistently, and those who had experienced unintended pregnancies. The focus groups were designed to elucidate the target audience's decision-making process related to contraceptive use and its thinking about unintended pregnancies. The project recruited participants directly from the family planning clinics, through flyers on college campuses and in county social service offices, and through advertisements in local and campus newspapers. In Butte, the family planning clinic recruited students from the local alternative high school, which served many women who had already had unintended pregnancies or were at risk of doing so.

The key findings from the focus groups were as follows:

- Target audience members experience ambivalence about birth control. They know that it is the smart thing to do, but they have many excuses for their failure to use it.
- Many of the women engage in irrational thinking such as "It can't happen to me" and "We'll be okay just this once."
- Target audience members do not learn much about how to prevent pregnancies in school or from their parents. They need basic facts about contraception and a place where they can receive nonjudgmental information.
- Women who had babies as a result of unintended pregnancies said that if they had known how difficult it would be to raise a baby and everything they would have to give up, they would have been more careful about using birth control.
- The support of male partners and their cooperation in using condoms is needed. Target audience members need help in talking about this issue with their partners.

Strategy

In addition to the primary target audience, the contractors decided to address a secondary audience as well: male sexual partners from 18 to 24 years of age. The key behavioral objectives developed to support the goal of reducing the number of unintended pregnancies throughout the region included that after the campaign's completion, (1) target audience members will use an effective form of contraception every time they have sex, (2) target audience members will seek information on their birth control options, (3) target audience members will initiate discussions with their sexual partners regarding the use of birth control, and (4) male partners will use condoms every time they have sex. Attainment of the objectives were to be assessed through the detection of statistically significant increases in responses between surveys administered before and after the campaign.

Because the research showed that friends were the group most often consulted about sexual issues, peers would model the desired behaviors and help establish social norms. The strategy also included getting target audience members to think about what it would mean for them to become parents at this point in their lives. The campaign would provide basic information about birth control options and where to go for more assistance. Other secondary messages included the notions that men should be responsible and informed about contraception and that these issues should be discussed with the women's sexual partners.

CREATING A WORKPLAN

By now, you should have a good idea of the task you have before you. The final step in the planning stage is to create a workplan for program development, implementation, and evaluation. *If you have not created a workplan already, then read the rest of this book before proceeding so that you know what to include in the workplan.*

The workplan should be as detailed as you can make it, including the following for each objective:

- Tasks and subtasks
- Person responsible
- Deadline
- Resources needed

You also can identify the estimated costs for each task, potential roadblocks, and the evaluation criteria for each objective.

The workplan should help to keep the project on schedule by making sure that all staff know their roles and how they relate to the tasks others are performing. Deadlines can provide the motivation to complete each task on time. As with all things in life, however, whatever can go wrong will go wrong, so make sure to budget additional time and funds to accommodate Murphy's law. You might need to be somewhat flexible and readjust the schedule as the situation requires. The workplan also can serve as a way of tracking progress as you move through the program development process.

SECTION II NOTES

1. Alan Andreasen, *Cheap but Good Marketing Research* (Homewood, IL: Business One Irwin, 1988).

2. Gary Stern, *Marketing Workbook for Nonprofit Organizations* (St. Paul, MN: Amherst H. Wilder Foundation, 1994).

3. Adapted from Table 1 in Terrance Albrecht and Carol Bryant, "Advances in Segmentation Modeling for Health Communication and Social Marketing Campaigns," *Journal of Health Communication* 1 (1996): 65-80.

4. Alan Andreasen, *Marketing Social Change* (San Francisco: Jossey-Bass, 1995).

WORKSHEET 6:
Preliminary Social Marketing Strategy Worksheet

Target Audience

1. **What are the primary target audience segments you have chosen?**

   _____

   _____

   _____

   _____

2. **What are the secondary target audience segments you have chosen (if applicable)?**

   _____

   _____

Goals and Objectives

3. **What is the overall goal of your program?**

   _____

   _____

4. **What are the key objectives of your program? Add as many as necessary on a separate sheet of paper.**

   a. _____
   _____ *Who?*

   will _____
   _____ *What?*

   by _____ by _____
   When?   *How much?*

   b. _____
   _____ *Who?*

   will _____
   _____ *What?*

   by _____ by _____
   When?   *How much?*

   c. _____
   _____ *Who?*

   will _____
   _____ *What?*

   by _____ by _____
   When?   *How much?*

(continued)

WORKSHEET 6:
Preliminary Social Marketing Strategy Worksheet *(continued)*

Social Marketing Mix

5. Product

   a. What is the product or behavior you are asking the target audience to adopt?

_____

_____

_____

   b. What are the key benefits the target audience would receive from adopting the product?

_____

_____

_____

   c. What is the competition for your product in the target audience's eyes?

_____

_____

_____

   d. How is your product different from and better than the competition?

_____

_____

_____

6. Price

   a. What are the costs or other barriers that the target audience associates with the product?

_____

_____

_____

   b. How can you minimize the costs or remove the barriers?

_____

_____

_____

(continued)

WORKSHEET 6:
Preliminary Social Marketing Strategy Worksheet *(continued)*

7. Place

a. What are the places in which the target audience makes decisions about engaging in the desired behavior?

_____

_____

_____

b. Where do target audience members spend much of their time?

_____

_____

_____

c. What distribution systems will be most efficient for reaching target audience members?

_____

_____

_____

8. Promotion

a. Which communication channels do target audience members pay the most attention to and trust the most?

_____

_____

_____

b. What promotional techniques are the best for conveying your message?

_____

_____

_____

c. Who are the most credible spokespeople to address your target audience?

_____

_____

_____

(continued)

WORKSHEET 6:
Preliminary Social Marketing Strategy Worksheet *(continued)*

9. Publics

a. Who are the people or groups (in addition to your primary and secondary target audiences) outside your organization that you need to address for your program to be successful?

_____

_____

_____

b. Who are the people or groups inside your organization whose support you need for your program to be successful?

_____

_____

_____

10. Partnership

Which are the most promising organizations to join forces with for the social marketing program?

_____

_____

_____

11. Policy

What types of policies (organizational or governmental) should you address in your social marketing program?

_____

_____

_____

12. Purse strings

From which organizations will you seek further funding, if necessary?

_____

_____

_____

13. Now go back through each element of the social marketing mix and put an asterisk by the most promising ideas to use for developing messages and materials.

(continued)

Workplan

Task	Subtasks	Person Responsible	Deadline	Resources Needed	Evaluation Criteria
1.	1.				
	2.				
	3.				
	4.				
2.	1.				
	2.				
	3.				
	4.				
3.	1.				
	2.				
	3.				
	4.				
4.	1.				
	2.				
	3.				
	4.				

WORKSHEET 6:
Preliminary Social Marketing Strategy Worksheet (continued)

Workplan

Task	Subtasks	Person Responsible	Deadline	Resources Needed	Evaluation Criteria
5.	1.				
	2.				
	3.				
	4.				
6.	1.				
	2.				
	3.				
	4.				
7.	1.				
	2.				
	3.				
	4.				
8.	1.				
	2.				
	3.				
	4.				

STEP 2: MESSAGE AND MATERIALS DEVELOPMENT

Section Overview

In Step 1, you put in a lot of hard work. Now comes the fun part. Step 2 focuses on developing communications—the social marketing messages as well as the materials to convey them. You will combine the results of your previous research with some creativity to design a campaign that motivates your target audience to adopt your product. This section leads you through the process of identifying appropriate channels, developing effective messages, and transforming those messages into draft materials. The section consists of the following chapters:

■ Chapter 9: Identifying Appropriate Channels
■ Chapter 10: Developing Effective Messages
■ Chapter 11: Producing Creative Executions

IDENTIFYING
APPROPRIATE CHANNELS

"Channel" in social marketing does not mean the television station on which you air your commercials. The term refers to the medium that delivers your program's messages. This involves the marketing mix ideas of "place" and "promotion." Which methods will you use to get the message out or distribute the product to the target audience? Before thinking more specifically about which radio stations to use or how many colors your poster will be, consider whether those are really the most appropriate methods for your audience and message. For example, an Internet Web site is a great way in which to disseminate information to a computer-savvy audience but not for people without access to computers or for those who still have not figured out how to program their VCRs.

CHANNEL CRITERIA

There are a nearly unlimited number of channels that you can use. The key is to carefully select the most effective and efficient methods of reaching each target audience segment. *Effective* means that the way in which you convey the message attracts attention and inspires behavior change. *Efficient* means that you reach the most target audience members per dollar expended. If you are trying to reach a very small audience segment such as parents of fifth graders in a particular school district, then using television might be overkill; the message will reach many people, but the efficiency of the medium is low relative to the number of target audience members. A more efficient channel might be sending information home through the students themselves, having teachers or school administrators contact parents directly by phone, or using direct mail.

To identify the best channels to use, find out where target audience members spend their time and get their information. They will not go out of their way to find your message; you must go to them. Through the research you conduct with the target audience, you will learn which channels it pays attention to and trusts. Among different segments, you might find that certain channels are more popular or credible. Remember that there is no one right answer, but there will be better and worse choices based on your target audience and program budget.

Some channels that are commonly used in social marketing include the following:

- Mass media (e.g., television, radio, newspapers, magazines)
- Outdoor advertising (e.g., billboards, transit ads)
- Brochures, posters, and newsletters
- Comic books or fotonovellas (i.e., comic books using photos instead of drawings)
- Direct mail
- Interpersonal communications (e.g., doctors, peer counselors, telephone hotlines)
- Music videos and songs
- Dramatic presentations
- Community events
- Workplace events
- Point-of-purchase materials
- Yellow pages
- Internet

Each type of channel may serve a different role in the campaign. For example, a poster or radio ad is a good way in which to raise awareness about an issue, and a brochure can provide more in-depth information, but it might take a conversation with a clinician to finally motivate someone to act. Combining a number of approaches also helps you appeal to people who absorb information in different ways—by seeing it, by hearing it, by experiencing it, or by discussing it with others. Each channel has its own strengths and weaknesses, and the trick is to use several methods that complement each other. The more times someone is exposed to a message in different ways, the more likely it will stick.

OUTLETS

Once you have identified the channels that are most appropriate for the target audience, the next step is to think about the particular outlets you might use. Outlets are the specific television or radio stations, newspapers,

COMPARING CHANNELS

Channel	Pros	Cons
Television	• Can reach many people at the same time • Can have ads aired free as PSAs • Repetition of messages • Can provide follow-up through toll-free number • Visual medium provides more impact and the ability to demonstrate a behavior • Can reach specialized audience through cable stations or particular programs	• Expensive to produce and buy time • If a PSA, cannot control when it is run • Short format does not allow for more than awareness • Message can be obscured by commercial clutter • Target audience might not be watching when commercial is aired
Radio (most of the pros and cons listed under television apply to radio as well)	• Can narrowly target specific audiences • Often playing while people are engaging in other activities • Less expensive to produce and buy time than television	• Smaller audiences reached than with television • Does not work as well as television to demonstrate an activity
Print media (e.g., newspapers, magazines)	• Can provide more detailed information than broadcast, but still limited • Can tailor messages for specific audiences for different publications • Goes beyond building awareness by providing detailed information • Good for reaching more educated audiences • Audience can clip, reread, and think about the material • Might provide more credibility	• PSAs often not accepted • Not good for less literate audiences • Small ads might get lost
Print materials (e.g., brochures, fact sheets, newsletters)	• Can convey in-depth information, especially about complex issues • Often low cost (with unit prices decreasing with quantity) • Good to use as follow-up to requests for more information (resulting from other promotions) • Not competing with ads for audience attention • Good for how-to information, answering frequently asked questions	• Audience must have the interest and will to pick it up and read it • Not good for less literate audiences

NOTE: PSA = public service announcement.

(continued)

COMPARING CHANNELS *(continued)*

Channel	Pros	Cons
Posters and flyers	• Good for generating awareness • Can be placed in high-visibility/high-traffic areas • Can be put in places where decisions whether or not to perform the behavior are made • If attractive and eye-catching, people will want to put them up in their homes or offices	• Posters can be expensive to produce (relative to other print media) • Cannot provide detailed information • May need to be reposted often
Direct mail	• Can get mailing lists of very specific types of people • Allows you to contact target audience directly, personalize the message • Relatively low cost • Can easily test how effective your promotion was • Can send out catalog of other informational materials • Can send promotional items with your message that people will keep and continue to use (e.g., calendar, key chain)	• If mailing list is old or inappropriate, then it might not be successful • Envelope must stand out and say "open me," otherwise may be tossed
Outdoor media (e.g., billboards, transit ads)	• Great for reaching commuters • Very noticeable, not competing with other ads • Repetition • Relatively inexpensive way in which to reach many people	• Cannot provide very much information • Message must be understood within seconds
Interpersonal communications/ informal networks	• One-on-one communication can be very effective, especially if the person is seen as credible to the target audience member • Questions can be answered immediately • Message can be personalized to address particular benefits and barriers important to that person	• Not very efficient for mass audiences • Person might be mistrustful, wonder what the communicator has to gain from this • People with the most potential influence might not have time or interest to be involved

(continued)

COMPARING CHANNELS *(continued)*

Channel	Pros	Cons
Professional or organizational channels	• Trade associations are a good way in which to reach professionals with a credible message (e.g., mailings, ads in their magazines, conferences) • Affiliation provides a connection that makes target audience more likely to pay attention to message • Conference sessions can persuade and provide information in a memorable way • Materials can be distributed efficiently • Receiving endorsements from heads of key organizations can do a lot to advance the message	• There is not always an appropriate organization to work with, or one might not be willing to participate • Not all members of target audience may be affiliated with an organization
Internet/e-mail	• Beyond initial investment, very inexpensive to send e-mail messages or provide information through a Web site • Instantaneous method of delivery, good for time-sensitive issues • Messages may be sent and forwarded many times from colleague to colleague • Can send messages through listservs to reach many people with similar interest or profession at once	• Not everyone is Internet accessible • Might be difficult to compile an e-mail list of target audience members • People may automatically delete messages from addresses they do not recognize
Point-of-purchase materials (signs, displays, "take one" materials, or live demonstrations where the product is being promoted or sold)	• Catch people with your message when they are thinking about the product or a related topic • Convenient for target audience • Presence of your materials provides tacit endorsement of your message by the store	• Might be difficult to convince businesses to participate • Must regularly refill or restock materials
Yellow pages	• Your message will be there when someone is looking for a particular service (e.g., weight loss, family planning) • Ad is there for an entire year • You can reach people looking for your product's "competition" (e.g., putting reminders about picking a designated driver by the section listing bars and clubs)	• Relevant category might not exist • Might be somewhat expensive

**SOURCES OF DATA ON
AUDIENCE MEDIA HABITS**

The Arbitron Company
142 West 57th St.
New York, NY 10019
(212) 887-1300
http://www.arbitron.com
Provides market data on radio, network television, and cable television audiences

Nielsen Media Research
299 Park Ave.
New York, NY 10017
(212) 708-7500
info@nielsenmedia.com
http://www.nielsenmedia.com
Offers data on audience size and
composition for television programs

Mediamark Research Inc.
708 Third Ave., 8th Floor
New York, NY 10017
(212) 599-0444 or (800) 310-3305
info@mediamark.com
http://www.mediamark.com
Includes media use data on print
publications, radio, television, cable, pay-per-view, online services,
yellow pages, and other categories

Scarborough Research
11 West 42nd St.
New York, NY 10036
(212) 789-3560
info@scarborough.com
http://www.scarborough.com
Provides detailed audience data
on media including broadcast and
cable television, radio, newspaper,
online, city/regional magazines,
outdoor advertising, yellow pages,
and direct mail

(continued)

magazines, and other alternatives within each channel that will promote your message.

Although at this point you do not yet need to specify which media outlets you will use, you can start gathering information for when you reach the implementation phase. The most efficient method is to ask members of your target audience which radio stations they listen to and when, which sections of the newspaper they read, or which streets are best for billboards. You can ask these questions in your initial research or during pretesting in Step 3.

In addition to the target audience input, you can get information directly from the media outlets themselves. Your local public or university library's reference desk should have books listing media outlets of every type in your community or nationally (try *Gebbie's All-in-One, Bacon's Publicity Checker,* or the *Gale Directory of Publications and Broadcast Media*). Contact the outlets that look like good candidates for your target audience and have them send you media kits. A media kit usually will include information about the station or publication, audience demographics, a rate card, and information on special issues or advertising opportunities that are coming up. If you tell them who your target audience is, they often can provide specific ratings or subscriber demographics information that will help you to decide whether they are appropriate. If the outlet can send you Arbitron (for radio) or Nielsen (for television) ratings that show its market rank compared to other stations, look on that list for the other stations that reach your target audience to narrow down your search.

Local advertising agencies, public relations firms, advertising clubs, and even local libraries might have additional sources of information you can use to assess audience media habits. They might have the latest Arbitron or Nielsen surveys, market reports on audience demographics, product use and media habits, or information on media rates and circulation. Some of this information can now be found on the Internet as well. In Step 4, you will learn how to choose appropriate outlets and place your advertisements or public service announcements.

FORMATS

The format is the way in which the message is delivered via a media outlet—as an advertisement, a news story, an opinion piece, and so forth. Or, if you are using a nonmedia channel, then the format could refer to the size of the poster, the type of brochure, or creating a comic book versus a fotonovella. The format you choose will help shape the message and will affect your budget.

If, for example, radio is popular among your audience, then you can use several different communication formats through that media channel. You could produce radio advertisements for airing as public service announcements or paid commercials, you might appear on a station's talk show as a guest, you can pitch a news story to the station about your topic, or you could even create a popular song containing your message to be played in the station's regular rotation. Find out which formats appeal most to your target audience and use those.

Your communications can take many different forms, which are limited only by your imagination (and budget). Some ideas include the following:

- Daily and weekly newspapers (e.g., paid advertisements, public service advertisements, news stories, feature articles, inserts)
- Radio and television stations (e.g., paid advertisements, public service advertisements, guest on a talk show, news stories, entertainment programming, public access cable)
- Billboards and transit ads (e.g., outside and inside buses, taxis, subways)
- Movie theater slide ads before the show
- Bathroom stall posters
- Parade float
- Sponsorship of the local high school sports team
- Advertisements in a professional sports game program or announcements on the giant scoreboard screen
- Hand out flyers at a large event (e.g., concert, sports competition)
- Sponsor a contest
- Create videos and give them to video stores for free public service rentals or mail them to your target audience
- Design and publicize a Web site on your topic

MESSENGERS

A key part of channel selection involves considering who will deliver the message. The chosen messenger can have a great impact on whether the message is perceived as credible, important, and relevant to the target audience. Messengers such as physicians, health educators, hairdressers, and peers could speak to individuals or groups personally, although their effectiveness might depend on the relationship the individuals already have

---

SOURCES OF DATA ON AUDIENCE MEDIA HABITS
(continued)

Simmons Market Research Bureau Inc.
309 West 49th St.
New York, NY 10019
(212) 373-8900
simmonsres@aol.com
Offers data on audience characteristics for most types of media formats

Standard Rate and Data Service
1700 Higgins Road
Des Plaines, IL 60018
(800) 851-7737
http://www.srds.com
Provides data such as target demographics, audience size/circulation, and advertising rates for business publications, consumer magazines, major newspapers, community publications, direct marketing lists, radio, television and cable, and out-of-home media.

established with the persons delivering the message. If target audience members tend to trust their physicians or talk to their hairdressers about personal issues, then they might respond favorably to an interpersonal approach.

More often, the messenger will be someone the target audience does not know personally. The person might be a recognizable celebrity or public figure, or he or she might portray a generic figure such as a doctor or peer role model. The messenger might not even be a person at all but rather an animated character or an organizational endorsement. Depending on the purpose or style of the message, certain messengers will be more appropriate than others.

To determine who should deliver the message, consider the following criteria:

- Does your research from Step 1 provide any clues about who influences the target audience's behavior on this issue?

- Who does the target audience admire or seek to emulate?

- Who does the target audience trust to give it accurate information?

- To whom does the target audience usually ask questions about the topic?

- Will the target audience respond better to an authority figure? Peer? Celebrity? Animated character?

- Will the target audience immediately recognize who a potential messenger is or who he or she is supposed to represent?

- Is there a celebrity or public figure that is already associated with your issue?

- If a potential messenger is a celebrity or public figure, is he or she a role model on the topic? Might this person have anything in his or her past that could contradict your message (e.g., domestic violence, drug use, arrests)?

- Would you be able to get that person as your spokesperson? If so, is this person worth the money it would require (if his or her service is not volunteered)?

WORKSHEET 7: Channel Selection Worksheet

1. Which channels are most likely to reach your target audience? (check all that apply)

☐ Television

☐ Radio

☐ Newspapers

☐ Magazines

☐ Billboards

☐ Transit ads

☐ Posters/flyers

☐ Brochures/fact sheets

☐ Newsletters

☐ Comic books

☐ Fotonovellas

☐ Direct mail

☐ Interpersonal communications

☐ Community events

☐ Workplace events

☐ Point-of-purchase materials

☐ Internet

☐ Yellow pages

☐ Professional/organizational channels

☐ Music or dramatic presentations

☐ Other _____

☐ Other _____

2. For each channel you selected, note how you will find information on available outlets:

    a. Channel: _____

        Source(s) of information: _____

    b. Channel: _____

        Source(s) of information: _____

    c. Channel: _____

        Source(s) of information: _____

    d. Channel: _____

        Source(s) of information: _____

(continued)

WORKSHEET 7: Channel Selection Worksheet *(continued)*

3. For each channel you selected, what formats should you use to deliver your message to the target audience?

   a. Channel: _____

   Formats:

   _____

   _____

   _____

   b. Channel: _____

   Formats:

   _____

   _____

   _____

   c. Channel: _____

   Formats:

   _____

   _____

   _____

   d. Channel: _____

   Formats:

   _____

   _____

   _____

4. To what types of messengers would your target audience respond best?

_____

_____

_____

_____

DEVELOPING EFFECTIVE MESSAGES

Social marketing messages are not just clever slogans but rather well thought-out communications based on theory and research. To effectively change health and social behaviors, you will need to combine an understanding of behavior change with interpretation of your research results.

However, be sure to consider other approaches in addition to communications when designing your social marketing program. You might be able to avoid the need to convince your target audience to change its behavior altogether if you can create structural changes that bring about the same result. For example, passing a regulation requiring all residential pools to have childproof fences might be far more effective at preventing drownings than changing the daily behavior of parents and children. Altering the physical or social environment also can either make it easier for someone to perform a desired behavior (e.g., vehicles with built-in child safety seats) or make it more difficult to perform an undesirable behavior (e.g., prohibiting smoking in restaurants and workplaces). When these types of approaches are not possible, you must turn your attention to changing individual behavior—usually a more difficult proposition.

THEORIES OF BEHAVIOR CHANGE

To create messages that produce lasting positive effects on your target audience, you should first understand theories of how behavior change occurs. Although some programs use theory as window dressing to show that they were developed "scientifically," a well-designed program uses theory as the support beam on which everything else is hung. A solid theory gives shape to the messages, and without it the program might fall flat.

On the surface, behavior change appears to be a single-step occurrence; either someone engages in a behavior or not. But a major change in a person's lifestyle, such as quitting smoking or adopting an exercise routine, involves a complex thought process. So much so, in fact, that researchers have proposed many different models to explain the transition from nonadoption to adoption and, more important, to elucidate how to affect that process. These theories also are useful for thinking about changing complex social behaviors as well as those that affect an individual's health.

This section briefly touches on five current theories of behavior change to highlight key issues to consider when developing messages. You may decide to follow a single theory, or you can refer to the synthesis at the end of the section to determine the theoretical elements appropriate to your program. The implications of each theory for message development are illustrated using examples.

The most common theories used to explain health and social behavior are the following:

- Health Belief Model
- Theory of Planned Behavior
- Social Cognitive Learning Theory
- Transtheoretical Model (Stages of Change Theory)
- Diffusion of Innovations Model

Health Belief Model

The Health Belief Model[1] attempts to explain the conditions that are necessary for behavior change to occur. The model states that an individual will take action to prevent, screen for, or control a disease or condition based on the following factors:

1. *Perceived susceptibility:* The individual must believe that he or she is susceptible to the condition.
2. *Perceived severity:* The individual must believe that getting the disease or condition leads to severe consequences.
3. *Perceived benefits:* The individual must believe that engaging in the preventive behavior will reduce the threat or provide other positive consequences.
4. *Perceived barriers:* The individual must believe that the tangible or psychological costs of performing the behavior are of less magnitude than the benefits.
5. *Cues to action:* The individual must encounter something that triggers readiness to perform the behavior.
6. *Self-efficacy:* The individual must believe he or she can take action.

As an example, let us get into the head of Julia, a 21-year-old woman in the target audience of a skin cancer prevention campaign. She is blond with pale skin and loves to lie in the sun at the beach. When she remembers to do so, she puts on a sunscreen of SPF 8 so that she does not burn too badly (she says higher SPFs are too "goopy") but longs for a deep tan like that of her friend, Eileen. In fact, most of her friends go without sunscreen and even use baby oil to try to enhance their tans. She certainly has heard of skin cancer but thinks that it only happens to older people and can be removed without any major problems.

Using the Health Belief Model, behavior change messages would include several elements. The campaign would need to convince Julia that she is at high risk for developing skin cancer because of her skin type and sun-related behaviors. She must realize that some types of skin cancer, particularly melanoma, often are deadly and can develop at a young age. Once she is aware of the risk and its severity, a cue to action should take place such as an advertisement urging her to call a toll-free number for a brochure. Julia already knows that sunscreen prevents sunburns but does not appreciate its efficacy for preventing skin cancer or know about other behaviors that can reduce her risk such as wearing a hat and avoiding the sun during peak ultraviolet hours. She needs more reasons to use a sunscreen of SPF 15 all the time (benefits could include avoiding wrinkles and preventing her skin from aging) that will outweigh her desire for a tan and her perception of the discomfort of more protective sunscreen.

Theory of Planned Behavior

According to the Theory of Planned Behavior,[2] behavioral intention is the most important determinant of behavior. If someone plans to perform a behavior when in a particular situation, then the behavior is much more likely to occur. Intention is influenced by three main factors:

1. *Attitude toward the behavior:* The individual's beliefs about the likely positive and negative consequences of the behavior and the relative weight of importance of each
2. *Subjective norms associated with the behavior:* The individual's beliefs regarding what significant people in his or her life think about the behavior and how strongly that individual is motivated to meet their expectations
3. *Perceived behavioral control:* The individual's perception of the strength of external factors that make it easier or more difficult to carry out the behavior

If the skin cancer prevention campaign is to reach Julia using the Theory of Planned Behavior, then it will need to build her intention to take preventive action. To change her attitude toward protective sunscreen, messages should emphasize the positive consequences of regular use (e.g., younger looking skin, cancer prevention) and downplay the negative consequences (e.g., feelings of discomfort, pale skin). In addition, by finding out whose opinions Julia values most, the program can work with key opinion leaders to change subjective norms about sunscreen use. She might be more easily persuaded to wear sunscreen if she feels that her female peers think it is a good idea or if a doctor recommends it. So long as Julia believes that the norm among her friends is to work hard for a deep, dark tan, she is unlikely to change her behavior. Methods to facilitate the prevention behaviors, such as free samples of sunscreen, skin check reminders for the bathroom mirror, and the presence of beach umbrellas, might help to overcome the factors working against taking action.

Social Cognitive Learning Theory

Social Cognitive Learning Theory[3] states that behavior change is influenced by factors within the individual and the environment. As in the Theory of Planned Behavior, the individual will be motivated to act if he or she believes that the expected positive outcomes of a behavior outweigh the expected negative outcomes. If someone has not previously performed the behavior, then these beliefs generally derive from observation of what happens when others do so. When people similar to the individual perform the behavior and are rewarded for doing so, the individual will be more inclined to follow the role models' example. The individual can learn how to do the behavior by watching someone else model the process. He or she also will be more likely to adopt a behavior if the individual has a sense of self-efficacy—the belief that one has the skills and abilities to perform the behavior.

Because Julia respects the opinions of her peers most about things such as fashion and skin care, she might be receptive to a peer role model who displays sun-protective behaviors. The role model could be a beautiful woman with light, untanned skin who wears a fashionable, wide-brimmed hat to the beach, makes sure to wear sunscreen, and receives compliments on her skin. Although the actual behavior of putting on sunscreen is not difficult, Julia's self-efficacy will be heightened if she knows exactly when she needs to wear it, what type (SPF) to use, how much to apply, and how often to reapply it. She also may improve her self-efficacy regarding skin cancer prevention by learning what a potentially cancerous skin lesion or mole might look like.

Transtheoretical Model
(Stages of Change Theory)

Rather than noting the necessary elements for behavior change, the Transtheoretical Model (also known as the Stages of Change Theory)[4] describes the stages that an individual passes through on the way to adopting a behavior. This model has been used in many social marketing programs for topics ranging from tobacco use to safer sex.

The five stages are as follows:

1. *Precontemplation:* An individual is not aware of the potential problem and does not consider himself or herself at risk. At this stage, messages about behavior change will not receive much attention, and the main goal should be to raise awareness about the problem.

2. *Contemplation:* The individual realizes that he or she might be at risk and begins to consider whether to do something about it. At this stage, emphasizing the benefits of the behavior is likely to move the person to the next stage. Increasing the perceived social pressure for behavior change also will help.

3. *Preparation:* The individual has decided that he or she should take action and learns more about what is involved. If the person encounters many barriers to changing his or her behavior, then the process might stop at this point. Therefore, messages to move the person into action should minimize the perceived barriers where possible and also convey necessary skills.

4. *Action:* The individual performs the behavior once and determines for himself or herself whether it was worthwhile. Positive reinforcement at this stage would make the person more likely to do it again.

5. *Maintenance:* The individual continues to perform the behavior in the appropriate situation. Messages should provide reinforcement and tips on maintaining the commitment such as help with goal setting and overcoming potential barriers.

With any given behavior, an individual might stop at a particular stage in the process or even revert to a previous stage. Someone might move back and forth between preparation and action many times over the course of his or her life, particularly for behaviors requiring long-term lifestyle changes such as weight loss and smoking cessation. Using the stage model, you can segment your target audience by stages and address the segment(s) that most of the target audience falls into or target each segment sequentially over different phases of the campaign.

Julia still is in the precontemplation stage. She does not consider skin cancer as something that could happen to her or believe that she is at risk. Although she uses some sunscreen, the type she uses will not protect her enough from the sun. According to the Stages of Change Theory, intervention efforts should focus on raising Julia's awareness that she is at risk for skin cancer because of her light complexion and sun exposure. She also needs more information about skin cancer and how it could affect her personally. Not until she realizes that she is at risk and can do something about it will she move on to the contemplation stage.

Diffusion of Innovations

Whereas the Transtheoretical Model follows an individual moving through time, the Diffusion of Innovations Model[5] describes a particular innovation moving through a population over time. With any new product or practice, some people will be the first to adopt it, others will wait until most of their peer group has already accepted it, and others never will change their ways. For a particular innovation, individuals will fall into one of the following groups based on when they accept the new idea or practice: innovators, early adopters, early majority adopters, late majority adopters, and laggards.

Social marketing programs often end up targeting the late majority adopters and laggards—the hardest people to reach and convince to change their behavior—because the people in the earlier groups have already made the change.

According to this model, the most effective communication channels for disseminating information about a new idea or practice are opinion leaders and peer-to-peer social networks. An individual's decision to accept or reject an innovation encompasses the following issues:

- Is the innovation better than what the individual currently is using or doing?

- Is the innovation easy to use or understand?

- Are other people in the peer group using the innovation? If so, what has been their experience with it?

- Does the innovation fit in with the person's value system and self-image?

- Is it possible to try the innovation first before committing to it?

- How much of a commitment is necessary to use the innovation?

- How much risk (monetary or emotional) is involved with adopting the innovation?

In her peer group, Julia would be among the early adopters of using sunscreen because most of her friends do not use it. Being the first in a group of friends to do something can be scary, and it can be hard to convince someone to lead. In this group, however, Julia is well respected and considered very smart. If the social marketing campaign can get her to start taking protective action, then she might be able to start the diffusion process in her own social circle. By answering some of the questions she might be asking herself about the new behaviors, the campaign will be more successful.

Synthesis: Relief From Theory Overload

If the dizzying array of different theories intimidates you, this synthesis provides the essential ideas you need to know. Based on the preceding models and other theoretical composites of behavior change theory,[6] the following list distills the key elements necessary to effect behavior change.

If you do not choose to follow one of the preceding theories strictly, then ensure that the following elements are addressed in your program's messages and interventions if they are not already present in the target audience. To achieve behavior change, the target audience must possess the following traits:

- Believe that it is at risk for the problem and that the consequences are severe

- Believe that the proposed behavior will lower its risk or prevent the problem

- Believe that the advantages of performing the behavior (benefits) outweigh the disadvantages (costs)

- Intend to perform the behavior
- Possess the skills to perform the behavior
- Believe that it can perform the behavior (self-efficacy)
- Believe that the performance of the behavior is consistent with its self-image
- Perceive greater social pressure to perform the behavior than not to perform it (social norms)
- Experience fewer barriers to perform a behavior than not to perform it

MESSAGE CONCEPTS

Before you jump right into writing a script or designing a poster, spend some time thinking about the basic elements of your message based on the theoretical constructs you chose. The concept development stage determines what you will say in your communications rather than how you will say it (the execution). What will be the main selling point for your product? What are the ideas the target audience needs to come away with? Specify goals for each communication piece you will develop. Make sure that you know exactly what you want to accomplish from the start.

To assist in developing your message concepts, you can use a process called "consumer-based health communications"[7] (although its effectiveness is not limited to health-related issues). This approach poses six questions for which the answers will form a creative strategy. The resulting strategy statement will guide the development of your executions—whether advertisements, brochures, one-on-one presentations, or health care services.

1. *Who will be the target consumers, and what are they like?*

Go back to your research and identify what you have learned about your target audience members by answering these questions:

- What are the most important benefits they see to adopting the product or behavior?
- What are the biggest costs of adopting the product?
- What are the most salient consequences of not adopting the product?
- What do they feel they need to adopt the product?
- What are the greatest social pressures relating to the issue?
- What is their perceived risk of being affected by the problem?
- What misperceptions do they have about the issue?
- What language do they use to talk about the issue?
- What special communication needs does the target audience have (e.g., low literacy level, non-English speaking, cultural speech patterns)?

Use this information to paint a portrait of your target audience members. Construct an identity for them by thinking about who a typical audience member might be—his or her name, information about job and family, current behavior, and feelings about adopting a different behavior. Create as rich a description of this person as you can so that he or she will feel real to you as you develop your campaign.

2. *What action should the target person take as a direct result of the communication?*

Make clear what "action step" you are asking the target audience members to take. Do you want them to call a phone number for more information? Make an appointment with a doctor? Eat less fat? The person who is motivated by your message is primed to take action; do not lose that opportunity. Include a way for people to follow up on your message, whether it is by providing a phone number, an address, or a Web site or by directing them to the appropriate professional.

Think about different scenarios in which the target audience might perform the desired behavior. Identify the points along the way at which individuals could choose the competition instead. If, for example, you are promoting the reduction of household solid waste, then the action you advocate will be different based on the stage in the purchase and disposal process you target. One possibility would be to urge the consumer to buy products that come in recyclable containers (vs. nonrecyclable containers). Another approach would be to focus on the repurchase point and promote buying refills for old containers that use minimal packaging materials (vs. a new container every time). Or, looking at the point of disposal, the action could be either recycling appropriate nonorganic refuse or composting organic materials (vs. sending it to the landfill).

The approach you select will provide the direction for developing your messages. Some actions will not be appropriate or doable for your target audience. Be realistic in the behaviors you choose to promote.

3. *What reward should the message promise the consumer?*

If target audience members perform the action you advocate, then what will they get out of it? There are several ways of presenting the "reward":

Highlighting benefits of the product. Show the good things that will happen if target audience members use the product. Consider the competition and what makes your product stand out. They need to see the product as the solution to a problem or issue that affects them; the benefits should be relevant and believable. To identify benefits, figure out what makes the attributes of the product relevant and "ladder" the benefits, as discussed in Chapter 3.

Reducing the barriers to adopting the product. Several types of obstacles may create resistance to adopting the product among the target audience. They must be minimized or removed so that the reward clearly outweighs the costs. These barriers may include the following:

- *Physical barriers* (e.g., inaccessibility of services, lack of transportation, monetary cost)

- *Emotional or psychological barriers* (e.g., fear of social disapproval or rejection, fear of failure, dislike of the product)

- *Social or cultural barriers* that may prevent someone from adopting a behavior because it goes contrary to "how things are done" or affects something with symbolic importance (e.g., promoting abstinence from alcohol in a college fraternity, suggesting that Los Angeles residents give up their cars)

If major barriers exist, then you will need to change the target audience members' perceptions by either removing the barrier or minimizing it in their minds. If they do not know how to perform the behavior, then give them the skills. If they think the product is too expensive, then either reduce the price or show why it is worth the money. If they do not think that people like themselves use the product, then show that they do.

Portraying the consequences of not adopting the product. Showing what might happen as a result of choosing your product's competition can bring your point home to target audience members. The consequence must, however, be meaningful to them. For example, the threat of death often is not enough to prevent drunk driving by teenagers; they believe that they are immortal. By focusing on more immediate concerns, such as the loss of their driver's licenses and thus their independence, messages may have more impact.

The "consequences" approach requires several caveats. The consequences must be believable; do not exaggerate to make your point or else the audience will dismiss the entire message. Also, using "fear appeals," or trying to scare the audience into doing something, often can backfire. People might become paralyzed by fear and shut out the message. This technique works best when you provide a solution or an action that they can take within the same message. Of course, any fear appeal you use must be something that the target audience can do something about.

Select the three or four key concepts that you think will be most compelling to the target audience and write them in the form of a statement to guide your thinking. Here are some examples for a sexually transmitted disease prevention campaign targeted at single adult men:

Benefits: "A man who uses condoms shows that he cares about his partner."

Barriers: "Condoms are not just for AIDS prevention."

Consequences: "You can prevent years of problems by taking a moment to put on a condom."

In your pretesting, you will determine which of the approaches is most effective with your target audience.

4. *How can the promise be made credible?*

You can promise your target audience members everything they desire, but if they do not believe you, then your message is moot. Credibility can come from the scientific facts you use to back up your message, although not all will be equally relevant to the reward highlighted in the communication. You also can show the truth of your message through demonstrations or testimonials as to the benefits of adopting the behavior.

Target audience members rely on many different characteristics of the execution to determine the believability of your message. The manner in which you deliver the message, as well as the messenger used, helps to establish credibility. Will you use an authority figure? A celebrity? A target audience member? Will you present a "slice of life" scenario in which actors talk about the product in an everyday setting? Or, will you use animation or a catchy jingle to convey information? Visual and auditory cues, as well as the quality of the execution, provide the target audience with reasons to believe you or discount your message. Be careful not to let the presentation interfere with the content or undermine the believability of your message.

5. *What communication openings and vehicles should be used?*

In deciding which vehicles to use to deliver your message, consider the concept of "aperture."[8] Just as a camera's lens opens and shuts very quickly to capture a picture, your opportunities to "capture" the target audience's attention might be fleeting. People are more likely to pick up on messages when they are already thinking about the subject or involved in some way. When you were last considering buying a car, how much more attention did you pay to automobile commercials than you would normally? Your target audience might have similar windows of opportunity through which you can get your message.

To improve your chances of success, try to expose target audience members to the message at a time that they will be most receptive and able to act on it. This might be when they are already thinking about the subject, when they are in a position to take some type of action, or just before they need to make a decision. For example, messages about healthy snacking may be effective at grocery stores, when people are making decisions about the foods that they will have available at home; on afternoon drive-time radio, as people are coming home from work hungry; or perhaps on magnets or stickers that people will see each time they go to the refrigerator or vending machine.

6. *What image should distinguish the action?*

Every communication conveys its message in a particular style. Whether it is the dry formality of a letter from the Internal Revenue Service or the heart-tugging sentimentality of a phone company commercial, the delivery affects how the recipient perceives and responds to the message. Before you proceed to turning your messages into finished products, you will need to decide the feelings and image you want to evoke with your communications.

The image that your audience has of the target behavior guides its response to your communications. An established, well-known type of behavior such as exercise might already hold a particular image for your target audience (although it could be different for each segment). For example, individuals might think of exercise as being for people who already have active lifestyles, who are younger and healthier, or who are obsessed with their looks. If the image of the desired action is negative or neutral, then your communications might seek to change it or, for a previously unfamiliar behavior, to create a new image. The image must be consonant with the target audience's perception of itself and should be appealing and accessible to it.

Every element of your communication executions contributes to the image that an individual forms of your product. This includes the tone, graphics, wording, music, messenger, and even paper stock used. The image should be distinctive and consistent throughout your campaign materials.

Tone refers to how the message is presented. The words and delivery style could be serious, humorous, dramatic, hip, friendly, folksy, stern, understanding, street-smart, frightening, cynical, or any other descriptive adjective. The tone must be appropriate for the subject matter, audience, and format. When the message itself is very serious, a humorous tone might contradict the meaning of the words. On the other hand, humor can be very effective in drawing someone in to your message. The tone you use can help establish a "personality" for your product.

At this point in the development process, you should formalize your creative strategy, although elements may change as others are modified. Pretest your message concepts before you turn them into executions; getting the "what to say" right at this stage is more important than the "how to say it" (see Section IV for information on pretesting). The concepts that are not received favorably by the target audience should be eliminated, retaining only those that are effective in developing your executions.

WORKSHEET 8:
Applying Behavior Change Theories

This worksheet will help you to identify information you might need to gather and give you a starting point from which to build your messages around a theoretical framework. Select one theory, or take appropriate elements from more than one.

1. Health Belief Model

   a. What is the level of perceived susceptibility among your target audience to the problem you are addressing?

   ☐ High   ☐ Medium   ☐ Low

   b. How severe does the target audience think the consequences of the problem are?

   ☐ Very severe   ☐ Somewhat severe   ☐ Not severe

   c. Does the target audience believe that engaging in the preventive behavior will lower its risk of the problem?

   ☐ Yes   ☐ Uncertain   ☐ No

   d. What are the benefits and barriers of engaging in the behavior, as perceived by the target audience?

   Benefits:

   _____

   _____

   _____

   _____

   Barriers:

   _____

   _____

   _____

   _____

   e. How can you help the target audience believe it can perform the behavior correctly (self-efficacy)?

   _____

   _____

   f. What "cue to action" will you use?

   _____

   _____

(continued)

WORKSHEET 8:
Applying Behavior Change Theories *(continued)*

g. How can you address the above elements to motivate behavior change?

_____

_____

_____

2. Theory of Planned Behavior

a. What are the positive consequences target audience members expect from the behavior, and how important is each to them?

Consequence	*Importance* *(high, medium, or low)*
_____	_____
_____	_____
_____	_____

b. What are the negative consequences target audience members expect from the behavior, and how important is each to them?

Consequence	*Importance* *(high, medium, or low)*
_____	_____
_____	_____
_____	_____

c. Who are the most socially influential people in the target audience members' lives, and how does the target audience think they perceive the behavior?

Person/Type of Person	*Perception of Behavior* *(positive, negative, or neutral)*
_____	_____
_____	_____
_____	_____

d. What external factors make it easier or more difficult to carry out the behavior?

Factor	*Perception of Factor* *(easier or more difficult)*
_____	_____
_____	_____
_____	_____

(continued)

WORKSHEET 8:
Applying Behavior Change Theories *(continued)*

e. Based on your answers to the above, how can you increase the target audience's intention to perform the behavior?

_____

_____

_____

3. Social Cognitive Learning Theory

a. Based on the above lists of expected positive and negative consequences of performing the behavior (Items 2a and 2b), which outweighs the other?

☐ Positives   ☐ Negatives   ☐ About equal

b. Does the target audience possess the skills needed to perform the behavior?

☐ Yes   ☐ Uncertain   ☐ No

c. Does the target audience believe that it has the skills and ability to perform the behavior?

☐ Yes   ☐ Uncertain   ☐ No

d. How can you teach the skills or have someone model the behavior for your target audience?

_____

_____

_____

4. Transtheoretical Model (Stages of Change Theory)

a. If the target audience is in the precontemplation stage, how can you raise its awareness of the problem?

_____

_____

_____

b. If the target audience is in the contemplation stage, which benefits should you emphasize and how can you increase the perceived social pressure regarding the behavior?

Benefits:

_____

_____

_____

(continued)

WORKSHEET 8:
Applying Behavior Change Theories *(continued)*

Increase social pressure by the following:

_____

_____

_____

c. If the target audience is in the preparation stage, how can you remove the perceived barriers and teach the necessary skills to perform the behavior?

Remove barriers by the following:

_____

_____

_____

Teach skills by the following:

_____

_____

_____

d. If the target audience is in the action stage, how can you reinforce the behavior to make it likely that it will be repeated?

_____

_____

_____

e. If target audience members are in the maintenance stage, how can you help them to continue their commitment?

_____

_____

_____

5. Diffusion of Innovations

a. Who are the main opinion leaders for your target audience, and what peer-to-peer networks can you use to spread your message?

_____

_____

_____

(continued)

WORKSHEET 8:
Applying Behavior Change Theories *(continued)*

b. How is the desired behavior better than what the target audience is already doing?

_____

_____

_____

c. Is the behavior easy to perform or understand?

☐ Yes   ☐ Somewhat   ☐ No

d. What experiences have others in the peer group had with performing the behavior?

_____

_____

_____

e. How can you make the behavior fit in with the target audience's value system and self-image?

_____

_____

_____

f. How can you reduce the monetary or emotional risk or level of commitment required for the target audience to adopt the behavior?

_____

_____

_____

WORSHEET 9: Creative Strategy Worksheet

In addition to the elements of the theories you decided to use in Worksheet 8, consider the following questions for each segment to help develop your creative strategy:

1. **Who will be the target consumers, and what are they like? (Describe each target audience segment as one person. What is his or her life and personality like? What does this person think, feel, and do in relation to your issue?)**

_____

_____

_____

_____

_____

_____

2. **What action(s) should the target person take as a direct result of the communication?**

_____

_____

_____

3. **What reward(s) should the message promise the consumer? (Consider benefits, barriers, and consequences.)**

_____

_____

_____

4. **How can the promise be made credible?**

     a. Facts to highlight:

_____

_____

     b. Manner of message delivery:

☐ Testimonial by peer

☐ Celebrity spokesperson

☐ Authority figure

☐ Dramatic vignette

(continued)

WORKSHEET 9: Creative Strategy Worksheet *(continued)*

- ☐ Animation
- ☐ Musical/jingle
- ☐ How-to demonstration
- ☐ Imagery
- ☐ Other _____
- ☐ Other _____

5. What communication openings and vehicles should be used?

a. At what times, places, or situations will the target audience's "aperture" be most open to your message?

_____

_____

_____

b. Which communication vehicles will help you best reach the target audience at those times, places, or situations?

_____

_____

_____

6. What image should distinguish the action?

a. What adjectives can you use to describe the image you wish to convey?

_____

_____

_____

b. What tone will you use in your communications to achieve that image? (The list includes common responses, but do not limit yourself to these.)

- ☐ Serious
- ☐ Humorous
- ☐ Dramatic
- ☐ Friendly
- ☐ Hip
- ☐ Folksy
- ☐ Frightening

(continued)

WORKSHEET 9: Creative Strategy Worksheet *(continued)*

☐ Cynical

☐ Businesslike

☐ Emotional

☐ Other _____

☐ Other _____

c. How else can you convey the desired image in addition to using words (e.g., music, graphic design, characters' appearance)?

_____

_____

_____

7. **How can you creatively present your messages (e.g., wording, positioning, use of emotion)? Use the space below to brainstorm some ideas (see Chapter 11 for suggestions about brainstorming techniques):**

_____

_____

_____

_____

_____

_____

_____

_____

_____

_____

_____

PRODUCING CREATIVE EXECUTIONS

Using the messages you developed and tested in Chapter 10, you will now take all of the elements of the creative strategy and turn them into executions, the actual communications pieces that will carry your message. Consider the capabilities and limitations of the channels and vehicles you have selected to use as you develop your materials.

BRINGING OUT YOUR CREATIVITY

The creative process can be the most difficult part of social marketing for some people. If you have not hired an outside agency to assist you in developing your program, then this is a point at which you can consider bringing one in to help with final message development, production, or graphic design. Of course, if you have the resources within your own organization or through freelancers, then you might be able to coordinate this process yourself. You also might consider adapting materials from other organizations that match your needs; you do not always have to reinvent the wheel.

Although there are no formulas or cookbook solutions, some guidelines can help direct your creative thinking. To be most effective, your communication should have three characteristics[9]:

1. It must be relevant and meaningful to the target audience.
2. It must be original, stating the message in a new way.
3. It must "break through the clutter" and be noticed.

Of course, while meeting these criteria, the material also must fit the goals and objectives originally specified as well as the overall creative strategy. You could have a brilliant idea, but if it does not meet your objectives, then you must set it aside.

Often, the best way in which to get your creative juices flowing is a brainstorming session, either by yourself or with a group of people working on the project. If in a group, you might want to also include people such as your receptionist, interns, and the human resources director—anyone who has a creative spirit or is willing and able to come. Have plenty of butcher paper or flip chart pages available so that you can record all the ideas that emerge during the session.

Pick an idea to concentrate on for a set amount of time (5 to 10 minutes) such as a slogan or campaign name or scenarios for a radio ad. Call out ideas as they come, and do not censor yourselves. Free-associate from other ideas that have already been put on the table. The time limit will provide a sense of urgency and force quick thinking. When the time is up (unless great ideas still are coming), look back over everything that was written and cull the most promising ideas. Spend more time elaborating on those and developing them into whole concepts.

Here are some ideas for getting started on your brainstorming:

- What do people expect to hear about your product? Now, think about what would be unexpected. Are there dramatic visuals you can use? Refutation of "common knowledge"? An unusual way in which to present the facts?

- How can you evoke an emotional response to your message? Which emotions are appropriate? What types of people should be portrayed? What type of situation would make sense?

- Play with the words associated with your product. Can you discover any double meanings that could change the interpretation of a common saying or phrase?

- If your product were a person, what would its personality be like? What would it look like? What would a cartoon character representing your product look like?

- Ask "what if?" questions that are contrary to how things are. "What if men had babies instead of women?" "What if we had transparent skin and could see our internal organs?" "What if time ran backward instead of forward?" "What if there were 'health police'?" Answer the questions in as many ways as you can.

As you brainstorm and develop your messages, remember this thought from French philosopher Emile Chartier: "Nothing is more dangerous than an idea when it's the only one you have." There is no such thing as one right answer, so keep looking from different angles until you have several right answers from which to choose.

LANGUAGE ISSUES

The language you use in your communications will affect how well the target audience comprehends and processes the ideas. Here are some suggestions for helping the audience pay attention to your message and act on it:

- Personalize the message by addressing the individual directly through the use of the word "you" and the imperative verb tense when appropriate (as in Nike's "Just Do It"). For example, use "Ask your physician about your medications" rather than "People should ask their physicians about their medications."

- Give the feeling of immediacy by using the present tense and words that make the subject of the sentence feel closer such as "this" instead of "that" or "here" instead of "there." For example, use "This pill keeps you from getting pregnant" rather than "That pill would keep you from getting pregnant."

- Starting off with a question will pull people in if they can answer "yes." Examples include "Do you wish you could cook healthier meals but don't know how?" and "Do you have high blood pressure? If so, you should know. . ." If you have done your research, then you should know what questions will draw in your target audience members. If you are not sure that they will say "yes" or your anticipated answer to the question, then do not ask.

- Use positive appeals rather than negative messages to effect attitude change about your product. Show why condoms are beneficial rather than just saying "Don't have unprotected sex." Or, highlight the benefits of exercise instead of discussing the problems associated with obesity. This approach works best when the audience has mixed feelings about the behavior.

- Be careful when communicating about risks; it can be easy to misunderstand probabilistic concepts. Refer to risks built up over time rather than single incident probabilities because people often underestimate cumulative risk. For example, the risk of contracting HIV in a single sexual act is fairly low but increases substantially over hundreds of encounters.

- If you want to compare the risks of one activity to another, then choose a comparison risk similar in factors such as whether it is voluntary, the level of dread associated with it, the amount of control someone has over its occurrence, and the level of knowledge about it. It would be more appropriate, for example, to compare the risk of contracting AIDS through sharing intravenous drug needles with the risk of contracting lung cancer from smoking rather than the risk of contracting breast cancer (which is not clearly linked to risky behaviors).

- In print materials, write at the reading level of your target audience. All too often, people who are used to writing in a professional style in their jobs forget that the people they are writing for might not have a college degree or even a high school diploma. Define any words that the audience might not know, and minimize the use of technical jargon. Use simple English whenever possible, keeping the number of multisyllabic words down. In

WRITING TELEVISION AND RADIO SCRIPTS

Writing scripts for television or radio ads is not magic. You just need to know the basics and follow them. Do not try to pack too much into your ads. Focus on one or two key points. Limit the number of characters to avoid confusion. Stay away from wild special effects or music that will detract from your message. Your ad also must capture the audience's attention immediately and hold it.

Television spots generally are either 15 or 30 seconds long, whereas radio spots are 30 or 60 seconds long. Although not the case for television, radio time often is sold in 60-second blocks, with the same price for 30- or 60-second spots. If you are submitting a public service announcement (PSA) to be read live on the air, it can be as short as 10 seconds long; you can provide several differently timed versions of the PSA for the station to use as time allows. In writing your scripts, try to use the shortest amount of time to get your message across. Generally, 5 syllables equal 1 second, and a 30-second spot can fit about 75 words.

The scripts for radio and television ads are similar, with one major exception. On the radio, you need to create a picture in your listeners' minds through words, sound effects, and music. Television provides that picture, so you must think visually as you develop the script. In addition to writing the dialogue for each shot, describe how the characters look, the location of each scene, key props (objects) that are included in each scene, and any special camera angles or effects. The dialogue must sound believable; remember that you are writing for the ears of your target audience members, not for readers of your organization's annual report. If you are providing a phone number or address on television or radio, repeat it verbally or make sure you leave it up on the screen for a long enough time for someone to copy it down.

Here is an example of a 30-second radio script developed for the "Don't Kid Yourself" campaign:

Jason and Miranda

SFX (SOUND EFFECTS): AUDIO HAS SLIGHTLY TINNY SOUND, AS THROUGH TV SET SPEAKERS	"JASON": Miranda. I've waited so long for this. . .
	"MIRANDA": Oh Jason, me too. . .
PASSIONATE SOUNDS, SOAP OPERA MUSIC SWELLS	TV ANNOUNCER: "The Greedy and the Gorgeous" will be back after these messages.
MUSIC ABRUPTLY CUTS OUT, AS WITH MUTE BUTTON	VIEWER #1: Do you believe Miranda is going to bed with Jason? He's been with half the women on the show.
	VIEWER #2: And you never see him take out a condom. Lucky Miranda lives in TV-land, or she'd end up with AIDS.
	VIEWER #1: Yeah, or a baby spitting up on her beautiful clothes.
	VIEWER #2: Wait, they're back.
MUSIC SWELLS	"MIRANDA": Oh, Jason, come to me now, now. . .
MUSIC DUCKS UNDER, FADES OUT	NARRATOR: In real life, sex has real consequences. Don't kid yourself. Call 1-800-230-PLAN.

Chapter 13, you will learn how to assess the readability level of print materials.

- Keep the materials focused on one or a small number of points, particularly if dealing with a time- or space-limited medium. If you are developing a series of materials, such as radio or newspaper ads, then base each one on a single message and use the same identifier to show they are all part of the same campaign.

- If you are designing a billboard or poster that will be read quickly and from a distance, keep the number of words to a minimum. Eight words is about the most that someone can read as a billboard whizzes by. A poster can have more words if people will have time to look at it. The letters also must be large enough to be legible from a distance.

CREATING DRAFT MATERIALS

Now is the time to put it all together by creating drafts of the materials including the words you will use and the graphic design or other production formats. These will serve as stand-ins for the finished materials as you pretest them with the target audience. By making these prototype materials look as close to their final forms as possible, you will get a better idea during the pretesting of which elements work and which do not. You might find out that the colors you used have negative connotations or that the audience cannot tell what the person in the picture is doing. By making any needed changes before going into production, you will know that your materials are as good as they can possibly be. These changes will be much less costly than if you had already printed up 100,000 brochures or produced a television ad and then found a problem.

Of course, you should not spend an excessive amount of money on creating prototype materials, particularly if your budget is tight. A television ad does not need to be fully produced for viewers to understand the concept. The people pretesting the materials need to have a good idea of what the finished product will look like, but this can be accomplished without having the final piece on hand.

For print materials, many desktop publishing (and even word processing) programs will let you easily lay out a brochure, flyer, or rough draft of a poster. Even if you do not have the artwork yet, you can arrange the text and create "dummy" spaces for the graphics. Work with a graphic artist to come up with sketches of visual concepts to go along with the words you will use. If you want to design the materials yourself with your own graphic software, you can buy high-quality computer clip art, photographs, or preprinted papers that look like they were created just for your project.

For broadcast materials, you first will need to develop a script. The script should include the lines for each character or the announcer, any actions they will take, sound effects needed, and/or special visual effects. You can

"DON'T KID YOURSELF" CAMPAIGN MESSAGE
AND MATERIALS DEVELOPMENT

Once the "Don't Kid Yourself" campaign developers had decided on the project's target audience and objectives, they were ready to begin thinking about the messages and materials they would use to encourage the regular use of contraception. Based primarily on the information gathered during the focus groups, they selected appropriate channels, developed message concepts, and created executions of draft materials.

Channels

Radio was selected as a key element of the campaign for many reasons. First, in the focus groups, nearly all participants said that they listened to the radio regularly. Second, radio allowed the campaign to precisely target women from 18 to 24 years of age and to reach a large percentage of that population. Third, because radio is ever-present in many people's lives, target audience members might hear the messages in situations where the need for birth control is imminent; the radio spots might serve as a reminder and make it more likely that they use birth control. The spots also could promote conversations about birth control issues when friends or partners were together. Finally, older people who might be more likely to be offended by the ads were less likely to be listening to the same stations as the 18- to 24-year-olds.

The focus group research showed that many of the women read particular types of newspapers or sections of the newspaper. Newspaper ads were used to reach those who respond better to visual information or do not hear the radio ads. They also provided the phone number and campaign messages in a form that could be cut out and kept until someone was ready to call. In Salt Lake City, women said that they read the alternative and college newspapers geared toward young adults rather than the main newspapers. In Butte, they read certain sections of the main newspaper—"Dear Abby," horoscopes, comics, birth announcements, and the crime report. Ads would be placed as close to these sections as possible.

A set of posters was planned to get the campaign message out through community organizations including clinics, schools, businesses, government agencies, recreational facilities, and local "hangouts."

The focus group participants identified a need for information best provided via two brochures. One would help women understand their birth control options, and the other would assist in bringing up the issue of using birth control and condoms with the women's sexual partners.

Drink coasters also were chosen to communicate the campaign's message because focus group participants said that bars, clubs, and coffeehouses were good places to reach women 18 to 24 years of age. In Butte in particular, drinking was one of the primary social activities; those under 21 years of age did not have any problem being admitted into bars or purchasing alcohol. In these venues, potential sexual partners or groups of friends drinking together could use the coasters as a method of initiating conversations about birth control.

Messages

The initial message strategy was based on a combination of elements from various theories. From the Health Belief Model, the messages would include information on the risks of having sex without contraception and the consequences of having an unintended pregnancy. The "cue to action" would be a toll-free phone number included in every communication. From the Theory of Planned Behavior, the campaign would seek to change the perception of social norms. From the Social Cognitive Learning Theory, the approach would include an emphasis on peer role modeling as well as providing skills to build self-efficacy. From all of these theories, the messages would promote the benefits of the behavior and reduce the barriers to adopting the use of contraception.

The key message concepts that the campaign needed to convey were as follows:

- You are likely to become pregnant if you do not use birth control consistently.
- Birth control helps you wait to have a baby until you are financially and emotionally ready.
- If you are sexually active, then get the facts about birth control.

(continued)

**"DON'T KID YOURSELF" CAMPAIGN MESSAGE
AND MATERIALS DEVELOPMENT** *(continued)*

▓ Sure, birth control can be a hassle. But what about the alternative?
▓ Birth control is something you should talk about with your partner.

A factual and straightforward tone, along with a dose of friendly empathy, would be used to urge the target audience to seek more information through a toll-free number or at a family planning clinic. The campaign would get its messages across through peer testimonials, dramatic vignettes, visualization of consequences, and straight facts presented in a nonjudgmental style using audience members' own words as much as possible. These elements, along with distinctive graphics and typefaces, would project a young, hip image for the campaign.

Executions

A total of 11 different radio spots were created, using both written scripts and dialogue taken directly from taped interviews with men and women in the target audience. Each spot had a separate objective and a distinct target audience segment. The campaign created this number of spots in case some needed to be eliminated based on pretesting and also to have a variety to choose from over the course of the campaign.

An artist produced a series of visual concepts to go along with the campaign messages. The project staff designed a variety of draft posters using the artist's drawings and a word processor. A set of four newspaper ads also were designed in several different sizes along with different versions of the drink coaster.

The brochures were laid out using a word processing program to pretest the text before going on to the graphic design. These provided in-depth information and skills-building content at an appropriate reading level, using the target audience's own language.

Once the draft materials were produced, the campaign developers were ready to pretest them with the target audience.

---

create a rough version of a radio spot by drafting amateur actors, co-workers, or friends with some acting ability to record the script onto audiotape. You can do this at a local recording studio or, if necessary, in a quiet room with a tape recorder.

Create a rough version of a television spot by making a storyboard that depicts each scene through drawings or photographs, with the appropriate part of the script displayed underneath each panel. From this, you can create a "real-time" version by videotaping each picture in time with a soundtrack of the script; if you use drawings, this is called an "animatic," whereas for photographs it is called a "photomatic." Another option is to videotape people (actors or otherwise) acting out the script in a setting as close to the final set as possible.[10]

If you will be placing your message on other types of materials, then you should create a mock-up of the piece. For a water bottle, buy a plain water bottle and glue the design onto it. If you are having keychains made, then cut out a piece of cardboard in the right shape, paste or draw on the design, and put it on a key ring. You can make a prototype of nearly anything with a little ingenuity or assistance from an artist.

When you pretest your materials, the target audience must be able to visualize them in their final form. With concrete details to comment on (rather than a vague description), the feedback will be much more helpful. After pretesting, you most likely will need to return to the message and materials development stage to refine your product based on the response from members of the target audience.

SECTION III NOTES

1. Victor Strecher and Irwin Rosenstock, "The Health Belief Model," in *Health Behavior and Health Education: Theory, Research, and Practice,* 2nd ed., eds. Karen Glanz, Frances Marcus Lewis, and Barbara Rimer (San Francisco: Jossey-Bass, 1997).

2. Itzak Ajzen, "The Theory of Planned Behavior," *Organizational Behavior and Human Decision Processes* 50 (1991): 179-211.

3. Albert Bandura, *Social Foundations of Thought and Action: A Social Cognitive Theory* (Englewood Cliffs, NJ: Prentice Hall, 1986).

4. James Prochaska and C. C. DiClemente, "Stages and Processes of Self-Change of Smoking: Toward an Integrative Model of Change," *Journal of Consulting and Clinical Psychology* 51 (1983): 390-95.

5. Everett Rogers, *Diffusion of Innovations,* 3rd ed. (New York: Free Press, 1983).

6. National Commission on AIDS, *Behavioral and Social Sciences and the HIV/AIDS Epidemic* (Washington, DC: National Commission on AIDS, 1983).

7. Sharyn Sutton, George Balch, and R. Craig Lefebvre, "Strategic Questions for Consumer-Based Health Communications," *Public Health Reports* 110 (1995): 725-33.

8. William Wells, *Planning for ROI: Effective Advertising Strategy* (Englewood Cliffs, NJ: Prentice Hall, 1989).

9. Ibid.

10. See Appendix D in National Cancer Institute, *Making Health Communication Programs Work: A Planner's Guide* (Washington, DC: U.S. Department of Health and Human Services, 1992), for an excellent step-by-step guide on how to create rough drafts for broadcast materials.

WORKSHEET 10: Materials Production Worksheet

1. Audiovisual Materials

   a. Type of materials to be produced:

Medium	Length	Number of Spots
☐ Television	_____	_____
☐ Radio	_____	_____
☐ Other _____	_____	_____

   b. Production assistance needed:

     ☐ Producer

     ☐ Director

     ☐ Actors/voiceover talent

     ☐ Camera operator (for television)

     ☐ Studio technician (for radio)

     ☐ Video/audio editor

     ☐ Music composer

     ☐ Additional production crew members

     ☐ Other _____

     ☐ Other _____

   c. Television/radio production tasks:

Task	Person Responsible	Deadline
Writing script	_____	_____
Creating draft materials for pretesting	_____	_____
Selecting producer and crew	_____	_____
Securing production facilities	_____	_____
Hiring actors/voiceover	_____	_____
Scouting locations	_____	_____
Coordinating props and wardrobe	_____	_____
Creating or choosing music	_____	_____
Copying the script for all involved	_____	_____
Coordinating rehearsals	_____	_____
Directing production	_____	_____
Editing video or audio	_____	_____
Duplication of final tapes	_____	_____

(continued)

WORKSHEET 10: Materials Production Worksheet *(continued)*

d. Television/radio production budget:

Item Description	Unit Price (per day, copy)	Quantity	Total Cost
Production facility	_____	_____	_____
Producer	_____	_____	_____
Director	_____	_____	_____
Production crew:	_____	_____	_____
_____	_____	_____	_____
_____	_____	_____	_____
_____	_____	_____	_____
Actors/voiceover talent	_____	_____	_____
Music	_____	_____	_____
Materials/props/wardrobe	_____	_____	_____
Draft materials for pretesting	_____	_____	_____
Tape duplication	_____	_____	_____
Miscellaneous expenses	_____	_____	_____
Other expenses:			
_____	_____	_____	_____
_____	_____	_____	_____
_____	_____	_____	_____

TOTAL TV/RADIO PRODUCTION EXPENSES $_____

2. Print and Other Media

a. Type of materials to be produced:

Medium	Size	Number of Versions
☐ Posters	_____	_____
☐ Brochures	_____	_____
☐ Newspaper/magazine ads	_____	_____
☐ Billboards	_____	_____
☐ Other _____	_____	_____

(continued)

WORKSHEET 10: Materials Production Worksheet *(continued)*

b. Production assistance needed:

☐ Artist

☐ Graphic designer

☐ Photographer

☐ Copywriter

☐ Publication writer/editor

☐ Printer/production facility

☐ Other _____

☐ Other _____

c. Print/other media production tasks:

Task	Person Responsible	Deadline
Selecting production team	_____	_____
Developing visual concepts	_____	_____
Creating artwork	_____	_____
Copywriting ads	_____	_____
Writing/editing publications	_____	_____
Creating overall graphic design	_____	_____
Creating draft materials for pretesting	_____	_____
Determining specs and quantities	_____	_____
Soliciting bids from printers	_____	_____
Selecting printer	_____	_____
Coordinating printing process	_____	_____
Spot-checking printed materials	_____	_____

(continued)

WORKSHEET 10: Materials Production Worksheet *(continued)*

d. Print/other media production budget:

Item Description	Unit Price (per day, copy)	Quantity	Total Cost
Artist	_____	_____	_____
Graphic designer	_____	_____	_____
Photographer	_____	_____	_____
Copywriter	_____	_____	_____
Publication writer/editor	_____	_____	_____
Draft materials for pretesting	_____	_____	_____
Printing of each piece:			
_____	_____	_____	_____
_____	_____	_____	_____
_____	_____	_____	_____
_____	_____	_____	_____
_____	_____	_____	_____
Miscellaneous expenses	_____	_____	_____
Other expenses:			
_____	_____	_____	_____
_____	_____	_____	_____
_____	_____	_____	_____

TOTAL PRINT/OTHER MEDIA PRODUCTION EXPENSES $_____

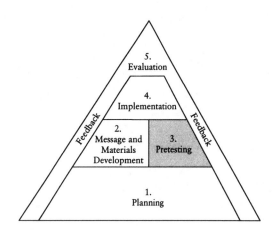

STEP 3: PRETESTING

Section Overview

If a tree falls in the forest but nobody is there to hear, did it make a sound? Likewise, if you conduct a campaign but the target audience members do not understand or notice, does it make a sound? Of course, you hear it because you are there with your chainsaw, yelling "Timber!" and watching one tree fall after another. But is it possible that you are living in a different forest from the target audience?

An essential part of developing a social marketing program is pretesting your campaign with the target audience. That way, you will know how to get its attention and ensure its comprehension of the messages so that your target audience will hear the trees fall.

The extensiveness of your pretest activities will depend on your situation. If you have very limited resources, do not skip this step; just use some less costly pretesting methods. If you are spending a great deal of time and money on the development of your campaign, then a comprehensive pretest period before implementation will help you to get the most out of your investment. Ideally, you would have two phases of pretesting: the first to test messages and concepts, and the second to test materials based on the concepts that were well received.

This section consists of the following chapters:

- Chapter 12: Pretesting Principles
- Chapter 13: Conducting the Pretest
- Chapter 14: Using the Pretesting Results

chapter twelve

PRETESTING PRINCIPLES

Pretesting will help you to know whether the materials you have developed will generate the effect you desire. This is an essential part of the social marketing process and is a hallmark of a well-designed program.

WHY PRETEST?

Pretesting might seem like an "extra"—nice to be able to do but not feasible given your time or budgetary constraints. But there are many reasons to pretest your materials or other elements of your social marketing mix with the target audience before finalizing them. By pretesting, you can accomplish the following:

- *Ensure that the target audience comprehends the messages.* Although you understand all the words you used, the target audience might not. Your materials might be at too high a reading level, the announcer might speak too quickly, or a concept might not be explained clearly. You might not notice, but your audience will.

- *Detect other interpretations of your message.* The campaign slogan might seem clever to you, but the words might mean something completely different to the target audience. This might be due to slang words used in that group or ambiguous wording on your part. Chevrolet found this out the hard way when the automaker introduced the Nova in Latin America (*no va* means "doesn't go" in Spanish).

- *Catch potentially costly mistakes.* By having many people look over your materials, potential problems will more likely be found—anything from minor typos to mistakenly using a picture of someone from a nontargeted ethnic or socioeconomic group (e.g., Japanese instead of Chinese). Having other professionals conduct a review as well will increase the chances of the content being accurate. Pretesting helps you to avoid the cost of completely redoing unusable materials after production.

- *Tune back in to the "real world."* You might develop messages based on points in your research that you think are critical, only to find out in pretesting that the target audience does not respond to your brilliant insights. You might be told that your humorous approach is too "corny." Or, some people might find your messages too graphic or offensive. The target audience will serve to check ideas that seem good in theory but do not work in practice.

- *Make the materials more appealing.* Depending on the audience, certain visual or other design elements, such as bright colors, a compelling graphic, and a musical style, will make it more likely they will pay attention to your campaign. The pretests will help to identify whether the target audience would pick up your materials or notice your messages in the media.

- *Identify details that subvert the message.* In pretesting, you will ensure that each element of the presentation supports and reinforces the message. You might learn that the background music is distracting, that the person in the picture looks too happy, or that the footage includes people wearing unwanted gang symbols.

- *Select from among several potential approaches.* If you developed more than one version of your messages or materials, then you can determine which approach works best by pretesting each with the target audience.

The benefits of pretesting are well worth the slight delay in implementing your campaign. It is better to have excellent materials later than to provide mediocre materials immediately. If these are materials you will be using for years to come, then a difference of a few weeks in development will not mean much in the long term. Build a pretesting period into your project timeline to ensure that you have plenty of time to get feedback and make changes (if needed).

If you have sufficient resources, then you may wish to divide pretesting into two phases. The first phase would involve pretesting the messages and concepts once you have developed them to identify those that are most effective. The second would pretest the materials developed based on the selected messages and concepts to determine how best to execute the idea. Using this method allows you to concentrate on one element at a time, building up the materials in a sequential manner.

PRETESTING PITFALLS

Although pretesting can do a lot to improve your materials, it is not infallible. The results are only as good as the quality of the research and interpretation. Even when pretesting is performed well, however, there are no guarantees that the program will be successful. Pretesting can give you an indication of the strengths and weaknesses of your materials, but it cannot definitively determine what will work.

Qualitative research methods, such as focus groups, are the most common form of pretesting. These methods help you to learn what the target audience members think about all aspects of your campaign, using their own words. You must be able to interpret the aggregated results to decipher what it all means. When you find many different opinions on the same issue, it might be difficult to know what to do with the information.

Be careful when interpreting qualitative research results, for they are not as straightforward as cold, hard numbers (although the latter can be tricky as well). You cannot necessarily extrapolate your results to the target population as a whole. If 3 out of 10 people in a focus group say the same thing, this does not mean that 30% of the people in the target audience feel that way. Picking up on group consensus or key points takes skill and discernment. Having a nonrepresentative sample of focus group participants also can cause skewed results.

Watch out for other types of bias that might be introduced into the research situation. For example, participants might provide the responses that they think you want to hear, or they might indicate agreement with the more outspoken members of a group even though they really feel differently. Testing might occur in an unnatural setting, different from the way in which people normally experience the particular campaign element you are testing. Or, the draft materials you use in your pretesting research might be so dissimilar from the final version that the feedback you received no longer is valid.

You also can run into problems when using the results of pretesting to revise your materials. Although you might think that you understand what the participants were saying, it is possible to misinterpret their comments, leading to changes that do not address the real issue. In another scenario, you might clearly understand the point made in pretesting but execute the change poorly from the target audience's point of view.

By now, it should be ingrained that the program development revolves around the target audience members. Do not, however, let them dictate every change that is to be made in your materials. Their word is important, but it is not gospel. Some of the suggestions you receive might be good but do not fit your campaign strategy, some might be unfeasible given your budget, and some might be just plain bad advice.

Avoiding these pretesting pitfalls might not be easy, but being aware of them will help. One way in which to minimize problems of unclear directives from the target audience is to pretest your materials with as many people as possible. After a while, a clear consensus might emerge. Using multiple pretesting methods, you may elicit different types of information, which can help you to better understand the responses you receive. With data from several sources, you can compensate for the weaknesses of each method.

You might want to convene a group of people working on the project to assist with interpreting the results rather than one person being solely responsible. This can check any biases a single researcher brings into his or her interpretation and also can bring in more heads to help decipher unclear points. To be extra careful, you can pretest the materials again once you believe that they are in their final form. This is especially important if you tested materials in a format that is substantially different from the way in which the target audience will experience them in the real world such as using storyboards for a television ad or black-and-white sketches of a poster.

PRETESTING CRITERIA

What criteria will you use to assess whether your materials meet your objectives? How will you define "effectiveness"? The following list suggests some of the measures you can use to determine whether you need to make changes in your overall campaign, in particular elements, or in minor details:

- *Comprehension.* Do target audience members understand the main points and secondary information? Do they understand every word being used? Are there any difficult concepts that need clearer explanations?

- *Relevance.* Do target audience members feel that the materials were made for people like them? Can they use the information in their own lives?

- *Noticeability.* Do the materials attract attention and jump out at the target audience? Will they break through the clutter?

- *Memorability.* Do target audience members remember the messages and materials after they have been exposed once? Several times?

- *Credibility.* Do target audience members think that the messages are credible? Do they recognize and trust the spokesperson or perceived source of the materials?

- *Acceptability.* Are the materials and messages acceptable to the target audience? Do they fit within the target audience's values and culture? Are controversial or uncomfortable topics dealt with in a sensitive manner?

- *Attractiveness.* Do target audience members think that the materials are attractive? Would they pick up the brochure, stop to read the poster, or watch the television commercial?

- *Knowledge, attitude, and/or belief change.* After being exposed to the materials, did the target audience increase its knowledge about the subject or change its attitudes or beliefs? Did the intention to adopt the behavior change?

- *Strong and weak points.* According to target audience members, what are the best things about your materials? If they had to change something, what would it be?

CONDUCTING THE PRETEST

Some planning is essential before starting any pretest activities. First, decide which pretesting methods you will use. Then, prepare for the pretests by developing the appropriate type of questionnaire and recruiting the participants. Interviewers or focus group moderators also will need to be trained or brought on board for the project. This section places particular emphasis on focus groups because of their importance in pretesting and in social marketing research in general.

FOCUS GROUPS

Focus groups are the research method most often associated with social marketing programs. They are used to obtain insights into people's perceptions, beliefs, and language related to a particular issue. Focus groups can be used at several points in the social marketing process—to conduct preliminary research for strategy development, to test messages and concepts, to pretest draft executions, and to evaluate the target audience's response to the social marketing program. This section provides in-depth information on how to set up and conduct focus groups yourself, particularly in the context of pretesting.

Participants

Focus groups generally involve 8 to 10 participants but may be as small as 5 or 6 people when you want more in-depth participation or if the subject is very sensitive. With groups larger than 10 people, not everyone may get a chance to talk, or getting through the questions might take too long. Do not have more people than you can comfortably fit around the table you will use.

To be most effective, each focus group should be comprised of people who are similar to each other in ways that correspond with your audience segmentation criteria. By separating each segment of your target audience into its own focus group, you can identify any differences that might exist among subgroups. Putting similar people together also will help them feel more comfortable speaking candidly. For this reason, avoid putting people of different social or professional status in the same group (e.g., labor and management, physicians and laypeople). If appropriate, you might want to do focus groups with your program's secondary target audiences as well.

The participants should not know each other too well, although they do not need to be strangers. Preformed groups or sets of friends might have their own way of communicating with each other that an outside observer might not pick up on, leading to misinterpretation or missing pieces of information. You also should exclude people who work in marketing or advertising or who work on the issue under investigation in some way. Focus groups should have some spontaneity to them, and people who know what to expect might not respond candidly.

To ensure that the participants are fairly representative, conduct at least two or three focus groups with people from each segment. When you start hearing the same ideas over and over with no new insights emerging, you have achieved saturation with that segment. You probably will not gain much by doing more than three or four focus groups per segment.

If you were developing a program to promote mammography, for example, you might conduct a set of focus groups with three different categories of women over 50 years of age: those who receive mammograms every year, those who have had at least one mammogram but not on an annual basis, and those who never have had a mammogram. You could divide those segments still further by age, by family history of breast cancer, by socioeconomic status, or by whatever attributes are important to your program. But be careful not to subdivide the segments too much because each new characteristic multiplies the number of focus groups you must do and might not make a big difference.

Recruitment

Where will you find the people to participate in your focus groups? You have several options:

- *Get them to contact you.* Use communication channels, such as radio public service announcements, newspapers, and flyers in waiting rooms, to get the word out about the focus groups. Use a financial incentive or the promise of an opportunity for people to voice their opinions as the reason for potential participants to call you to sign up. Using this method, however, will primarily bring in people who have strong feelings on the issue or who are more outgoing.

- *Contact them directly.* Recruit target audience members proactively by approaching people in a shopping mall, purchasing a commercial marketing list, or using random telephone screening.

- *Get referrals.* Perhaps a community organization or health clinic can refer people to you. You also can use a technique called "snowballing" by asking the people you recruit to give you names of other friends or acquaintances in the target audience who might be interested in participating.

Create a short questionnaire that you can use to screen interested potential participants as they contact you. Make sure that they fall into the right categories for the target audience and the particular segments you are researching. You also can find out when they would be available for the focus groups and either assign them to a group on the spot or wait to select a time that works for most people in that segment and call them back. Appendix C provides a sample focus group recruitment questionnaire.

Because 8 to 10 people generally is the right number for each focus group, recruit at least 10 people to make up for the inevitable no-shows. Recruit people about a week in advance of the focus group sessions. If you have enough time, send each person a letter confirming the date and time of the focus group along with directions to the facility. Call participants the day before to remind them and to confirm their attendance.

Participants should not know too much about what they will be discussing in advance. You can tell them something like, "You will be participating in a group discussion about health issues" or "We want your opinion on some advertisements we've developed for a new campaign." If you get too specific, they might think of what they want to say in advance, inhibiting the spontaneity of the group. Do not be too evasive, however, or else they might think you are hiding something for a nefarious reason.

Focus groups should last between $1\frac{1}{2}$ and 2 hours but no longer than that (or else the quality of responses will decline). When you sign up the participants, tell them the focus group will last for 2 hours and plan to use only $1\frac{1}{2}$ hours. You will then have the extra time if you need it, or the participants will be pleasantly surprised to get out early.

Depending on how you are gaining access to your participants, you most likely will need to provide an incentive to get people to participate. If you are working with a captive audience such as at a workplace or in a school, then you might not need to "bribe" them to attend. But if your participants have a choice whether to attend or not, then you should offer an incentive as an indication that you know their time is valuable. This can be in the form of cash (usually at least $25) or another item of value to the target audience members such as dinner, a gift certificate to a local store, movie tickets, or something else that appeals to them. Appropriate incentives may vary among audiences; a physician might feel that his or her time is worth more than a "paltry" $100, whereas teenagers might be thrilled with a pizza party. You also might need to consider basics such as offering child care during the focus group and providing transportation for people to get there.

ASSISTANT MODERATOR DUTIES

▨ Take responsibility for all equipment and supplies:

- Tape recorder, microphone, tapes, batteries, extension cords
- Name cards, markers, pens, handouts
- Honoraria
- Refreshments

▨ Arrange the room before participants arrive.

▨ Sign people in as they arrive. Take care of latecomers unobtrusively.

▨ During the focus group, sit off to the side, out of the sight lines of the participants. If possible, sit at a different table with the tape recorder.

▨ Take notes during the discussion, including main points and well-said quotes, as close to word for word as possible. Also note nonverbal activity such as nods, laughs, and agreement or disagreement among participants.

▨ Make a sketch of the seating arrangement to help the moderator remember participants' names afterward and to assist the transcriber.

▨ Monitor the recording equipment. Know how it works; make sure that the correct buttons are pushed, make sure that the microphone is turned on, and check periodically that the reels are moving. Label the tapes with identifying information including Tape 1 and Tape 2 if two tapes are used. Turn the tape over or put a new tape in quickly and without drawing attention to the recording equipment.

(continued)

Environment

Many communities have special facilities designed specifically for conducting focus groups that are rented out to market research firms. These are conference rooms, often located in shopping malls, that have one-way mirrors behind which researchers can observe the group and videotape the proceedings. You most likely will not need to go to these lengths for your research if you have an appropriate location to hold the focus groups.

The focus groups should be held in a neutral and comfortable setting such as a conference room or a community center. Use a room that has minimal distractions (e.g., ringing phones, people walking through) and has a door you can close for the privacy of the participants. Set up the room with a round table or U-shaped seating so that the focus group moderator can have eye contact with everyone.

Record the session to allow the moderator to focus on the group without taking notes on what is being said. Audiotaping is less obtrusive and threatening than use of a video camera. You will need a good tape recorder with a table microphone to pick up voices from all directions. The moderator should explain to the group why the session is being recorded and how the tape will be used—to ensure participants of their privacy.

You might wish to have someone serve as the assistant moderator to help check people in, monitor the tape recorder, and coordinate logistics. This allows the moderator to focus his or her attention on the group itself. Others working on the project who wish to observe the focus groups can take turns serving as the assistant moderator. Having additional observers in the room can make the participants feel self-conscious and undermine the informal character of the group.

Make the room as comfortable and friendly as possible. You can offer refreshments, such as soda and coffee, but avoid crunchy foods that can drown out the voices on the tape. As people come in, have them make name cards for themselves (by folding a piece of card stock in half) and put them on the table in front of their seats.

Questions

As simple as a focus group might seem to an outside observer, in reality it is the result of hours of preparation. The process begins with the development of a topic guide—a sort of "road map" for the moderator to follow. The topic guide provides an outline of the topics to be covered, which helps to keep the discussion on track and makes sure nothing is left out. See Appendix D for a sample focus group topic guide.

The questioning approach generally flows from general issues to the more specific or sensitive questions. The questions do not necessarily need to be followed in the original order if the discussion naturally leads to a different topic, but everything should be covered eventually. With a good topic guide, key issues will emerge naturally, without the moderator bringing them up. You might need to design different topic guides for each focus group segment; not all questions might make sense in each group.

Focus groups generally start with an introduction by the moderator explaining what will happen and laying down some general rules. The goal is to create an open, comfortable atmosphere and to let the participants know that they can trust the moderator.

Tell the participants why you have brought them together and why what they are doing is important. Although you still might not want to "show all your cards," you can give them general information about what they will be discussing. If knowing the organization sponsoring the focus groups would bias people's responses, then you can use other honest subterfuges. If your program is, for example, the county's Drug Abuse Prevention Project for High-Risk Youth, then you can say you are with the county health department. A well-known provider such as Planned Parenthood could call itself a women's health organization. Or, you can hire an independent moderator who will use his or her own company's name without giving an indication of who the research is for.

The ground rules should cover the following issues:

- Confidentiality (use first names only)
- What you will do with the results
- Who will hear the tapes
- Importance of one person speaking at a time within the group discussion
- Encouragement of different points of view
- Desirability of both positive and negative comments
- Neutrality of moderator (feelings not hurt by negative comments)
- Duration of focus group and when "honoraria" or incentives will be received

> ### ASSISTANT MODERATOR DUTIES
> *(continued)*
>
> ▩ Do not participate in the discussion unless invited to do so by the moderator. Save questions or responses to the participants' discussion until the end. The moderator may ask the assistant to summarize the main points that came up or to refer back to the notes for clarification.
> ▩ Hand out the honoraria at the end, and have participants sign that they received the money or incentive.
> ▩ Debrief with the moderator afterward.

FOCUS GROUP QUESTIONING STRATEGIES

■ Start with more general questions and funnel down to more important specifics.

   ■ What issues related to your health have been on your mind the most lately?

   ■ What does the term "heart disease" mean to you?

   ■ What is the first thing you think of when I say "cholesterol"?

   ■ What do you like most about exercise?

■ Use open-ended questions, not yes-or-no questions. These can be discussion stoppers.

■ Do not ask too many "why" questions. They make people feel like they have to be able to defend their answers. Instead, ask what features they like or what influenced them to do something.

■ Have preprepared "probes" to find out more information about people's answers to a particular question (e.g., "What are you basing that on?," "Which is most important?," "What do you think is ideal?").

■ Ground people by using questions about their past experiences rather than asking about future intentions (e.g., "Think back to the last time you had an appointment at the clinic. What would you have changed to make it better?").

(continued)

To begin, have the participants go around the table and introduce themselves. Ask them to provide their first names and any other relevant information that will establish them as peers of the other participants and might help in interpreting their later comments. This may include their ages, whether they are married, whether they have any children, where they live, and/or the types of work they do. You also can ask them to answer an easy question to get everyone talking. The question should be relevant to the purpose of the focus group but not necessarily "on topic" (e.g., what they do in their free time, their favorite radio station or television show, their health-related goals, their pet peeves about doctors).

Designing effective questions for the main section of the focus group takes strategic thinking. The questions you ask will depend on your purpose; exploratory focus groups will be very different from pretesting focus groups. Separate the questions that are nice to know from the ones that you need to know. Make sure that you have a purpose behind every question you ask. Use the idea of "backward research" to identify all the information you need to make decisions in your program. Design questions to get that information in the most effective way.

Although your inclination might be to get as much information from your participants as possible, do not try to fit too much into the time you have available. Asking too many questions on different topics can make the participants bored or fatigued. As a rule of thumb, you probably can fit about 8 to 12 main questions (with several follow-up questions each) into 2 hours. If necessary, you can have the participants fill out a short written survey at the end to collect demographic information, quantitative responses to very specific questions, and/or information that might not be appropriate to ask during the focus group. During the focus group, you also can have participants provide anonymous written responses to key questions that they might not be comfortable revealing to others.

Moderating Skills

The person who serves as moderator ideally should be trained in conducting focus groups or experienced in group facilitation. This does not mean that you cannot moderate your own focus groups if you do not have these skills. Many organizations offer training in focus group moderation, or you can refer to one of the books listed in Appendix A for assistance. Moderating focus groups well is a skill that is learned and developed through practice.

Consider training target audience members or people from the same community to moderate the groups. They might be able to elicit more honest or extensive responses than would a moderator who is noticeably different from the target audience members. Using more than one person to moderate a series of focus groups has advantages and disadvantages; with more people, you can complete more groups in a short period of time, but you might not be able to easily compare the results from each group because of differences in style and questioning techniques.

Prior to the first focus group, if you will be the moderator, memorize the topic guide. Knowing the questions in advance helps you to lead from one question to the next when the time is right without having to refer to the guide. You should be alert and focused, so take some quiet time alone before the group starts. As participants arrive, greet them and engage in small talk to make them comfortable.

The moderator's role during the focus group is that of a neutral referee, keeping the discussion on track without doing much of the talking. Participants should be encouraged to talk to each other rather than solely to you. In addition, avoid showing any personal reactions to what the participants say; they should perceive you as being completely nonjudgmental. That includes both verbal and nonverbal responses—head nodding, raising eyebrows, saying "That's right" or "Hmmm."

As the moderator, you will need to actively listen and ask questions about what the participants say. You can ask for clarification, probe for more information, or point out contradictions to explore what participants really mean to say. Make sure that you bring back the discussion if it wanders too far afield, although letting it digress briefly can be useful; you might learn things you would not have thought to ask about.

If you have problems getting the discussion going, or if certain people appear reticent, you can encourage them to talk through nonverbal cues. Eye contact can help bring people into the group and make them feel comfortable speaking. You also can use silence as a tool to facilitate participation. After asking a question, or after someone else has spoken, wait for at least 5 seconds before continuing. Although that pause might feel like a long time, it gives the participants a chance to think about what was said and to respond. If you move on to the next item without leaving any lag time, then you risk missing a thought that has begun to percolate. Finally, be sensitive to the group's receptiveness to discussing the topic. If you encounter

---

FOCUS GROUP QUESTIONING STRATEGIES *(continued)*

- Other types of questions you can use include the following:
  - *Role-play.* "Pretend I'm a friend of yours who has been having sex without birth control. What advice would you give me?"
  - *Project traits onto other people.* "How would you describe a person who carries a gun?"
  - *Hypothetical situations.* "In what types of situations would you bring your child to the doctor?"
  - *Top of mind associations.* "What is the first thing you think of when I say 'cigarettes'?"
  - *Meaning of the obvious.* "What does confidentiality mean to you?"
  - *Chain of questions.* "Why is that important to you?"
  - *Sentence completion.* "The best thing about this product is. . ."

PRETESTING MATERIALS IN A FOCUS GROUP

If you are using the focus groups to pretest your materials, then keep these points in mind:

- Be sure that everyone can see or hear the materials or media. Make copies for all participants if they need to be able to read the text, or read the words aloud for them. Pass around illustrations or sample prototypes of your materials.

- Rotate the order in which you present different versions of the materials in each focus group. This will reduce any bias that might arise based on comments made about the versions that were seen first.

- Ask for general reactions first before you focus on specific design or text elements of the materials.

- Encourage negative reactions if only positive ones are emerging. Participants might be hesitant to criticize the materials, especially if they think you were involved in their development. Ask a question such as "If you had to change one thing about this, what would it be?"

- After showing all versions, you can ask the participants to rank them in order of preference. This can be done as a group or written down and turned in individually.

resistance, then you might need to adjust the topic guide accordingly or perhaps consider conducting one-on-one interviews instead.

Try not to become an authority figure in the group by answering questions if they come up. Ideally, wait until the end of the group to answer questions or to correct information that is wrong or harmful. Often, other people in the focus group will provide answers. This also lets you see how well they understand the topic.

At the end of the focus group, thank everyone for their participation and give them their promised incentive. Afterward, go over the discussion with the assistant moderator to identify the "big ideas" that emerged and to confirm that your understandings of what transpired correspond. You might wish to make notes of your immediate impressions while they still are fresh in your mind. If necessary, make changes to the topic guide based on spontaneous discussions that you found useful during the session.

Analysis

Interpreting focus groups involves several levels of analysis. Within each focus group, look at the words spoken by individuals as well as the key points made by the group as a whole. Also, compare the main ideas that emerged across all the focus groups to identify similarities and differences in the findings.

Before beginning the analysis phase, have transcripts made from the tapes of the focus group proceedings. Although it is not always necessary, ideally a word-for-word transcript of each group would be provided by a professional with experience transcribing focus groups. This ensures that you will not lose potentially valuable information—in the form of an idea, the words that are used, or the context of a given remark. But this method can be expensive if you are doing a large number of focus groups.

In the more common approach, you can listen to the tapes yourself and transcribe all of the contents or just key sections, or you can rely on the notes taken by the assistant moderator and fill in missing information as you listen. This also can serve the purpose of refreshing your memory about what happened in each session before you start your analysis. The main advantage of having a professional transcribe the tapes is that it will save you time; every hour of focus group tape time can take about 3 hours to transcribe.

Begin by reading over all the transcripts and any notes you and your assistant moderator took during each session. As you read, look for trends and strongly or frequently held opinions. Go through question by question and note the main points emerging across the groups. Also, make a note of any quotes that support the points you see emerging.

Keep the following points in mind:

- Do not take responses out of context. Remember that respondents were reacting to a particular question or a comment from another person.

- Note the words that people use to talk about the issue, particularly if they tend to use different words than you do (e.g., "protection" vs. "contraception").

- Do not quantify the responses you receive or generalize them to a larger population.

- Try to remember as you read the transcripts whether there were sounds of agreement or disagreement from the rest of group that did not get written down. Only one person might have said an important quote, but if everyone agreed nonverbally at the same time, then it might have been missed in the transcription.

- Comments that are specific and based on someone's own experiences should be given more weight than those that are general and impersonal.

- There is no one right way in which to analyze qualitative data, but there are wrong ways.

Before preparing a report of your findings, determine who will be reading the report and how it will be used. A more informal report would include a short summary of key findings, perhaps in a bulleted list. If you need to create a more formal report, then provide a point-by-point analysis with selected quotes to back up your findings.

OTHER PRETESTING METHODS

Pretesting ideally should include both qualitative and quantitative research methods. The strengths of one method can help to compensate for weaknesses of another.

Other common pretesting methods besides focus groups include the following:

- Intercept interviews
- Self-administered questionnaires
- Theater or natural exposure testing
- Readability testing
- Expert and gatekeeper review

FOCUS GROUP MODERATOR QUALITIES

A good focus group moderator should have the following qualities:

- Experienced in doing focus groups (or at least have some training)
- Familiar with the topic
- Similar to the participants or at least comfortable interacting with them
- Able to put others at ease
- A good listener
- Nonjudgmental
- Able to ask questions in a way that will not bias the answers
- Able to think on his or her feet
- Flexible

The following subsections provide guidance on using these methods to pretest your materials.

Intercept Interviews

Intercept interviews (sometimes called "central-site" or "central location" interviews) are an efficient way in which to collect quantitative data, particularly for pretesting. Trained interviewers are stationed at a location commonly visited by the target audience such as a shopping mall, street corner, or supermarket. The interviewer then approaches people who appear to fit the target audience definition and asks them whether they would take a few minutes to answer some questions. If so, the interviewer first asks the respondent several questions (called a "screener") to determine whether he or she is a member of the target audience or specific segment you are researching. If all of the criteria are met, then the interviewer takes the respondent to a separate room or a quiet place to sit during the interview.

The interview generally lasts no longer than 15 to 20 minutes. If it will take any more time than that, you might need to offer an incentive for the person to continue such as money, a gift certificate, or food. Read the message concepts or show the draft materials to the respondent, and then ask for his or her reactions.

The questions should be in primarily multiple-choice (e.g., "Do you think the situation in the ad was *very believable, somewhat believable,* or *not at all believable*?") or short-answer format (e.g., "Where would you go for information about your health?"), with a minimal number of open-ended questions (e.g., "How would you describe the message of the ad?" or "What do you like and dislike about this poster?"). Open-ended questions, which allow the interviewee to answer a question at length, take more time and thought to answer and can be more difficult to transcribe. When pretesting several different versions of message concepts or materials, rotate the order in which you present each piece. This helps to avoid any systematic bias based on whether the materials are seen first or last.

Intercept interviews are a way of reaching a large number of people quickly and relatively inexpensively. But because the respondents are not selected randomly from the population, this method is not necessarily statistically representative or projectable to the entire target audience. You can get a good idea of which elements work and what needs to be changed as well as preferences among different versions of an ad. You should do as many interviews as necessary to begin to see patterns emerge; if most people agree on the same points, then 50 interviews with each segment might suffice, but if there are major disagreements, then you might need to conduct about 100 interviews with each segment.

If you will be conducting your intercept interviews on privately owned property such as a shopping mall or fast food restaurant, then obtain the consent of the management from the outset. Some market research companies have offices in shopping malls and specialize in intercept interviews and focus group recruitment. If you do not have a small army of volunteers or staff who can be trained as interviewers, then consider whether contracting with one of these companies is a more efficient use of your time and money.

Self-Administered Questionnaires

Self-administered questionnaires are a pretesting method that gathers responses from many people simultaneously without requiring a large investment in staff time. These questionnaires can be administered to a group of people to fill out and return on the spot, to individuals in intercept interviews, or to a large sample through the mail. If you use this method to pretest, then either show the respondents the materials in person or mail them along with the questionnaire. This method might not be feasible for testing certain types of materials by mail (e.g., television and radio ads), because of the costs of duplication and mailing, unless it is used for only a small number of people.

Consider using this method when you do not have the staff to conduct individual interviews or when you cannot meet with people in person because of time or distance. Self-administered questionnaires also allow for anonymity, which might be necessary in the case of highly sensitive topics.

Pilot test the questionnaire with 5 to 10 members of the target audience before using it to ensure that the questions and answers are clear and understandable. If you will distribute the questionnaires by mail, then you must provide very explicit instructions because there will be no one to answer questions that might arise. Respondents will be more disposed toward filling out a short questionnaire with primarily multiple-choice questions than a 10-page survey with many spaces for long answers. Also, keep in mind the reading level of your respondents as you design the questionnaire.

Along with the instructions on reviewing the materials and filling out the questionnaire, be sure to include a date by which it should be returned. A self-addressed stamped envelope in which to return the questionnaire will make it more likely that the respondents will comply.

The main disadvantage of using self-administered questionnaires through the mail is the probability of a low response rate. There are several ways in which to increase the number of responses:

- Contact the potential respondents before sending out the questionnaires to request their participation and to tell them to watch for the packet in the mail.

- Follow up with the respondents by mail and/or telephone after they have received the packets and encourage them to return the questionnaires.

- Overrecruit a higher number of respondents than is statistically necessary so that if many do not return their questionnaires, you still will have the numbers you need for analysis.

■ Provide an incentive for the individuals to respond such as a dollar bill enclosed with the survey or a chance to win a prize in a drawing of all respondents.

As with any survey, there is a possibility that the people who did not respond are different in some way from those who did; this is called nonresponse bias. You can reduce this bias by following up with interviews of a small sample of the nonrespondents and analyzing their answers. If there is no difference from the main sample, then nonresponse bias probably is not a problem. But if there is a difference, then you can extrapolate from that sample to the larger group of nonrespondents and add those responses back into the analysis.

Usually when using quantitative methods for pretesting, you are most interested in the numbers and percentages of people who think or respond in a particular way. If you do not have statistical expertise or statistical software, then you can tally up the responses to each multiple-choice question manually. If you have more statistical resources, then you also can compare whether people in a particular category differ from those in other categories (e.g., males vs. females, different ages, different segments). For open-ended questions, look at all of the responses together and create categories of similar answers. You can tally the categories and perform a more detailed qualitative analysis.

Theater or Natural Exposure Testing

The drawback of many pretesting methods is that the target audience does not experience the materials in the same setting as it would during the actual campaign. Theater testing and natural exposure testing are more sophisticated means of assessing the effectiveness of campaign materials such as television, radio, and magazine ads. These methods present the campaign's advertisement in the midst of other ads without telling the audience what they are evaluating. These techniques might not be practical if you have a small budget or lack the technical expertise to execute them well.

Theater (or "forced exposure") testing involves the recruitment of target audience members to a central location to ostensibly preview and evaluate a new television program (for radio, the process is essentially the same). During the session, respondents see a television program interspersed with advertisements for various products and services, either once or a number of times. The ad being pretested is inserted in the middle of the other commercials. At the end of the program, participants are given a questionnaire and asked some standard questions about their opinions of the program to continue the ruse. Then, they are requested to recall and write down the ads that they saw and the main message of each ad. At the end, the facilitator shows the test ad again and asks questions specifically about that item.

"Natural exposure" testing occurs when respondents view or hear the ad in a normal setting such as on their own television or radio at home. Day-after recall tests are one such method in which respondents are asked about the ad after it has run. On the day after it airs, a sample of approximately 200 people who saw it are interviewed, after having been told that they will be reviewing the program in which it was embedded. The questionnaire determines how many people who saw the program remembered seeing a particular commercial and whether they can remember any of the specific messages. In a variation of this approach, respondents might be prerecruited on the day the program will be aired and asked to watch. They are contacted the following day to answer the questionnaire. Cable systems in some communities will allow you to air television advertisements in specific blocks of households, so you can limit your follow-up to those that you know received the ad in their homes.

Readability Testing

In printed materials, the readability of the text is critical, particularly for audiences that are likely to have lower reading levels than the general population. You can assess the readability of printed text either by hand (using a standard formula called the SMOG Readability Formula) or through a computer program (some grammar checkers and word processors provide this feature). This will tell you the approximate level of education needed to understand the material.

Readability testing is a quick and easy method that does not require involvement of the target audience. However, it should be used as an adjunct to, rather than a replacement for, pretesting with the intended users. The results do not guarantee that an audience of a certain reading level will understand the material, but it can give you an indication of whether it is appropriate. Readability testing generally is recommended for materials that have a lot of text such as longer print ads and brochures.

Readability tests analyze the number of polysyllabic words and/or sentence length in a particular document. Longer sentences and more syllables mean that a higher reading level is needed by the intended audience to fully understand the material. Keep in mind that if the text includes many medical words, even if they are defined and understandable to the target audience, the score will be higher.

These tests look only at the basic structure of the text, that is, the technical details. However, making text more readable also involves the logic of each sentence; how the sentences flow into each other; the use of headings, subheadings, and bullet points; and the use of active verbs. For less literate audiences, pictures illustrating the text also might increase comprehension of the text. There is no substitute for pretesting with the target audience to assess all the different factors contributing to readability. See Appendix E for the SMOG Readability Formula.

COMPARING PRETESTING METHODS

Pretesting Method	Pros	Cons
Focus groups	• Group interaction might encourage more discussion and responses • Excellent technique for obtaining qualitative information from many respondents at once • Can gather information relatively quickly	• Should not be used when you need quantitative data • Participants might feel inhibited about expressing opinions if different from others • Participants might not be representative of target audience as a whole • Can be expensive
Intercept interviews	• Quick and relatively inexpensive method • If location is chosen well, can interview many target audience members • Interviewer can clarify responses if necessary	• Not true random sample • Can be difficult to tell who is target audience member • Interviews must be short • Might need permission to do interviews on private property
Self-administered questionnaires	• Inexpensive and easy to gather many responses • No need for interviewers • Can distribute by mail • Respondents can remain anonymous	• May be difficult for low literacy populations to read and fill out • Low response rate probable • Cannot clarify meaning of responses • Cannot control how participants are exposed to materials
Theater or natural exposure testing	• Exposure to materials similar to actual campaign	• Can be expensive • Requires special screening facility or service
Readability testing	• Cost-free and easy to use • Does not require involvement of target audience	• Only checks text • Cannot be used by itself
Expert and gatekeeper review	• Helps ensure factual accuracy and effectiveness • Might increase chances of public service announcements being run by an outlet or of participation by partners	• Professionals might be too busy to assist • Does not substitute for target audience feedback

Expert and Gatekeeper Review

In addition to testing the materials with the target audience, it often is helpful to include professionals in the field and representatives of intermediary organizations in the review process. The "experts" might include people with extensive knowledge of the subject matter to ensure that the information provided is technically accurate or professionals with health communication and social marketing expertise to assess the effectiveness of the product design. They can help identify any potential trouble spots that might not be brought to light with other forms of pretesting.

"Gatekeepers" are those you must work with to reach the target audience. They might be the staff of a partner organization that will be distributing the materials to their clients or members. They might be the physicians who have agreed to urge their patients to quit smoking. Or, they might be the public affairs directors at the television stations on which you plan to air your public service announcements. Without the cooperation and support of these people, you could have a difficult time distributing your materials and getting your message out to your audience. The nurse who is supposed to give his or her patient your campaign materials probably will not do so if the nurse thinks they have major problems. This goes back to the idea of who your internal and external publics are. You might need to get the "buy-in" of several different groups, each of which might want to review the materials.

Provide the draft versions of the materials to the experts or gatekeepers you deem most relevant to your project, along with a questionnaire on the aspects on which you want their opinions. You also can gather this information through telephone or in-person interviews and meetings. Have the reviewers evaluate the materials on accuracy, comprehensiveness, appropriateness for the target audience, clarity, and design.

WORKSHEET 11: Pretesting Planning Worksheet

1. Which of the following methods will you use to pretest your messages and materials? (check all that apply)

☐ Focus groups

☐ Intercept interviews

☐ Self-administered questionnaires

☐ Theater or natural exposure testing

☐ Readability testing

☐ Expert and gatekeeper review

☐ Other _____

2. Focus group planning

a. Who will moderate the focus groups?

_____

_____

b. Who will serve as assistant moderators?

_____

_____

_____

c. Where will the focus groups take place?

_____

_____

d. With which segments will you do separate focus groups?

Segment 1: _____

Segment 2: _____

Segment 3: _____

e. When will each focus group take place?

Segment 1: _____

Date: _____ Time: _____ to _____ a.m./p.m.

Date: _____ Time: _____ to _____ a.m./p.m.

Date: _____ Time: _____ to _____ a.m./p.m.

(continued)

WORSHEET 11:
Pretesting Planning Worksheet *(continued)*

Segment 2: _____

     Date: _____ Time: _____ to _____ a.m./p.m.

     Date: _____ Time: _____ to _____ a.m./p.m.

     Date: _____ Time: _____ to _____ a.m./p.m.

Segment 3: _____

     Date: _____ Time: _____ to _____ a.m./p.m.

     Date: _____ Time: _____ to _____ a.m./p.m.

     Date: _____ Time: _____ to _____ a.m./p.m.

f. How will you recruit participants for the focus groups?

    _____

    _____

    _____

g. What will you offer people as an incentive to participate?

    _____

h. Workplan:

Activity	Who	Deadline
Develop topic guide	_____	_____
Locate facility	_____	_____
Set dates/times of groups	_____	_____
Select/train moderator(s)	_____	_____
Recruit participants	_____	_____
Confirm attendance with participants	_____	_____
Conduct focus groups	_____	_____
Transcribe tapes/write up notes	_____	_____
Analyze results	_____	_____
Write report	_____	_____

3. Intercept interview planning

a. Who will serve as interviewers?

    _____

    _____

    _____

(continued)

WORKSHEET 11:
Pretesting Planning Worksheet *(continued)*

b. What location(s) will you use to find participants and conduct the interviews?

_____

_____

_____

c. Between what dates or on which days will you conduct the interviews?

_____

_____

_____

d. What will you offer people as an incentive to participate?

_____

e. Number of responses needed: _____

f. Workplan:

Activity	*Who*	*Deadline*
Develop questionnaire	_____	_____
Develop "screener"	_____	_____
Test questionnaire	_____	_____
Select/train interviewers	_____	_____
Select site/get permission	_____	_____
Conduct interviews	_____	_____
Input data	_____	_____
Analyze data	_____	_____
Write report	_____	_____

4. Self-administered questionnaire planning

a. How will you select potential respondents?

_____

_____

_____

b. How will you distribute the questionnaires to potential respondents?

_____

_____

_____

(continued)

WORKSHEET 11:
Pretesting Planning Worksheet *(continued)*

   c. What will you offer people as an incentive to participate?

      _____

   d. Number of responses needed: _____

   e. Workplan:

Activity	Who	Deadline
Develop questionnaire	_____	_____
Test questionnaire	_____	_____
Write introductory letter	_____	_____
Send out/distribute questionnaires	_____	_____
Compile questionnaires	_____	_____
Input data	_____	_____
Analyze data	_____	_____
Write report	_____	_____

5. Theater or natural exposure testing planning

   a. Which type of testing will you use?

      ☐ Theater   ☐ Natural exposure

   b. How will you recruit participants for the tests?

      _____

      _____

   c. What will you offer people as an incentive to participate?

      _____

   d. Between what dates or on which days will you conduct the tests?

      _____

      _____

      _____

   e. Number of responses needed: _____

(continued)

WORKSHEET 11:
Pretesting Planning Worksheet *(continued)*

f. Workplan:

Activity	Who	Deadline
Develop test materials	_____	_____
Develop questionnaire	_____	_____
Test questionnaire	_____	_____
Recruit participants	_____	_____
Set date(s)	_____	_____
Locate theater facility	_____	_____
Select theater test facilitator	_____	_____
Contract with testing service (if using natural exposure test)	_____	_____
Input data	_____	_____
Analyze data	_____	_____
Write report	_____	_____

6. Readability testing planning

a. What is the approximate reading level of your target audience?

_____ grade

b. Using the SMOG Readability Formula, what is the approximate reading level of each of your print materials?

Material	Grade Level
_____	_____
_____	_____
_____	_____

7. Expert and gatekeeper review planning

a. Which experts will you ask to review your materials?

_____

_____

_____

_____

(continued)

WORKSHEET 11:
Pretesting Planning Worksheet *(continued)*

b. Which gatekeepers will you ask to review your materials?

_____

_____

_____

_____

c. How will you collect the feedback from the reviewers?

☐ Mail

☐ Telephone

☐ Individual interviews

☐ Group meetings

☐ Other _____

d. Workplan:

Activity	Who	Deadline
Develop questionnaire	_____	_____
Identify potential reviewers	_____	_____
Contact potential reviewers	_____	_____
Compile questionnaires/feedback	_____	_____
Analyze data	_____	_____
Write report	_____	_____

USING THE
PRETESTING RESULTS

With all of the feedback about your materials that you have gathered from the target audience and other sources, you might be wondering, "Now what do I do?" The results might conflict with each other, there might be no consensus, or you might simply not be sure where to start. At this stage, you will analyze and interpret your pretest results, make changes to the materials based on the feedback, pretest the new versions (if necessary), and then finalize the materials.

INTERPRETING PRETEST RESULTS

Looking at all the reactions, insights, and advice you collected, sift through and categorize the information into appropriate topics (e.g., text, visual design, message concepts). In each topic, label each idea as "definitely change," "possibly change," or "do not change." Try to look at the items objectively, setting aside your own feelings about which elements you like or dislike. In addition, keep in mind that you do not have to make every change that was mentioned during the pretesting.

In your analysis, the "definitely change" items should include the following:

- Factual errors
- Unclear sentences or words
- Changes noted by a clear majority (so long as the changes are reasonable)
- Easy changes (e.g., wording, colors, layout)
- Elements or versions that definitely do not work

FINAL MATERIALS PRODUCTION ISSUES

Radio and television advertisements

■ Contact the stations on which you will be running the ads to find out their format requirements. They might require your ads to be provided on a particular size or type of tape such as reel-to-reel or digital audiotape. Some stations have the capability of downloading the ads from a satellite transmission done by your production facility, eliminating the need for sending a tape at all.

■ If you are considering using a cable television production facility, then check with your chosen stations whether the quality will be sufficient. The quality of spots taped by public access channel facilities is not necessarily high enough for regular broadcast television.

■ Determine the final number of copies you will need of the ads for duplication purposes. Also, think about whether you want the cases in which the tapes will be delivered to provide any information about your campaign beyond your organization's name, spot titles, and times.

(continued)

Throughout your pretesting activities, you probably will have noted items for this category without much problem. Many of the necessary changes will be obvious as you look at the results. The "do not change" ideas also will be fairly clear in the responses you receive from your pretesting respondents.

However, there will be many other changes suggested by the target audience and/or professional reviewers that are not as clearly necessary. The "possibly change" items might include the following:

■ Elements that some people suggested changing but with no clear consensus

■ Elements that confused a few people but were understood by most people

■ Elements that might cost a lot of money to change (e.g., redoing an entire television spot, hiring a different spokesperson, using special effects)

In these cases, you will need to use your judgment as to whether the materials will really be more effective with these revisions. If so, are there ways in which you can use the suggestions without altering the elements that worked? Or, can you figure out a way in which to reduce the amount of money it would cost to implement the suggestion (if that is the concern)? You might need to prioritize the opinions you have received from different groups involved in pretesting such as target audience members, professional reviewers, and campaign partners. If there is substantial disagreement, then the target audience generally should be the ultimate arbiter (except in cases of factual error), but recognize that internal politics within the program might dictate some decisions as well. You might need to concede some points if you encounter resistance from gatekeepers or others who must provide their approval to go forward with the campaign.

WHEN ARE YOU DONE PRETESTING?

The pretesting stage can go on indefinitely, moving back and forth from message and materials development to pretesting until your results show that not a thing should be changed. For those of us in the real world, however, there soon comes a point of diminishing returns. You probably will not have enough time or money to continue the cycle for very long, and more pretesting does not guarantee effectiveness.

If pretesting elicits substantial changes in the look of the materials, messages, or medium, then you might need to go back and pretest the essentially "new" materials. If the materials do not change extensively as a result of pretesting, then you probably can assume that you are done. You will have to draw the line somewhere between the pretesting and redesign stages.

FINALIZING THE MATERIALS

After you have determined exactly how the materials will look or sound, you will need to finalize the design and produce the materials in sufficient quantities for the campaign. This includes printing posters, brochures, or other written material; duplicating television or radio tapes; and manufacturing other types of items. Solicit bids from different printers or production houses to find the most affordable vendor for your needs. You might be able to procure in-kind donations of materials/services or receive discounts if you are a nonprofit organization or can convince the vendor that yours is a worthy cause. Do not be afraid to ask; the worst vendors can do is say no, and they might even say yes.

Leave plenty of time for printing and other production work. Deadlines are notorious for being broken, and the people providing various pieces might not finish them on time, so your products might be finalized only shortly before implementation is set to begin. If necessary, you might be able to submit a rush job and pay a premium for the convenience, but advance planning will save you money and headaches.

Review all materials before they go into final production. Check the "blueline proofs" from the printer to catch any final errors or misalignments of the color plates. Do not decide to make major alterations in the text or graphics at this stage because such changes will be much more expensive to make. Also, listen to or watch the master audiotape or videotape before duplication to ensure that everything is in the proper order and was created exactly as you want it.

All individuals appearing in any of your materials (e.g., photographs, videotape, audiotape, personal stories) should sign a release form. This will allow you the unrestricted use of the materials in which they are involved so that you can use them indefinitely and in whatever fashion you deem appropriate. Professional actors and other talent might have restrictions because of union rules, but try to secure a "buy-out" through a one-time fee that allows you to use the materials indefinitely.

FINAL MATERIALS PRODUCTION ISSUES
(continued)

Print

- For printed materials, you will need to work with the printer to determine the process it will use, the ink colors (the price generally increases with the number of different colors), and the quality of paper you need.
- When the materials require folding, stapling, or other special treatment, it usually is more efficient to have the printer use its machines than for you to do it yourself.
- If you plan to ship large quantities of the materials to other locations and your printer is not local, then it might be more cost-effective to have the printer send the materials directly to the other sites than to have your organization ship them again.
- For newspaper or magazine ads, find out the desired format from each publication. This includes the advertisement sizes, image type (positive or negative), resolution quality (dots per inch), and type of paper or film the publication requires.

PILOT TESTING

The best way to gauge the potential success of your social marketing program is through pilot testing (also known as "test marketing"). This is the ultimate pretesting method. By bringing together all of the elements of the marketing mix in a real situation, the pilot test provides a "dress rehearsal" before launching the program in all locations. But if the campaign is designed for one city or community, then a pilot test might not make as much sense as it would for a statewide, regionwide, or national program.

Before you spend a substantial sum on a program that might not work in the real world, a pilot test allows you to work out the kinks and to assess the effectiveness of the marketing effort. Commercial marketers often try out a new soft drink or shampoo in a few cities around the country to gauge consumer response before introducing it nationwide; that way, if it bombs, they can quietly withdraw the product and go back to the drawing board having spent thousands rather than millions of dollars. They also can test different pricing, packaging, and distribution strategies to see which work best.

The key to getting projectable results is in the selection of the test markets. Without pilot sites that are representative of the demographics and geographic area of the campaign, the findings might be skewed and inapplicable to the region as a whole. For example, if one of the cities used as a pilot site has a large college, then the 18- to 24-year-old population might respond differently from how it would in a primarily working-class town.

Select representative communities for the pilot sites using criteria such as the following:

- Demographics (including percentage of the target audience)
- Population size
- Resources (e.g., community organizations, funding availability)
- Prevalence of the disease or problem
- Willingness of community organizations to participate
- Political climate
- Ease of travel by program staff to site
- Media available in community

You might need to use several pilot sites to test the effects of the campaign in different types of environments and population mixes such as in metropolitan cities, smaller cities, rural areas, college towns, and cities with large numbers of retired people. If there are striking cultural differences within the geographic scope of the program such as among the West, Midwest, Northeast, and South of the United States or even between northern and southern California, then you should choose pilot sites in each region to detect any salient differences.

"DON'T KID YOURSELF" CAMPAIGN PRETESTING

Once the messages and materials were drafted for the unintended pregnancy prevention campaign, the project contractor pretested them in several ways. The Salt Lake City and Butte family planning clinics again brought together focus groups, including some with young men, to test the messages, visual concepts, radio spots, and brochures. The materials were reviewed by members of the project steering committee, who knew the subject matter and were familiar with the target audience. All print materials also were tested for readability using the SMOG Readability Formula. Later drafts of the brochures were tested in individual interviews with family planning clinic clients in each state as well.

Although the pretesting results were very positive overall, the focus groups and expert reviewers identified areas in many of the materials that required modification. Some examples of the changes made based on the pretesting feedback include the following:

- The "Jason and Miranda" radio spot (see sidebar on page 114 for script) originally had the soap opera actors behind the camera shift to speaking out of character during a break from filming and commenting on how irresponsible and unsafe their characters were being. The focus group participants found this too confusing, so it was changed to viewers of the soap opera making the comments. This spot also used old-fashioned soap opera music that reminded many in the focus groups of a recent margarine commercial, so new music was created.

- Another radio spot highlighted the positive effects of oral contraceptives. Although it originally began by stating that "the pill" helps prevent cancer of the ovaries and uterus, focus group participants said that some of the other effects were more salient to them such as cutting down on menstrual cramps and PMS. These features were moved to the beginning of the spot.

- Some of the radio spots that used sound bites from interviews with real people were not totally clear because of problems with enunciation or confusing phrasing. These were retaped using actors when necessary.

- Out of the six visual concepts for posters, two were eliminated based on feedback from the focus groups. One idea of showing a lottery ball machine with pictures of babies on some of the balls did not go over well in Utah, where gambling is discouraged and which does not have a state lottery. On the other hand, a concept that visually depicted the statistic that 9 out of 10 young women will become pregnant in a year if they use no birth control resonated with nearly all of the participants.

- The focus group participants really liked the brochure on birth control options because of its nonmedical nature and use of their own slang words. Based on their suggestions, the contractor added information on the costs of each method and changed some wording to make it more clear.

The campaign tagline, "Don't Kid Yourself," also emerged from the pretesting focus groups. One participant in Salt Lake City, summing up the message in the poster visuals, said, "I think it should be something like 'Don't Kid Yourself.' These aren't accidents, they're excuses." This phrase was a nice double entendre that concisely stated the campaign's message in both of its meanings. The fact that it came from a target audience member was an added bonus.

Once the changes were made based on the pretesting feedback and the final materials were approved by the steering committee, the contractor had the materials printed and the radio ads taped and duplicated. The campaign was ready to be pilot tested in Salt Lake City and Butte.

The test market can help to diagnose strengths and weaknesses of the program so that each element can be fine-tuned. Pilot testing helps the staff become experienced in operating the program and in measuring real-life costs. The pilot test differs from the full program only in its scale; implementation and evaluation occur in the same way whether it is a test market or the full-scale program (see Sections V and VI for more information on implementation and evaluation). In fact, you might end up exploring more elements in the pilot test than you ultimately use in the regionwide implementation because you might drop some elements that did not work.

Monitor the process and outcome evaluation activities very closely to catch any potential problems or opportunities that should be addressed prior to the full implementation. Look for anything that could not be foreseen through pretesting such as problems with recruiting campaign partners, with distributing the materials, or with reading the phone number on the billboards. Qualitative information, such as interviews or focus groups with the target audience, can help you to know what those who have been exposed to the campaign think about it and whether they have any suggestions for improving the visibility and effectiveness of the campaign.

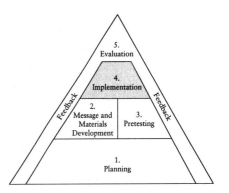

STEP 4: IMPLEMENTATION

Section Overview

The implementation phase is where all your hard work pays off. Everything that you have developed finally sees the light of day and has a chance to work its magic on the target audience. A well-planned implementation increases the probability of reaching the right people and having the desired effect on changing behavior.

Think about NASA preparing to launch a rocket into space. Long before the craft is revving on the tarmac at Cape Canaveral, Florida, years of research and testing go into its development. Scientists orchestrate every detail of the mission, from takeoff to landing. They anticipate possible problems and plan solutions in advance. Everyone knows his or her role and is ready when the moment comes.

If you could be even a fraction as prepared as NASA in the implementation of your social marketing program, then you would have a high likelihood of success (and you do not even have to be a rocket scientist). For a flawless launch of your program, consider the following analogy:

- *T minus 3.* Develop an implementation plan to guide you.
- *T minus 2.* Plan media buys and public relations strategies.
- *T minus 1.* Put monitoring systems in place and distribute materials.
- *T minus 0.* We have liftoff!

This section consists of the following chapters:

- Chapter 15: Developing an Implementation Plan
- Chapter 16: Planning and Buying Media
- Chapter 17: Generating Publicity
- Chapter 18: Monitoring Implementation

DEVELOPING AN IMPLEMENTATION PLAN

Rather than jumping into implementation as soon as your materials are ready, take some time to plan each necessary step. The implementation plan covers all of the preparatory activities as well as what will happen after the program is introduced. A comprehensive plan includes the following elements:

- Distribution plan
- Public relations plan
- Internal readiness plan

DISTRIBUTION PLAN

How will you disseminate the program materials to the target audience? A distribution plan will help you to think through all the steps involved in getting your materials from Point A to Point B (it is not always a straight line). The questions to consider in creating the plan include the following:

- *What are your dissemination channels?* Do you have partner organizations that will hand out brochures and put up posters? Do partners need to be brought on board? Do you have radio, television, or other media materials that will be placed with media outlets, either as public service announcements or as paid advertisements?

- *How many copies of each piece do you need?* Estimate the potential demand for items that will be requested or picked up by the target audience so that you know the quantities to print. Add enough extra leeway that you can replace materials if they are used up early in the campaign. For tapes of television or radio spots, print advertisements, or other media, create enough copies for all of the outlets you will use. If any of the radio stations on which you are placing ads are owned by the same company, then they might be able

MEDIA DIRECTORIES

Bacon's Newspaper/Magazine Directory
Bacon's Radio/TV/Cable Directory
Medical and Health Media Directory
Bacon's Information Inc.
332 S. Michigan Ave.
Chicago, IL 60604
(800) 972-9252
directories@baconsinfo.com
http://www.baconsinfo.com

Broadcasting & Cable Yearbook
Cahners Publishing
P.O. Box 7460
Torrance, CA 90504
(800) 554-5729
custserv@espcomp.com
http://www.cahners.com

Burrelle's Media Directory
Burrelle's Information Services
75 East Northfield Road
Livingston, NJ 07039
(800) 876-3342
directory@burrelles.com
http://www.burrelles.com

*Editor & Publisher International
Year Book*
Editor & Publisher Co.
11 West 19th Street
New York, NY 10011
(212) 675-4380
edpub@mediainfo.com
http://www.mediainfo.com

(continued)

to share one tape (check with the stations). Make extra copies for yourself and your partners to have on hand in case additional opportunities emerge in which you can use them.

■ *How will you keep track of your inventory?* If you do not already have one, create an inventory tracking system. This might be as simple as creating a photocopied form that you fill out each time materials are sent out. Or, it might be as advanced as a computerized database that automatically deducts the number of materials sent from the total inventory. At the end of each week or month, assess whether you still have sufficient quantities to last through the campaign. You can give your campaign partners a reorder form to make the process as easy as possible when they need more materials.

■ *Does everyone know how to distribute the materials?* Whether your own staff or that of other organizations, ensure that all involved know what to do once they have the materials in hand. Provide very clear instructions as to how the materials are to be distributed. Will they be placed in waiting rooms? On countertops of local businesses? Will they be handed out directly to their clients? Spell out clearly what you want done with the materials, or they might end up sitting in the box.

PUBLIC RELATIONS PLAN

The media can be a very effective ally in getting your message out to your target audience. Use public relations strategies to attract coverage by the "free" media such as news outlets and talk shows. The particular methods you can use to generate publicity are covered in Chapter 17, but you can start to think about how to incorporate the media into your implementation.

Use a kickoff event to introduce your campaign to the media and the community. This could be a press conference in which you preview your ads and explain how and why the campaign was developed. Other ideas include the following:

■ Walk-a-thon or fun run

■ Health fair

■ Expert panel discussion

■ Concert

■ Disease screening

■ Celebrity appearance

The event you offer should meet three criteria. First, it must attract members of your target audience. Second, it must communicate your message. Third, it must be considered newsworthy enough by the media for them to cover it.

Your public relations plan also should specify which media outlets you will target. If your campaign covers a large city, state, or even more territory, then you might have an overwhelming number of choices of television, radio, newspapers, and magazines to sift through. You can narrow down your choices by consulting a directory of media outlets that identifies the audiences targeted or the type of programming each offers. Some cities also might have media directories specifically for their local areas; check your local library.

Build a media contact list that includes the critical information about each outlet. You should be able to get much of the data from a media directory, but to be safe, contact each station or publication to make sure that you have the most up-to-date information. Staff turnover is high in the media, and to have the best chance of getting your materials to the right person, you need to know who covers your topic. Keep an eye out for which reporters or columnists cover key "beats" (topics), such as health, children and families, metro (local issues), social issues, and government agencies, and for who the relevant people are in the newsroom, such as the assignments editor and editorial page editor.

Wire services, such as Associated Press, United Press International, and Reuters, are an efficient way of reaching many news organizations with your story at once. Most newsrooms subscribe to at least one wire service, through which they learn of breaking news as it happens. Some newspapers use stories they get off the wire word for word, whereas others use them as background for original articles. The wire services usually have bureaus in major cities, state capitals, and some smaller cities. There might even be an independent wire service that gathers and distributes information particularly for your state or region. Many wire services publish "daybooks," which provide details of upcoming events that their subscribing news organizations might want to cover. Your media contact list for the wire services should include most of the same people noted previously as well as the names of the relevant bureau chiefs.

INTERNAL READINESS PLAN

Because you probably have been the main person thinking about the social marketing program from Step 1 until now,

---

MEDIA DIRECTORIES
(continued)

Gale Directory of Publications & Broadcast Media
Gale Research Inc.
P.O. Box 33477
Detroit, MI 48232
(800) 877-GALE or (313) 961-2242
galeord@gale.com
http://www.gale.com

Gebbie's All-in-One Directory
Gebbie Press
P.O. Box 1000
New Paltz, NY 12561
(914) 255-7560
gebbie@pipeline.com
http://www.gebbieinc.com

Working Press of the Nation
R. R. Bowker
121 Chanlon Road
New Providence, NJ 07974
(888) 269-5372
info@bowker.com
http://www.bowker.com

you know the campaign's goals and objectives, target audience, main messages, and planned procedures inside and out. Do not forget, however, that others in your organization might have only a vague notion of what you have been doing. To prepare others in your organization for implementation and to bring them on as part of the social marketing team, educate your staff and volunteers about what you are trying to do. You can gather people for a half-hour meeting to explain the campaign or conduct an intensive training on social marketing and how the campaign was created.

Depending on how involved others in the organization will be in the implementation phase, you might need to spend time going over each person's role. If, for example, you are publicizing a toll-free number, then be sure that the people answering the phones know what to do, particularly with common questions or requests. Create a telephone protocol that makes it easy for the phone answerers to know what to say or key questions to ask. Or, if nurses are supposed to hand out an educational brochure from the campaign, talk to them about who the target audience is and how best to incorporate the brochure into the visit. Clinic managers might need to be explicitly told to put up posters and to set brochures on the tables in the waiting rooms. Do not assume that everyone knows what to do, even if it is obvious to you.

Be very clear in your expectations of what your partners will do. Work closely with them to prepare for implementation and ensure that they perform their roles correctly. Set discrete objectives for what you want to accomplish through the partnership, and give the partners tasks that are reasonable. The easier you make it for them to participate, the more likely they will do it right. Give them camera-ready copies of your materials, talking points, display racks for your brochures, and other aids. Listen to their suggestions and concerns, and address them whenever possible. Also, make sure to acknowledge your partners' contributions to the program and thank them publicly when possible.

During the campaign, you are likely to receive inquiries from the media for more information as well as reactions from the community, both positive and negative. To avoid panic-stricken receptionists and staff, have a plan in place prior to implementation to respond to these types of situations. Anyone who answers the phone or interacts with others outside of the program should know what to do if faced with a persistent reporter or an irate caller.

Designate one person in your organization to serve as the spokesperson for the social marketing program. This could be the project director or someone else who is comfortable with public speaking and knows the project well. You also can designate someone to serve as a backup in case the primary spokesperson is not available. All calls or communications requiring any type of public comment regarding the campaign should be directed to these people. They should be prepared to respond as needed and ideally should have some media relations training.

Create some talking points to help the spokesperson communicate the key ideas of the campaign to the media or others who might call with questions. These points should include the following:

- Facts about the problem including local statistics (if you have them)
- How your program is addressing the problem
- Why you chose to use that approach
- Responses to foreseeable objections to your program

The internal readiness plan focuses on the reactive side of your outreach efforts. This can be just as important to your campaign as other public relations activities, depending on who contacts you and what they do with the information. If your organization is unprepared when a reporter calls, then the headline story in the local newspaper the next day might feature your program's critics along with an inappropriate quote from your receptionist.

WORKSHEET 12: Building a Media Contact List

Use this worksheet as a model for your media contact list. You can photocopy one page for each entry or create a database that includes each field.

Broadcast Outlets

1. Date entered: _____

2. Station call letters: _____   Frequency or channel number: _____

3. Mailing address: _____

   _____

4. Main phone number: _____

5. Does the station accept press releases by: ☐ Fax?   ☐ E-mail?

6. Fax number: _____

7. E-mail address: _____

8. Newscasts:

Time of Broadcast	Relevant Segments (e.g., health, consumer news)	Deadline/ When to Call	News Director	Phone
_____	_____	_____	_____	_____
_____	_____	_____	_____	_____
_____	_____	_____	_____	_____
_____	_____	_____	_____	_____

9. Public affairs programs:

Day/Time of Broadcast	Name of Show	Deadline/ When to Call	Producer of Show	Phone
_____	_____	_____	_____	_____
_____	_____	_____	_____	_____
_____	_____	_____	_____	_____

10. Talk show programs:

Day/Time of Broadcast	Name of Show	Deadline/ When to Call	Producer of Show or Host	Phone
_____	_____	_____	_____	_____
_____	_____	_____	_____	_____
_____	_____	_____	_____	_____

(continued)

WORKSHEET 12: Building a Media Contact List *(continued)*

11. Notes/other information:

_____

_____

_____

Publications

1. Date entered: _____

2. Publication name: _____

3. Mailing address: _____

_____

4. Main phone number: _____

5. Does the publication accept press releases by: ___ Fax? ___ E-mail?

6. Fax number: _____

7. E-mail address: _____

8. Publication type:

    ___ Newspaper   ___ Magazine   ___ Journal

    ___ Newsletter   ___ Other _____

9. Publication frequency:

   ___ Daily   ___ Weekly   ___ Monthly   ___ Other _____

10. Deadlines (e.g., time, day of week, month): _____

_____

11. Best time to call: _____

12. Editors:

Title	Name	Phone Number
Assignments editor	_____	_____
Editorial page editor	_____	_____
Features editor	_____	_____
Metro editor	_____	_____
Political editor	_____	_____
_____	_____	_____
_____	_____	_____

(continued)

WORKSHEET 12: Building a Media Contact List *(continued)*

13. Reporters/columnists:

Beat/Column	*Name*	*Phone Number*
_____	_____	_____
_____	_____	_____
_____	_____	_____
_____	_____	_____
_____	_____	_____
_____	_____	_____

14. Notes/other information:

_____

_____

_____

_____

chapter
sixteen

PLANNING AND BUYING MEDIA

For those who have never done it before, buying print space or broadcast time on radio or television can be somewhat intimidating. But you do not have to be an advertising whiz to be able to place your own advertisements in the media. With an introduction to how it all works, you can navigate the world of media buys yourself to save your organization money and have more control over the process.

Traditionally, advertising agencies receive a 15% commission when they place an ad, which is paid by the media outlet. This no longer is always the case, but it still is quite common. The client pays the full cost (or "gross rate") to the agency, and the agency then pays the station or publication the "net" rate, which is 15% less than the gross rate. The 15% is built into the cost of the ad, so even if you are not working through an agency, you might be able to obtain that rebate. Print up some letterhead that includes the words "In-House Agency" after your organization's name to use when placing an ad and request the "standard 15% agency commission." This might not always work, but it is worth a try. Alternatively, you can work with an independent media service, which is staffed by experts in media placement and rate negotiation. These firms generally work for a commission of 10% or less or a fixed fee negotiated with you, which can save you money over the traditional commission structure.

PAID VERSUS FREE MEDIA

Why pay to place an ad when you can have it run as a public service announcement (PSA) for free? Generally, your campaign will benefit much more as a result of investing money into media buys. Of course, if you do not have enough money to pay for your media placements, then PSAs are the next best alternative.

(continued)

DETERMINING REACH AND FREQUENCY

The two main variables you need to consider as you plan your media buys are reach and frequency. Reach refers to the number or percentage of people who see or hear your ad at least once during a given period of time (usually 4 weeks). Frequency is the number of times the average person or household sees or hears your ad during that period of time. You might not be able to pinpoint your target audience segments beyond basic demographic descriptions unless the outlet providing the ratings information has additional variables available for analysis.

One way of comparing the relative efficiencies of various media vehicles in reaching your audience is by calculating the cost per thousand (CPM) to reach your audience for each station or publication. Just divide the cost for each option by the number of people you will reach through that medium (divide the number of people by 1,000 first). For example, a television ad that reaches 800,000 people at a cost of $10,000 (10,000 divided by 800 yields a CPM of $12.50) is less efficient than a newspaper ad that reaches 50,000 people at a cost of $300 (300 divided by 50 provides a CPM of $6.00).

To decipher the Arbitron and Nielsen printouts, you need to know that a rating point equals 1% of the total audience. Gross rating points (GRPs) are the total number of rating points in your overall advertising schedule, or the percentage of people you will reach. This is a function of reach multiplied by frequency; for the same amount of money, you can reach more people less often or fewer people more often.

The chief advantage of buying media time or space is that you can direct exactly when and where the ad runs. If you know that members of your target audience tend to listen to a particular radio station as they drive to work in the morning, then you can ensure that your ad will run at that time. Or, if you want to place your ad in the sports section of the newspaper, then you can guarantee that by purchasing the space. The more flexible you can be, the less the placement will cost, but you lose the benefit of targeting your audience precisely.

When you submit broadcast or print materials as PSAs, you are relying on the good graces of the media outlet to run them at all, let alone in a favorable position. If you have ever watched television at 3 a.m., you probably have seen several PSAs in the commercial breaks. But when was the last time you saw one during prime time? Unless your target audience includes a lot of insomniacs, you cannot count on reaching many people with PSAs. Once in a while, you might encounter a public service director who feels strongly about your message and schedules it in a prominent spot, but that is the exception rather than the rule. Developing long-term relationships with the public service directors at major media outlets and educating them about your issue can help improve the visibility of your PSA. Or, you might be able to obtain in-kind donations of media time from corporate or media partners. Repetition and access to the target audience are the keys to effective media placement, and these are hard to obtain through PSAs.

BROADCAST MEDIA BUYS

If you are not working through a media service, call the radio or television stations that you know or think that your audience watches or listens to. Ask to speak with someone in advertising sales, and talk to an account executive about what you wish to accomplish through your social marketing program. Tell him or her about the target audience you are trying to reach, particularly its demographics. Ask each outlet to send you a media kit, which includes information about the station, its rate card, and a printout of the latest Arbitron (for radio) or Nielsen (for television) ratings for your target audience. The ratings will give you an idea of where the station ranks compared to others in the same market (geographic area) for your audience's demographics at certain times of the day. Look at the rankings to see whether there are other stations listed near the top that you should consider.

You can purchase radio and television ad spots at particular times of day ("dayparts" in broadcast parlance) or for specific programs. Or, you can select "run of station" (ROS) programming, which means that the station determines when your spot fits into its schedule throughout its on-air time; this usually is the least expensive option and provides coverage throughout the day. Consider your target audience's lifestyle and when it is most apt to be listening to the radio or watching television. High school students are not likely to have access to radios during school hours but might listen while socializing after school or on weekends. Stay-at-home moms might have an opportunity to watch late morning talk shows on television but turn the tube over to the kids when they get home from school. The account executive can help you figure out the best times or programs for your needs.

If your campaign is nationwide, then you should work with the network salespeople who sell space at a national level. This means that you will not have to contact every station across the country but rather will deal with only a few people. More likely, you will want to reach people within a particular state or metropolitan area. In that case, you will buy spot television or spot radio by working directly with the stations in that market. In some cases, the same company might own more than one station in the area you want and could provide less expensive "combo" rates if you purchase ads on two or more of its stations. Do not forget about cable television; it allows you to reach a very specific niche (e.g., ESPN, MTV, Sci-Fi Channel) and to run commercials within a small geographic area. The disadvantage is that not everyone has cable (only about two thirds of households), and those without it might be the very audience you need to reach. Talk to a cable salesperson to determine the stations and programs that might work for you.

When determining how to structure your advertising schedule, consider whether you want to run your spots in rotation or in flights. Scheduling the ads in rotation means that the station airs them regularly during a specific period of time. The spots can rotate horizontally (scheduled at the same time each day to reach regular drive-time listeners or viewers of a particular program) or vertically (at different times throughout the same day to catch the audience members whenever they might tune in). Scheduling in flights means that the spots run for a set amount of time (whether 4 weeks, 6 weeks, or another period), then are not run for the same amount of

---

DETERMINING REACH AND FREQUENCY
(continued)

The printouts will show both the ratings for each station (the percentage of the audience who have watched or listened to a particular station at least once during that period of time) and the audience share of each station (out of all the people watching television or listening to the radio at that moment in time, the percentage who were tuned to a particular station). You probably will be more interested in the ratings so that you can determine the percentage of the total audience you are reaching, not just those who happen to be flipping the channels at a given moment. Target rating points (TRPs) refer to ratings based on your specific target audience.

The salespeople at each station can help you calculate when and how many times you need to run the advertisement to reach a certain percentage of the target audience. You can either ask them to suggest a schedule that will maximize the TRP you can achieve within your budget or tell them the percentage of the target audience you would like to reach, as well as how many times on average (in essence, the TRP), and they will provide a figure. Most stations and media services have computer programs that will help them determine the most efficient and effective schedule based on your specifications.

SAMPLE FLIGHT PLAN

Contact information:	Jane Smith
	The Health Council
	123 Main Street
	Springfield, XY 12345
	Phone: (123) 456-7890
	Fax: (123) 456-7891
Station:	KXYZ-FM 109.9
Spots:	"Save a Life"—30 seconds
	"Go for It"—30 seconds
Dates:	February 1 to March 28, 1999 and
	June 1 to July 26, 1999

Rotation:

Daypart	Number of Spots/Week	Daypart	Number of Spots/Week
Monday-Friday		_Saturday-Sunday_	
6 a.m-10 a.m.	6	10 a.m.-3 p.m.	3
10 a.m.-3 p.m.	6	7 p.m.-12 midnight	3
3 p.m.-7 p.m.	6		
7 p.m.-12 midnight	6		

Total ads per week:	30
Total weeks:	16
Total ads:	480
Cost per ad:	$25
Total cost:	$12,000

---

time, and then appear again for another flight. This helps stretch your budget by making it seem that the ads have been running during the entire period. Your ads should run a minimum of 10 times per week, although 18 often is used as the norm. Some times of the year are more expensive than others, such as the Christmas holiday season, so you might want to plan your campaign around those periods.

Once you have looked over the stations' rate cards or received price quotes over the phone and have narrowed down the most appropriate outlets to reach your audience, it is time to talk to the account executives again. Think of the price on the rate card as the "suggested retail price"; rates almost always are negotiable. Ask whether the station offers a nonprofit rate (if appropriate) or whether it can reduce the price because of the public service nature of the ads. You might be able to get a "buy one, get one free" rate, where for every ad you buy, you receive another ad as a PSA (which the station can place anywhere in the schedule). Or, the station might offer special promotional opportunities such as broadcasting live from your organization's event, including information about your program in its newscast, and naming your organization as a sponsor of one of its regular features (e.g., "This traffic report is brought to you by the Regional Bicycle Coalition. Bike to work tomorrow and leave the traffic behind.").

Once you are ready to make the buy, make a list of all the information you need to know or need to convey to each station so that you can keep it all straight. Talk to the salespeople at each station to find out what is available that meets your specifications and to try to bring the price down or get more value in other ways. Once they have provided a proposed package of spots that is acceptable to you in gross rating points (GRPs) and price, reserve the spots verbally. Within a day or so, the station will provide you with a written confirmation or contract detailing your agreement, or your contact might ask you to send a "flight plan" with all your specifications. Find out when the station needs to have the materials (usually at least 48 hours before the schedule begins) and what form it prefers (e.g., reel-to-reel, digital audiotape, satellite transfer).

After the ads have gone on the air, you will receive an affidavit of performance certifying when your ads were broadcast (generally at the end of each month). This should include any ads run as PSAs as well. Check the affidavit against your original order to make sure that the station delivered as promised. If new ratings have come out since you ordered the spots, you might wish to assess whether your ads achieved the GRPs originally promised. If you notice any problems, talk to the salesperson immediately to see whether they can rectify the situation through "make-goods" (running the ad again if it was not run correctly or at all) or credits for future advertising.

PRINT MEDIA BUYS

The process and principles involved in purchasing advertising space in a newspaper or magazine are very similar to those of broadcast media. The concepts of reach and frequency apply in the same way, but the audience reached is measured by the publication's paid circulation rather than by ratings points. Of course, more people might see the publication than are counted in the official circulation figure as a result of "pass-along" readership (others reading the same copy) and copies that are given away.

To identify the publications that will reach your target audience, you have several options. One source of information is the Standard Rate & Data Service (SRDS), which publishes several directories with information for advertisers on newspapers, consumer magazines, and business publications. The SRDS directories offer information on each publication's intended audience, circulation, rates, and produc-

---

RADIO AND TELEVISION DAYPARTS

Advertising rates generally are determined by the daypart in which the ad runs. (Please note that slight variations in times may occur according to station or region of the country.)

Radio Dayparts

Daypart	Time
Morning drive-time	6:00 a.m.- 10:00 a.m.
Midday	10:00 a.m.- 3:00 p.m.
Afternoon drive-time	3:00 p.m.-7:00 p.m.
Night	7:00 p.m.-12:00 midnight
Overnight	12:00 midnight-6:00 a.m.

Television Dayparts

Daypart	Time
Early morning	6:00 a.m.- 9:00 a.m.
Daytime	9:00 a.m.- 3:30 p.m.
Early fringe	3:30 p.m.- 5:30 p.m.
Early news	5:30 p.m.- 7:00 p.m.
Prime access	7:00 p.m.- 8:00 p.m.
Prime time	8:00 p.m.- 11:00 p.m.
Late news	11:00 p.m.- 11:30 p.m.
Late fringe	11:30 p.m.- 1:00 a.m.
Late night	1:00 a.m.- 6:00 a.m.

tion requirements as well as other useful pieces of information. Another helpful source is Mediamark Research Inc., which regularly publishes data on readership of consumer magazines according to demographics. If, for example, you wanted to know which publications reach a higher than average proportion of men between from 18 to 34 years of age who are married with no children and earning more than $40,000 a year, you might find that you should consider magazines such as *Fortune, PC Computing,* and *Men's Fitness.* Other media directories, such as those listed previously, will let you know what publications are published in a particular geographic area. Many public libraries have these directories available at their reference desks.

When you have an idea of the publications that are most likely to reach your audience, contact each newspaper's or magazine's display advertising department (display ads are provided in a graphical layout, as opposed to classified ads, which generally involve lines of print only). Ask an advertising salesperson to send you a media kit including a rate card, readership demographics, production requirements, and a few recent sample issues. When you receive the kit, look everything over and consider whether that publication is likely to appeal to your target audience and whether the editorial content is compatible with your advertisements.

Among the pieces of information in the media kit that are most important for you to note and understand are the following:

- *Publication schedule.* Is the publication daily, weekly, monthly, or quarterly? What day is each issue sent out? Is it different from the date on the cover?

- *Closing dates.* By when do you need to reserve the space verbally? What is the deadline for getting the ad to the publication? What is the space cancellation date (after which you must pay for the ad even if you decide not to run it)?

- *Size of advertising units.* Does the publication sell space by the column-inch (the number of columns wide by the number of inches deep), by another unit, or by preset modular sizes (e.g., one-half page, one-eighth page)? How wide are the columns in the publication? What is the size of the page?

- *Cost.* What is the price per column-inch (or other unit)? Does the publication offer nonprofit rates? Does it offer frequency discounts? If so, do you need to sign a contract to receive the discount?

- *Format.* Does the publication require the ad to be in a special format (e.g., positive, negative, electronic)? Can it lay out an ad for you if you supply the text? Can you supply preprinted inserts to disseminate in copies of the publication?

- *Placement.* Does the publication charge extra to place an ad on the page or in the section you request? What sections are available, and are there any special issues or advertorials coming up?

- *Geographic targeting.* Is it possible to place the ad in publications that will go to only certain parts of the metropolitan area or regions of the country?

SAMPLE PRINT INSERTION ORDER

Contact:	Jane Smith
	The Health Council
	123 Main Street
	Springfield, XY 12345
	Phone: (123) 456-7890
	Fax: (123) 456-7891

Publication:	The Springfield Gazette
Ad rate:	$5.60 per column-inch (nonprofit rate)
Instructions:	Please place the ads in the Sports section

Issue	Ad Size	Size Provided	Description of Ad	Price
March 25, 1999	3 columns × 7 inches	5 inches × 7 inches	"Safety First"	$117.60
April 11, 1999	2 columns × 4 inches	4.25 inches × 4 inches	"Go for It"	$44.80
April 30, 1999	4 columns × 5 inches	8.5 inches × 5 inches	"Save a Life"	$112.00
May 6, 1999	2 columns × 4 inches	4.25 inches × 4 inches	"Go for It"	$44.80
			Total:	$319.20

Call and speak with a salesperson at each publication to reserve space in the issues in which you would like to place your ad(s). Be prepared to provide the publication date(s), the size of the ad(s), and any special instructions you have regarding placement. Find out the closing date to get the materials to their offices (usually 2 or 3 days before publication for newspapers, 30 to 90 days for magazines), and get a final quote on the rate. Newspapers and magazines usually are not as willing to negotiate on their rates as are broadcast media, but you might be able to get a lower nonprofit rate or a frequency discount if you agree to buy a certain number of ads or amount of space.

Send the prepared ads, along with an insertion order, to the salesperson before the closing date in a sturdy, reinforced envelope. The insertion order should consist of a written version of the information you provided when you verbally reserved the space.

After your ads run, you should receive documentation of the fact. You do not need to purchase issues of each publication to check the ads; the publication will send you tear sheets of each page your ad is on. When you receive the tear sheets, check them to be sure that the ads ran as ordered and make sure that the reproduction quality is satisfactory. Any problems should be promptly reported to the salesperson so that he or she can provide a make-good ad or adjust your invoice accordingly.

OUT-OF-HOME MEDIA BUYS

Out-of-home (OOH) media include outdoor advertising such as billboards and painted signs, transit ads, and other types of displays. These media can reach a large proportion of the total population but are more difficult for narrowly targeting demographics below the level of neighborhood. The companies that own the billboards and other OOH media and provide the printed sheets, paint, and construction are called "plants." Different plants may specialize in particular media such as the following:

- Billboard posters
- Painted bulletins (signs)
- Bus and subway signs (inside and outside)
- Subway station and bus shelter displays
- Taxi advertising
- Airport terminal and shopping mall displays
- Restroom stall posters
- Postcard racks
- Aerial advertising

OOH media buys are sold based on packages called GRP showings, that is, the degree of market coverage you get when you buy a certain number of postings. The quantity you purchase depends on where the displays are located, how many people see them every day, and the percentage of the population you wish to reach. If, for example, you purchase a No. 50 GRP showing, then half the adult population of that market will be exposed to your message every day, and by the end of a month, your advertising will have reached 75% of the audience with a frequency of 15 times each.

Shapes and sizes vary depending on the type of medium. Billboard posters most commonly come in two sizes: 30-sheets (12 feet high by 24 feet wide) and 8-sheets (5 feet high by 11 feet wide). Painted bulletins can range from 10 to 20 feet high by 40 to 80 feet wide. Transit signs depend on the particular system and the location of the signs.

Speak with a salesperson or sales "rep" who sells the type of OOH media in which you are interested. He or she can provide detailed information on rates, where postings will be available, achievable reach and frequency, and demographic coverage. The OOH plant generally provides both the production of materials and ad space. Each plant has a rate card that explains the market and how GRP showings are priced. You also can refer to a publication called *The Buyer's Guide to Outdoor Advertising*,[1] which updates the current statistics on rates and markets for posters and painted bulletins twice a year. This directory also provides lists of OOH plants operating in each state for reference.

Once you have decided how you would like to proceed, ask the salesperson to take you on a "preride," in which he or she drives you around to view each location you are considering purchasing. This gives you an opportunity to see whether there are any problems (e.g., construction) that might interfere with your target audience seeing the ad.

Most types of OOH media are sold in 30-day increments, although some more permanent signs may be sold in 3-month to 3-year blocks. As with broadcast and print media, you can try to negotiate a better deal than that initially offered. For example, you might be able to get a bonus month or additional posters during the scheduled period. Or, the plant might agree to leave your posters up after your run until someone else purchases that location, which could be several months. You most likely will sign a contract committing your buy in writing.

Provide the OOH plants with complete posting and painting instructions, along with the produced materials, if you are producing them. Check with the plant for the best format in which to provide your artwork. Find out the deadlines for the posting dates you want and make sure that the plants have the materials in time. Once they are up, you can make a "postride" to ensure that the materials were posted as contracted and that they remain in good condition throughout their scheduled period.

chapter seventeen

GENERATING PUBLICITY

Just as you can get your message out by purchasing advertising time or space, you can promote your program in the spaces between the commercials (what people really want to pay attention to) through public relations. Although getting news coverage often is thought of as free publicity, those press conferences, news releases, and slick media kits are not cheap. The resources and effort your staff members put in make it "earned media" rather than "free." But when you compare the cost of these activities to that of creating a mass media campaign or that of buying airtime or advertising space, pitching stories ("selling" your story idea) seems like a bargain. Public relations can be a useful adjunct to your other communications activities if you are able to generate coverage by appropriate media outlets. On the other hand, if your target audience does not read the newspaper or watch television news, then these techniques might not be worthwhile for your program.

Using public relations strategies as part of your social marketing program accomplishes the following:

- Lends credibility to your program and message via news coverage
- Reaches many people at once
- Does not require purchase of media time or space
- Develops mutually beneficial long-term relationships with media
- Gets your message out quickly and efficiently

Public relations also has some potential disadvantages including the following:

- You have less control over how your messages are conveyed
- Media coverage is not guaranteed, no matter how good your public relations efforts
- You might not reach your target audience members with the media that cover your program

MEDIA ADVOCACY

Media advocacy is a tool that uses the media's power to bring about social change and to influence the public debate on an issue. Of course, political interest groups also engage in media advocacy, but the focus here is on public health. Practitioners use media coverage to present an issue from a public health point of view and to "frame" the issue in a different way from how people normally think about it. Ultimately, the goal is to put pressure on lawmakers to adopt a particular policy or on corporate entities to change something that they are doing that negatively affects people's health. A social marketing program may incorporate media advocacy techniques into its media strategy if its goals include changing public or corporate policy or countering unhealthful messages in the media.

Media advocates use a variety of skills, such as grassroots organizing, coalition building, lobbying, and media savvy, to create newsworthy events that get their points across. One useful means of getting attention is using what has been called "creative epidemiology" or "social math." This involves reframing statistics into a vivid image that is meaningful to the audience. Instead of saying, for example, that 400,000 Americans die from smoking-related causes each year, you can localize the statistic and give it more impact by stating that 3 people in your city die each hour because they smoked. Or, rather than relaying that college students drink 430 million gallons of alcoholic beverages per year, you can create an image by saying that they consume enough alcohol each year to fill 3,500 Olympic-size swimming pools.

(continued)

■ Big news developments might bump your story or take precedence over the press conference you planned for months

This chapter offers a set of public relations strategy questions to help you consider whether and how to use public relations in your social marketing program. Rather than regarding the media as a fearsome adversary, think of it as a potential ally. Before jumping in, there are certain questions you should ask yourself.

WHY DO YOU WANT MEDIA ATTENTION?

Determine exactly what you want to accomplish through your public relations efforts. Do you want to build awareness of your program within the community? Promote a particular attitude or behavior? Advocate for policy change? The answers to these questions will determine who you should try to reach with your message and which media outlets and vehicles you should target.

As with every aspect of your social marketing campaign, be strategic in your public relations plan. Set goals consistent with your overall program strategy. You can use public relations methods to accomplish the following:

■ Supplement and reinforce your campaign with the target audience

■ Reach your secondary audiences

■ Increase community awareness of your program

■ Put pressure on policymakers to address your issue

Select the target audience for your public relations efforts carefully. This may or may not be the same group you target in your other communications efforts. If you want to reach the same target audience, then refer back to your research on the group's media habits and work through those outlets to get your message to that group. For other audiences, research the media that will best reach them. You probably would not use the same media to reach members of Congress as to reach low-income parents of 2-year-olds. Be as specific in your public relations outreach as you are in the rest of the social marketing program. On the other hand, if your goal in attracting media attention is to publicize your organization and its services throughout the community, then you should contact as many outlets as you can for possible coverage.

WHAT IS YOUR "NEWS"?

Often, what we consider newsworthy and exciting in our own programs would make a reporter yawn. Why should people be interested in yet another project addressing AIDS? Or the fact that you just got funded for another year? Or your new toll-free phone number? The news media have their own criteria for judging what is worth covering, so to get their attention, you will need to frame the issue in an appealing way.

Find an angle that makes your idea stand out and grabs the reporter's interest. The media prefer stories that contain at least one of the following elements:

- *Timeliness.* Look for a news "peg" (an issue that currently is in the news) to tie your information into current events or upcoming holidays. If a well-known celebrity just died of the disease your program addresses, then you can use this window of opportunity to get information on that disease's prevention and treatment to your target audience and others. Or, if there is an annual day, week, or month set aside for your issue, such as Child Abuse Prevention Month, then use that as the peg (although you might need more angles than that to make your issue relevant).

- *General interest.* Make your issue as relevant to people in your own community as possible. Connect the information to a common situation that people encounter or an issue that nearly everyone must address. A stress reduction program might put out a list of "stress-buster" tips for dealing with traffic jams (because very few of us are lucky enough to avoid those). Or, a study showing which fast food restaurants offer the healthiest selections might attract many people's attention. Those living in colder climates might be eager to see a winter feature on back care tips for shoveling snow.

- *Local angle.* Provide local data or reactions to a national or international news event. People want to know how the big story relates to them. If the results of a national survey on homelessness are released, then provide information on the homeless problem in your community, how it compares to that in the rest of the country, and what people can do about it. If Congress is considering cutting funding for your program, then highlight the plight of some of the people in your community and what it would mean for them.

- *Conflict.* The media love a good conflict, whether it is good versus evil, big tobacco companies versus nonsmoking advocates, or school board members versus each other. Reporters tend to cover all sides of an issue, even when there might not necessarily be a valid second viewpoint. Make their job easy

---

MEDIA ADVOCACY
(continued)

Using symbolism is another effective tool in the media advocacy arsenal, as illustrated by the following example. When tobacco manufacturer Philip Morris Companies Inc. sponsored a 2-year tour of the Bill of Rights around the country in 1990, tobacco control advocates came together to address what they saw as a usurping of a national symbol to promote smoking and to improve the company's image.[a] At each stop on the tour, local activists garnered media attention by setting up "Nicotina," a figure modeled on the Statue of Liberty that symbolized the problems caused by tobacco. Nicotina held a cigarette in her upheld hand instead of a torch, had the phrase "Give me your poor, your tired, your women, your children yearning to breathe free" at her feet, and stood on a pile of cigarettes purchased by 14-year-old children. On the base of the statue was a running clock showing the number of people who had died of tobacco-related diseases since the beginning of the tour. The advocates also wore and handed out buttons that said "YES Bill of Rights, NO Philip Morris." At nearly every stop, the anti-tobacco protesters received some media coverage of their health messages and the controversy surrounding Philip Morris's sponsorship of the tour. In early 1991, Philip Morris quietly changed the tour schedule and shortened its length by 2 months.

a. This case study is described in Lawrence Wallack, Lori Dorfman, David Jernigan, and Makani Themba, *Media Advocacy and Public Health: Power for Prevention* (Newbury Park, CA: Sage, 1993), 183-188.

and cast your story, if appropriate, as a struggle of right over wrong. Try not to demonize your opposition, however, because this might make you look like an unreasonable fanatic.

- *Human interest.* Providing a human side to a disease or an issue creates emotional appeal. Telling the story of one person who is affected helps people to connect with the issue and think about it in relation to themselves, particularly if the person is similar to themselves in other ways.

- *Novelty.* When something has not been seen before or is an unusual occurrence, people pay attention. Whether it is a lemonade-powered car or a new advance in contraception, this is literally "news." Do not create a gimmick just to attract media notice, but if you truly have something that is new or different, then use that as your hook.

- *Celebrity.* The whole idea of being a celebrity is that people look at you as you walk down the street. They listen to what you have to say. If you can find a famous person who will serve as your spokesperson or will provide some comments about your issue, people will be more likely to listen than if your public information officer were speaking. The celebrity should be someone who appeals to your target audience and who the media would feel is worth covering.

- *Superlatives.* Do you have something that is the biggest? The best? The fastest? The most effective in clinical trials? The media do not want to know what is second best; they want to run screaming headlines about new breakthroughs or new highs and lows. Use this desire for superlatives to get your story noticed. Is the problem you are working to prevent the leading killer of young children? Does your city have the most low-birthweight babies in the country? But do not dig too far just to come up with a superlative; the world's biggest gall-stone might not be a very big draw.

WHAT TYPE OF MEDIA COVERAGE DO YOU WANT?

The term "media" refers to many different types of entities—radio, television, newspapers and magazines, computer software and the Internet—that vary extensively within each category. Each of these channels provides different opportunities to reach particular audiences with a specific type of message.

The standard media formats that you can use to promote your messages include the following:

- *News.* This is factual and timely information about important events or new developments. News stories generally would

---

WRITING OP-EDS

Op-eds provide your point of view on a particular issue. Use them to begin a community-wide discussion on a particular topic or to weigh in with your side's arguments in an ongoing debate. To make your op-ed as effective as possible, keep the following in mind:

- Present your opinion clearly and without ambiguity. Every sentence in the op-ed should bolster your case.
- Support your premise with facts and figures. Make statistics relevant to the people reading the article.
- Offer solutions. Do not just write about the fact that a problem exists.
- Keep the op-ed brief. It should be no longer than 800 words.
- Time the submission of the op-ed with a holiday or other event, such as the kickoff of your campaign, to make it more newsworthy.
- Have a recognized expert or someone with credentials related to the topic sign his or her name to the op-ed. This will increase the chances that the article will be printed and lends it more credibility.
- Send the op-ed to the op-ed page editor at larger newspapers or to the editorial page editor at smaller publications.

show up on a television or radio news program, on the front page or metro section of a newspaper, in a newsmagazine or the news section of another type of periodical, or through an Internet news service. A news format provides greater credibility to your information and attaches inherent importance to it. Because a reporter takes your information and rewrites it, you have less control over the content and slant of the story.

■ *Feature.* This is a story focusing on the human or emotional side of an issue. Feature stories are more like short stories than news, with an emphasis on helping the reader understand someone else's experiences, thoughts, and feelings. Although a feature story may contain facts and figures and be based on current issues, it generally is not as time sensitive as a news story. Features pop up all the time on television news and radio networks such as National Public Radio. You also can find them scattered throughout newspapers and especially in magazines, which, because of their weekly or monthly publication, prefer stories that are not time dependent.

■ *Editorial.* This is a short piece offering the opinion of an individual or organization on a particular topic. Editorials can be in the form of an op-ed (runs opposite the editorial page) by a well-known or well-qualified person, a letter to the editor responding to an article that was published previously, or a "community viewpoint" spot on television or radio. In an editorial format, you have more control over how your message is conveyed, although an editor might trim your words to make it fit the space.

■ *Entertainment.* This is a program or published item that people watch, hear, or read primarily for fun or diversion. Television or radio talk shows can be a forum in which you can provide information to a lot of people who might not relate to other formats (although a show with topics such as "My Lover Is an Alien" might not be appropriate). Network-produced programs, whether drama or comedy, provide many opportunities to provide pro-health or social messages if the producers are willing to build those in. Radio call-in shows can reach many active listeners who will pay close attention to what you have to say (whether they *agree* with you or not). "Dear Abby" has legions of people who hang on her every word. Working your messages into entertainment formats can be effective because the audience is not expecting to learn anything, yet many people form their opinions and attitudes based on what they are exposed to in the entertainment media every day.

■ *Public service.* This is information that most types of media provide as a courtesy to the community. Public service programming might include community calendar announcements to publicize upcoming events, a weekly nonprofit spotlight to

---

WRITING LETTERS TO THE EDITOR

A letter to the editor can be used in many ways—to respond to an article or editorial that you disagree with, to agree with a piece and provide supporting facts, or to comment on an issue relevant to your community that has not necessarily been covered by the publication. To increase the likelihood of your letter being published, keep the following in mind:

▥ Be brief and to the point. A good length for a letter to the editor is approximately 100 words.

▥ Do not personally attack the author of an article or write in an inflammatory tone. Provide a rational, well thought-out response to the points with which you disagree.

▥ Include your name, address, and phone number with the letter. An anonymous letter probably will not be published, and the editor might need to call to confirm that you are indeed the author before printing it.

▥ Your letter is likely to be edited or shortened to fit the space available, so try to preemptively edit out any unnecessary or redundant sentences before submitting the letter to make it as concise as possible.

▥ Include the name of your organization in the letter or below your signature if you think it will enhance your credibility.

describe the services of a community organization, public service announcements, or community access cable programming.

WHO WILL YOU CONTACT IN THE MEDIA?

The key to implementing your media strategy is getting your information to the right people at the right places at the right time. Use your media contact list to identify the appropriate person for your purposes at each outlet. If you have an idea for a story on your issue, then contact the reporter who covers that beat or the news director. When you plan an event that you want covered by the media, contact the assignments editor or news director. To be booked as a guest on a television or radio talk show, approach the show's producer or host.

For long-term relationship building, get to know the media gatekeepers at each outlet. These are the people who set the editorial tone of the publication or station and determine what types of stories are covered. At a newspaper or magazine, this is the editor-in-chief or managing editor. At a radio or television station, the key gatekeeper is the station manager, program manager, or public affairs director. Write a letter to the key media gatekeepers in your community introducing yourself and your organization. Explain your issue and why they and their audiences should be interested. Identify exactly what you would like them to do. Increase the number of stories on your topic? Sponsor a public service campaign? Write an editorial on your issue? Follow up with a call to set up a meeting and make your case in person. At the very least, your organization will stand out to them the next time you send a press release or hold a media event.

HOW WILL YOU CONTACT THE MEDIA?

In addition to the media gatekeepers, start to establish beneficial working relationships with the reporters and producers at key outlets before you need to pitch them a story. Write to those who cover your issues to give them reactions to their previous stories related to your issue and provide them with an information packet on your organization for future reference. If a reporter or producer knows that you are available as a source, then that person might call you the next time he or she is working on a related story.

WRITING A PRESS RELEASE

A press release is a succinct summary of the story you are "pitching" to a news organization. To prevent your release from being pitched right into the garbage can, keep the following hints in mind:

- Make the release as short as possible. Ideally, you should keep it to one page, but certainly no more than two pages. If you have more than one page worth of information, then consider turning some of the information into a fact sheet or backgrounder to supplement the press release.

- Grab the reader's attention with a strong headline (generally eight words or less) and compelling lead sentence.

- Use recent trends, upcoming holidays, or other "pegs" to establish the newsworthiness and timeliness of your release.

- Report your information as straight news, without any hype or too many adjectives.

- Do not forget to include the who, what, why, where, when, and how of the issue. Provide the information in descending order of importance, with the most critical facts at the beginning.

- Be accurate with your facts, and avoid typos or misspellings of names, to maintain your credibility.

- Use quotes from key people involved in the news story when appropriate.

- Provide contact information, such as your name and phone number, for a reporter to call with questions about the press release. You might wish to list more than one person in case the reporter needs to reach someone immediately.

- Use proper press release format, typed double-spaced and on one side of the paper. Include the date and city in which the news is taking place in the form of a dateline just before the opening paragraph.

When you have news that you want covered by the media, send out a press release to your media list. Never send a press release to more than one person at the same outlet; if two reporters find that they have started writing the same story, then you might ruin your chances of ever getting another story covered. Avoid addressing the release to "Editor" or "Health Reporter" because without a person's name on the envelope, it might get lost in the shuffle. If you must send it without a name, then be as specific as possible in the title. You generally can send your press releases in three ways: mail, fax, and e-mail. Individual reporters or outlets might have their own preferences about how they wish to receive releases, so include that information on your media list. When you have an event to promote, send out a media advisory that lists only the who, what, why, when, and where of the occasion; this is much briefer than a press release.

Follow up with a phone call to the person you sent the release to a couple of days after he or she would have received it. If following up on a media advisory, call close to the day of the event to personally invite the press to cover it. Most news organizations work under tight time frames, so be respectful of the reporter's time when you call. Try to phone in the morning before noon rather than in the afternoon, which is when the deadlines for most outlets fall. Ask whether the person is "on deadline" or if he or she has a few minutes before you go into your pitch. Explain who you are and why your news is important. Be ready to follow up with additional information, and be enthusiastic about the topic as you explain why it is newsworthy. If you are not excited, then why should the reporter be?

WHAT DO YOU HAVE TO OFFER?

Keep in mind that the news media need people like you to help them fill column-inches and airtime. You know the topic, you have ideas for interesting stories, and you have access to the people the stories are about. Although you should not contact a reporter every week with a story concept, do not feel intimidated about calling if you truly have a newsworthy idea.

The more you can do to help the reporter do his or her work, the more likely your story will be the one that gets covered that day. Succinct information, such as fact sheets and backgrounders (explaining the events, legislation, or scientific concepts behind your news story), helps the reporter to quickly understand the issue. Photographs or video footage related to the

---

EXAMPLE OF A MEDIA ADVISORY

MEDIA ADVISORY

HEALTHVILLE CANCER COALITION INTRODUCES SKIN CANCER PREVENTION CAMPAIGN

The Healthville Cancer Coalition, comprised of representatives from 10 local organizations, will introduce its new campaign to prevent skin cancer on May 5, 1999. The campaign includes television and radio advertisements as well as a school district-wide children's contest to design the campaign's poster. The most recent data on local skin cancer rates also will be announced at the event.

PARTICIPANTS: Susan McCall
Chairperson,
Healthville Cancer
Coalition

Dr. Patricia Smith
Chief of Dermatology,
Healthville
General Hospital

John Delancey
Executive Director,
Healthville
Community Foundation

DATE: Tuesday, May 5, 1999

TIME: 11:00 a.m.

PLACE: Healthville General Hospital
Auditorium
123 Main Street, Healthville

CONTACT: David Solomon,
Healthville Cancer
Coalition
(123) 456-7890

CONDUCTING A PRESS CONFERENCE

You might wish to hold a press conference to respond to negative publicity about your program, to provide additional information on how a current news event affects your organization or community, or to actively generate attention to an issue your program is addressing. If you do not have major news to announce but wish to inform the media about an issue, then consider conducting a more informal media briefing with a small number of reporters that cover your topic.

To plan and conduct an effective press conference, follow these steps:

1. Clarify your purpose and the key messages you wish to convey at the press conference. Use those guidelines to shape what the speakers will say.

2. Prepare a media list of the reporters and media outlets you wish to invite to the press conference.

3. Set the date, time, and place of the press conference. The best days of the week are Tuesday through Thursday; to increase attendance, try not to schedule a media event on a Monday or Friday, and definitely avoid the weekend. The best time to hold the press conference is in the mid-morning, between 9:30 a.m. and 11:00 a.m., to leave enough time for the reporters to make their deadlines for the day. The event should be held in a site that is convenient for reporters to get to and has appropriate accommodations for the needs of the press. There must be sufficient room and lighting to set up television cameras. You can use your organization's conference room, a local hotel or conference facility, a community center, or a visually interesting and related outdoor location such as in front of the state capitol building.

4. Select two to three speakers. They should be articulate, knowledgeable, and comfortable dealing with the media. In addition to your organization's spokesperson, you might wish to include an expert on the topic to provide technical explanations, such as statistics and medical information, or a person from the community who is affected by the problem. Limit each person's comments to 5 minutes or less, and roughly script what each will say to avoid duplication among the speakers.

5. Send out a media advisory to everyone on your media list. If you have time, send it out a week in advance. If the press conference was called on short notice, then fax the advisory. In either case, follow up with a telephone call the day before or the morning of the event to encourage attendance and to get an idea of who will be there. Make sure that the wire services include your advisory on their daybooks the day before and the day of your event.

6. Before the press conference begins, set up the room. Place a table and chairs at the front with a name card in front of each speaker (facing the audience). Chairs for the reporters should be arranged theater style. You probably will need a podium with a microphone for your speakers. To make it easier for the reporters to record the proceedings without placing their own microphones on the podium, you can rent a "mult-box" that they can plug into. Make sure you have signs directing people to the room, and have a sign-in table where you can greet the reporters and give each of them a press kit.

7. Keep the total length of the press conference to between 30 and 45 minutes. Leave time at the end for a question-and-answer period. Work with the speakers in advance to anticipate possible questions and how best to answer them. Reporters might wish to set up individual interviews with the speakers after the event.

8. Follow up with the media outlets that were not represented to see whether they are interested in receiving a press kit from the event and in interviewing the speakers. If you did not receive the turnout you expected, it might have been because another breaking news story was happening at the same time.

story also heightens your chances of coverage. Provide as many "pieces" of the story as you can—real people affected by the issue, experts willing to be interviewed, copies of relevant studies. If you want television coverage, then make sure that you have visuals to offer such as children playing at a family support center, a counselor speaking with parents, and other compelling action shots.

HOW WILL YOU RESPOND WHEN THE MEDIA CALL YOU?

Even if you do not actively seek them out, the media might come to you for information or your reaction to a news story. When this happens, do not panic. Your internal readiness plan should designate a contact who is comfortable talking to the media and has the authority to speak for the organization. If that person is not available, then the person answering the phone should know to ask the deadline for a response for all media calls and find someone else to call back. Otherwise, your organization might miss an important opportunity to provide comments, respond to allegations, counter misinformation, or build a positive relationship with a reporter. Often, there are no second chances.

When speaking to a reporter, always be honest. If you fudge an answer, then it might come back to haunt you and will damage your credibility. When you do not know the answer to a question, just say so. Find out the reporter's deadline and either call back with the answer or make a referral to other sources who could speak on that point.

Make yourself as understandable as possible. Speak in plain English, without jargon or acronyms; not everyone knows that CAPTA is the Child Abuse Prevention and Treatment Act or that the word "lacerations" refers to cuts on the skin. Avoid mumbling or speaking too fast when talking to a reporter, especially if you are being recorded for radio or television. Broadcast media require actualities—taped quotes from interviewees—interspersed with the narration throughout their stories. If your portion of the interview is not clear, then you might be cut from the story.

Know the main message you want to get across and repeat it in several different ways throughout the interview. Keep the

---

ASSEMBLING YOUR PRESS KIT

A press kit should contain all the information a media professional needs to put together a story about your issue or organization. Provide press kits to the media at a press conference or media briefing or when you pitch a story.

A good press kit might contain the following, placed in a folder with pockets and labeled with your organization's name on the outside:

- Current press release
- Fact sheet providing statistics and information on the issue
- Backgrounder explaining what has happened to date on the issue or technical details
- Literature about your organization
- Photographs or camera-ready charts, graphs, or other materials to help illustrate the issue
- Copies of past newspaper articles on your organization or issue
- List of experts or people affected by the issue who are willing to be interviewed by the media
- Biographies of your key spokespersons
- Statements of support from your partner organizations

THE INTERNET AS A PUBLIC RELATIONS TOOL

The Internet and World Wide Web offer many public relations opportunities that can make your job easier and more effective. Here are some ideas:

■ Create a Web site about your organization. Include many of the pieces of information you would put in your press kit such as information on the issue and your organization. Be sure to post contact information for e-mail and telephone inquiries.

■ List your Web site on as many Internet search engines as possible (e.g., Yahoo!, AltaVista, InfoSeek) to ensure that someone searching for information on your topic will find your organization's Web site.

■ Provide your e-mail and Web site address on your letterhead and all pieces of literature you send out.

■ Send out press releases by e-mail. Most media organizations are now online, and you can either use a commercial service to electronically distribute your materials or do the legwork yourself to track down the appropriate e-mail addresses for the people you want to reach.

■ Do not forget about online news services when you consider where to send your press releases.

■ Ask other related organizations to include links to your Web site in exchange for you adding them to yours.

■ You can put all your campaign materials on the Web, from text-based brochures to graphics of posters and even sound and video files. Even if your target audience is not likely to use the Internet, many others will see your materials and become familiar with your campaign.

---

sentences to short "sound bites" to make them more usable as actualities. As you answer the reporter's questions, do not limit yourself to the questions at hand; integrate your key points into the answers as well. The better able you are to articulate the main messages throughout the interview, the more likely they will come through in the final story.

WORKSHEET 13:
Implementation Planning Worksheet

I. Distribution Plan

Distribution Checklist

Date to Be
Completed by

Partners chosen to participate in dissemination of materials   _____

Correct quantities of materials ordered   _____

Materials ready to be distributed   _____

Materials distributed to partner organizations   _____

Partners received instructions on how to distribute materials   _____

Materials available to target audience   _____

Media materials distributed to media outlets   _____

Inventory tracking system in place   _____

Materials reordering system in place   _____

Partner Distribution Plan

Organization Disseminating Materials	Contact Name/ Phone Number	Item 1 Quantity	Item 2 Quantity	Item 3 Quantity
1.				
2.				
3.				
4.				
5.				
6.				
7.				

(continued)

WORKSHEET 13:
Implementation Planning Worksheet *(continued)*

II. Internal Readiness Plan

1. Program spokesperson: _____

2. Backup spokesperson: _____

3. Key talking points about social marketing program:

a. _____

_____

b. _____

_____

c. _____

_____

d. _____

_____

e. _____

_____

4. Procedure for dealing with comments or complaints about the social marketing campaign:

_____

_____

_____

_____

5. Other people/organizations to refer reporters to for more information on topic:

Name	Organization	Phone Number	Type of Information

(continued)

WORKSHEET 13:
Implementation Planning Worksheet *(continued)*

6. Partner roles:

Partner Organization	Contact Name/Phone Number	Role(s) in Campaign
1.		
2.		
3.		
4.		
5.		
6.		
7.		
8.		
9.		
10.		

(continued)

WORKSHEET 13:
Implementation Planning Worksheet *(continued)*

III. Media Buy Plan

1. Broadcast Media Buys

Flight dates:

_____ to _____

_____ to _____

_____ to _____

Station	Contact Name/ Phone Number	Rank for Target Audience	Ad Rate	Number of Ads	Total Cost

2. Print Media Buys

Ad publication dates:

_____ _____

_____ _____

_____ _____

_____ _____

_____ _____

Publication	Contact Name/ Phone Number	Ad Size	Ad Rate	Number of Ads	Total Cost

(continued)

WORKSHEET 13:
Implementation Planning Worksheet *(continued)*

3. Out-of-Home Media Buys

Type of out-of-home media: _____

Posting dates: _____ to _____

Out-of-Home Company	Contact Name/ Phone Number	Ad Size	Ad Rate	Gross Rating Point Showing	Total Cost

(continued)

WORKSHEET 13:
Implementation Planning Worksheet *(continued)*

IV. Public Relations Plan

1. What is your purpose in seeking media attention?

_____

_____

_____

2. What is your "news"?

_____

_____

_____

3. What type of media coverage will you seek? (check all that apply)

☐ News

☐ Feature

☐ Editorial

☐ Entertainment

☐ Public service

☐ Other _____

4. Which specific formats will you use (e.g., talk show, op-ed, letter to the editor)?

_____

_____

_____

5. How will you seek media coverage to kick off or promote the campaign?

☐ Press release

☐ Press conference

☐ Media briefing

☐ Other media event: _____

6. What items will you include in your press kit?

_____

_____

_____

_____

_____

_____

MONITORING IMPLEMENTATION

Before implementation even begins, put monitoring mechanisms in place to retrieve feedback on the program and to catch any problems in their early stages. Although you might not be able to anticipate every type of problem you will encounter, a monitoring system will at least help to identify problems as they arise during implementation. Most problems can be easily solved if you detect them early enough, but left unchecked, they can mean the difference between success and failure.

Tracking the progress of your program helps you to accomplish the following:

- Ensure that the elements of the program are being carried out as planned

- Ensure quality

- Address any potential problems that arise

- Alter the course of the program (if necessary)

- Keep staff and partners energized

- Know when you might be running out of materials for restocking

- Assess the results of your program

Monitoring may be as simple as asking callers how they found out about your program, counting the number of brochures that have been given out, or making sure that your partners are doing what they promised. If you find that most of your referrals are coming from just a couple of clinics, then follow up with the other clinics to learn why they are not referring more people to you. Or, if the phone calls in response to your ads suddenly slow down to a trickle, make sure that the radio station did not stop running the commercials too early. Effective monitoring involves staying on top of trends in your program's activities and ensuring that implementation is on the right path toward accomplishing program goals.

PROCESS EVALUATION

Process evaluation activities monitor the day-to-day operations of your program so that you can say with relative certainty what comprised the actual intervention. You can evaluate the effects and contributions of each piece of the program to change or remove elements that are not working as intended. By keeping your finger on the pulse of the program, you will be able to adapt and make necessary adjustments along the way.

Before putting monitoring mechanisms in place, determine your process evaluation objectives. What measures will tell you whether your program is on track? You should not necessarily measure something just because you can; measure it only if it will help you in your assessments of program success. Identify the pieces of your program that will provide an indication of whether the campaign is progressing as planned.

Internally, determine how closely the program is meeting the projected timeline and budget as well as whether staff members understand and perform their roles correctly. Externally, assess the effectiveness of each of your partners in disseminating campaign materials or making referrals to your program. Make sure that media buys are implemented as directed. Track the number of inquiries coming into your organization as a result of the campaign and how they were handled. The specifics of your program will determine the elements that are included in your process evaluation.

The information that a process evaluation provides can help with improving the program during implementation itself rather than waiting until the campaign is over to assess whether the program went as planned. Tracking activities during implementation helps to answer the following questions:

- How many people were reached through the media with your advertisements or public service announcements? How many were target audience members?

- How many target audience members and other people participated in your program activities?

- How many responses (e.g., phone calls, mail requests, new appointments) did you get as a result of the program? How do these compare to those in the months leading up to the campaign and the same months the previous year(s)?

- How did your program respond to the inquiries that were received? Was appropriate action taken in each case?

- How many materials were handed or sent out to the target audience by your organization? How many materials were posted or displayed to be picked up?

- How many media "hits" (or news stories) appeared as a result of your public relations efforts?

- How many materials were each of your partners given? How many were disseminated by these partners?

- Were staff and partners adequately trained to effectively carry out their roles in the program? Did they perform their roles correctly?

- Were all activities carried out on budget and according to the timeline? If not, why not?

- Did all paid media ads run as scheduled?

- Are there any current events or pieces of legislation pending that might affect the program?

TRACKING MECHANISMS

The mechanisms you can use to track the progress of program implementation range from simple counts of phone calls and materials to complex analyses of management practices. Monitor closely all aspects of your program throughout the course of the implementation period rather than waiting until the end to look at the results. Some items will need to be assessed once a week or month, whereas others should be tracked on a daily basis. Following are the primary categories for monitoring during implementation, with a brief description and suggested list of methods.

Outreach Activities

Purpose: To evaluate whether materials were distributed in the manner and quantities planned

Tracking methods:

- *Materials inventory.* Use tracking forms to keep an accurate count of how many of each type of material goes out and whether materials need to be reordered.

- *Distribution list.* Create a list to track which organizations help to distribute the materials and follow up with phone calls to ensure receipt and dissemination.

- *Materials placement audit.* Physically visit partner organizations or outreach locations to check whether posters are up, brochures are placed where people can pick them up, and other materials are being used correctly.

Target Audience Response

Purpose: To assess the number of target audience members responding
             to and participating in the program as a result of the campaign

Tracking methods:

- *Response tracking sheets.* Categorize the incoming phone calls or mail to tally important items such as the type of request and the answers to the question "How did you find out about us?" The same sheet can be used to track a day's or week's worth of responses.

- *Activity reports.* Determine the number of people participating in program activities through sign-up sheets or attendance records.

- *Public "diaries" or graffiti sheets.* Place blank journals or hang blank pieces of butcher paper up in places such as clinic waiting rooms, community recreation centers, and program events to collect feedback from target audience members about the program and their feelings about an issue.

Media Exposure

Purpose: To determine whether paid media ran as scheduled, whether
             and when media ran public service announcements, and
             whether your public relations activities yielded media coverage
             as well as the number of target audience members reached
             through all these methods

Tracking methods:

- *Television and radio logs.* If you purchased media time, you will receive a list of exactly when each ad ran including (usually) any extra spots the station provided as public service announcements. If you did not purchase spots, then the station may or may not provide this information.

- *Tear sheets.* When you purchase ad space in newspapers or magazines, each publication will provide you with a copy of the page on which your ad appeared.

- *Clipping services.* Clipping services scan metropolitan and local community newspapers, television and radio news, and news wire services to provide you with clippings or transcripts of all stories mentioning your organization, a specific event, or topics of interest. Hire a clipping service before you begin your campaign because most cannot locate articles retroactively. You can analyze the media coverage of your campaign to assess whether your main messages got through and whether it was generally positive, negative, or neutral coverage.

■ *Bounceback cards.* Enclose a postage-paid postcard printed with a few quick questions when you submit your public service announcement for the public service director to fill out and send back to you. You might be able to get an idea of which stations intend to use the public service announcement, although busy individuals might ignore the cards.

Management Effectiveness/Efficiency

Purpose: To assess whether the program was managed well from the standpoint of staff, partners, timeline, and budget

Tracking methods:

■ *Staff survey or focus groups.* Either anonymously survey staff involved in program implementation or conduct focus groups to determine ways in which program management or other processes are going smoothly or could be improved.

■ *Partner feedback.* Elicit input from program partners regarding the effectiveness of program processes and communication through phone calls or surveys.

■ *Timeline and budget assessment.* Compare the original program timeline and budget with the actual outcome and assess what could be done differently the next time to comply better with each (if necessary).

Issue Monitoring

Purpose: To stay on top of trends and developments in the field by tracking changes and events that have strategic implications for the social marketing program

Tracking methods:

■ *News and information searches.* Subscribing to a daily source of news and information such as the Associated Press wire, Nexis, or a clipping service will notify you of any new developments or news in the field that might affect how the target audience responds to your program or how you present the program. Reading a major newspaper daily or monitoring news over the Internet also can help keep you informed.

"DON'T KID YOURSELF" CAMPAIGN IMPLEMENTATION

Implementation of the "Don't Kid Yourself" campaign in the pilot cities occurred over the course of 2 months between May and July 1996. The implementation plan helped to identify what needed to be done before the campaign kickoff. The clinics in Salt Lake City and Butte developed dissemination plans for distributing the posters, brochures, and coasters throughout the communities. The people who answered the phones at each clinic were briefed on the campaign and provided with information on how to respond to community complaints about the campaign.

The contractor negotiated and purchased radio advertising time on several stations in each city that focus group participants had indicated were popular with their peers. In most cases, the stations provided free spots as public service announcements for each spot that was purchased for the campaign or at least lowered their normal rates. The newspaper advertisements also were placed at nonprofit rates in the alternative and college newspapers in Salt Lake City, in certain sections of Butte's main newspaper, and in its local shopper. In addition to the paid advertising, a press release was sent out to local media outlets announcing the "Don't Kid Yourself" campaign.

Prior to the beginning of implementation, several tracking systems were put in place to help assess the effects of the campaign. A caller tracking sheet was developed and used to tally how callers answered the question "How did you find out about us?" Surveys were distributed to target audience members at the clinics throughout the entire implementation period to assess whether respondents were exposed to elements of the campaign. Blank "diaries" were placed in the clinic waiting rooms with instructions on the cover about the types of comments that were sought along with a pen attached to each book. A press clipping service also was hired to track any resulting media coverage of the campaign.

Implementation ran fairly smoothly over the 2-month period. Many local businesses and other organizations were willing to participate in the campaign by putting up posters and using the coasters in the bars and clubs. One of the ads had to be pulled from the Butte newspaper because a local health official felt it was too explicit and he would not provide his approval to run it. Although there were some negative phone calls related to the campaign, many more positive comments were received. The tracking systems were not consistently used by the receptionists, so the results were somewhat spotty for the caller tracking sheets and clinic surveys; many receptionists found it difficult to add another procedure to their regular routine. Although entries in the clinic diaries did not usually refer directly to the campaign, most of the comments were very positive about the care received in the clinics, and this improved morale among the staff. In both cities, target audience patients provided positive feedback about the campaign when they came to the clinics.

- *Legislative tracking systems.* Electronic services such as Washington Alert will notify you of any legislative actions on the topics of your choice.

- *Attitude surveys.* Polling organizations such as Gallup and Louis Harris regularly conduct national surveys to assess general attitudes on particular topics. Knowing the results of any polls taken on topics relating to your program may assist you in adjusting your program during implementation.

SECTION V NOTES

1. Available from Leading National Advertisers, 11 West 42nd Street, New York, NY 10036, phone: (212) 789-1400, fax: (212) 789-1450.

WORSHEET 14:
Implementation Tracking Worksheet

1. **What are the key process evaluation objectives for your program? (Remember that they must be measurable, specific, and attainable.)**

   a. _____

   _____

   b. _____

   _____

   c. _____

   _____

   d. _____

   _____

   e. _____

   _____

2. **What types of mechanisms will you use to track progress of your implementation?**

   a. Outreach activities:

   ☐ Materials inventory

   ☐ Distribution list

   ☐ Materials placement audit

   ☐ Other: _____

   b. Target audience response:

   ☐ Response tracking sheets

   ☐ Activity reports

   ☐ Diaries/graffiti sheets

   ☐ Other: _____

   c. Media exposure:

   ☐ Television and radio logs

   ☐ Tear sheets

   ☐ Clipping services

   ☐ Bounceback cards

   ☐ Other: _____

(continued)

WORKSHEET 14:
Implementation Tracking Worksheet *(continued)*

d. Management effectiveness/efficiency:

___ Staff survey

___ Staff focus groups

___ Partner feedback

___ Timeline and budget assessment

___ Other: _____

e. Issue monitoring:

___ News and information searches

___ Legislative tracking systems

___ Attitude surveys

___ Other: _____

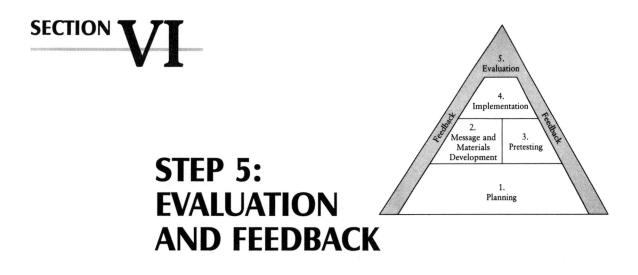

STEP 5: EVALUATION AND FEEDBACK

Section Overview

What if we never evaluated what we did in our daily lives? We might continually take the longest, most inefficient route home from work. We might lose a friend or spouse because we were unable to assess and correct the things that we did wrong in that relationship. Or, we might not realize that the medicine we were taking for an illness was ineffective and that we needed to try a different treatment. Just as we constantly evaluate our own actions based on their results, a social marketer must assess the effects that the program is having and make adjustments based on that information.

Although listed as the final step of the process, forms of evaluation and feedback occur throughout the life of a social marketing program. They are addressed here last because until you implement the program, you cannot assess whether it was successful in actually changing the behavior of your target audience and in meeting other objectives. To avoid a last-minute evaluation tacked on at the end of your campaign, build evaluation into the social marketing process from the very beginning.

This section consists of the following chapters:

- Chapter 19: Evaluation Basics

- Chapter 20: Evaluation Design

- Chapter 21: Evaluation Methods

- Chapter 22: Using Feedback to Improve Your Program

chapter nineteen

EVALUATION BASICS

The word "evaluation" often strikes fear in the hearts of program planners. However, with an understanding of why it is necessary and what it entails, you soon will see evaluation as an indispensable and not so daunting piece of a well-planned social marketing program.

WHY DO EVALUATION?

Increasingly, funders require that their grantees include an evaluation component in their programs. If this is your situation, then think of evaluation as something that you are doing for yourself rather than for your funders because you will benefit much more than they will. Even if you do not have an outside organization telling you to evaluate your program, it still is good social marketing practice.

Evaluation creates accountability. For this reason, many people are wary of having their programs evaluated and would prefer to rely on anecdotal evidence of success rather than actual data that may or may not reflect well on them. Do not be intimidated by evaluation; instead, see it as an opportunity to prove that your program has made a difference. Positive results also might assist you in securing additional funding in the future.

If done well, your evaluation activities also will help to improve your program while it is being implemented as well as in later incarnations. By identifying what does and does not work, you will be able to focus your resources on the most effective parts of the program and eliminate or reduce other components. A good evaluation is one that provides useful information, not just interesting statistics. Design your evaluation activities around the questions you need answered to improve your program. Remember the concept of "backward research"? This is the same idea.

Your evaluation need not be conducted by an outside evaluator, although if you lack research expertise on your staff or wish to ensure a totally objective

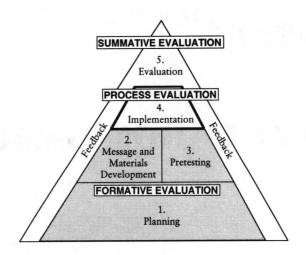

Figure 19.1 Evaluation in the Social Marketing Process

assessment, you will find a consultant quite useful. You can carry out most types of evaluation methods yourself or with volunteers, if necessary. Social marketing research does not have to be the type of research you learned about in school—with randomized treatment and control groups, complicated statistics, and primarily academic questions. There is a place for this type of research in social marketing, but for the most part, you can use relatively simple methods to get the type of information you need.

TYPES OF EVALUATION

When you begin to consider evaluation of your social marketing campaign, you might focus primarily on the question "Did the program work?" But evaluation entails more than this broad question. Several types of evaluation help to assess different aspects of program success throughout the life of the project, as depicted in Figure 19.1. Balch and Sutton[1] aptly pose three simple questions pertaining to each level of evaluation research:

- What should we do?

- How are we doing?

- Did we do it?

The first question—"What should we do?"—is answered through formative evaluation. Formative research is done to shape the program strategy and pretest the materials prior to implementation. You are already familiar with formative evaluation through your activities in the first three steps of the social marketing process: planning, message and materials development, and pretesting. This is the research you used to determine the messages, materials, and overall marketing mix that might work best for the target audience and then to narrow down the choices through pretesting.

During implementation, the second question—"How are we doing?"—assesses whether the program is executed as planned. *Process* evaluation, discussed in Chapter 18, determines what information or services were delivered as a result of the program and to whom. Understanding what actually happened during the course of implementation, as opposed to what was supposed to occur, can help identify why certain elements of the program were or were not effective. Process evaluation is especially useful for determining how to adjust the program in midstream or to improve implementation for the next time.

Answering the third question—"Did we do it?"—involves summative evaluation. This type of research investigates the effect that your program had on factors related to the problem or issue it was designed to address, and it is the focus of this chapter. Summative evaluation can be further separated into two different components: outcome evaluation and impact evaluation. *Outcome* evaluation occurs at the end of program implementation or periodically over the life of a campaign. Identifying the extent of attitude and behavior change in the target audience and correlating it with individual exposure to the campaign is an important measure of the program's effectiveness. Outcome measures are commonly used in summative evaluation to link achievement of the program's objectives to campaign activities. Pre- and postcampaign knowledge, attitudes, and behavior surveys to assess related changes are the most common type of outcome evaluation method.

Impact evaluation makes the leap from behavior change to health or social outcomes. This type of evaluation determines whether the people who adopt the behavior promoted by the social marketing program experience a subsequent reduction in morbidity or mortality (or improvement in quality of life) related to the overall goal of the program. The actual impact of the campaign often is difficult to assess accurately. Because many of the problems that are tackled by social marketers will not appear until many years after the campaign (e.g., heart disease, cancer), it might be impossible to determine the effect of a particular social marketing program on overall trends. Long-term prospective studies following participants over time often are necessary to assess the program's effects on these types of issues. However, for other outcomes that change relatively quickly (e.g., HIV

ETHICAL EVALUATION

Kotler and Roberto[a] propose another type of evaluation for social marketing programs— ethical evaluation. Whenever we strive to change people's behavior, we must do so responsibly and be accountable to the target audience members. Although in the end the results of the program are the final measure of success, the means to that end are just as important. Ethical issues should be considered at each stage of program development to ensure the integrity of target audience research and that the program itself does not encourage behavior change in an unethical way.

People never should be coerced into a behavior, even though it might be "for their own good." Making offers that the target audience members cannot refuse, such as large amounts of money, might be ethically suspect and counterproductive to long-term behavior change. Excessive incentives might encourage materialism and a disinclination for people to help themselves without an extrinsic reward.

Social marketing programs might have side effects or unintended consequences that are harmful in the long run. For example, a program intended to empower low-income women to use condoms resulted in beatings by several male partners who perceived the women's insistence on using condoms as an insult. Whenever possible, potential negative effects of the program should be identified and explored with the target audience during the initial formative research. Implementation of the program should be monitored to ensure that it "does no harm" so that changes can be made midstream (if necessary).

a. Philip Kotler and Eduardo Roberto, *Social Marketing: Strategies for Changing Public Behavior* (New York: Free Press, 1989), 352-363.

status, pregnancy), it is possible to track rates before and after implementation of the program.

(Note: Depending on your academic background, you might have learned different names for each type of evaluation. This book follows the standard used in the field of social marketing. The names are not as important as the concepts, so do not worry if you use a different set of labels to distinguish each type of evaluation.)

EVALUATION CHALLENGES

The anxiety often felt by new social marketers about evaluation is not entirely without basis. Done correctly, an evaluation can provide valuable data and feedback. Done poorly, an ineffective campaign might receive a glowing review, or the positive effects of a well-constructed program might go undetected. This is due to a variety of challenges to conducting a sound evaluation. These hurdles can best be overcome by recognizing and planning for them from the start.

The main challenges you might face in your evaluation include the following:

- ■ *Unrealistic expectations.* Communications alone can go only so far in bringing about reductions in morbidity and mortality, particularly for chronic diseases. Your social marketing program, in all likelihood, will not dramatically alter these rates in your community overnight or even after 1 or 2 years. When evaluating your communications activities, be realistic in what you can expect for your results. Awareness, knowledge, attitudes, intentions, and behavior all can be measured and linked to your program. Whether that behavior change actually affects the problem it is designed to address might be out of your control. An incorrect theory of causation of the problem (whether biomedical or psychosocial), additional campaigns being done by other programs, and delayed effects of the intervention that might not be evident for decades are among the factors that can conceal or confound the related morbidity and mortality data.

- ■ *Limited resources.* The most imposing barrier to conducting an evaluation can be lack of resources, whether in the form of funds, staff time, or expertise. Often, social marketing projects barely have enough money for formative research and materials production, so summative evaluation gets short shrift. There are, however, ways in which to stretch your project funds and use low-cost methods to ensure at least some evaluation of whether your program met its objectives. Universities can provide a wealth of evaluation expertise as well as potential free or low-cost labor in the form of a professor interested in combining his or her research with your campaign or a health education or research methods graduate student looking for a class project. Using secondary data from other sources, such as annual surveys or epidemiological surveillance systems already in place, is another way in which to minimize the costs involved with data collection.

- *Reliance on a single method.* Just like the six blind men feeling various parts of a pachyderm and coming to vastly different conclusions about what an elephant looks like—a snake (trunk), a tree (leg), a wall (side), a rope (tail), a fan (ear), or a spear (tusk) from each of their perspectives—you might find diverse results depending on the research methods you use in your evaluation. To avoid getting just one possibly skewed description of your program's effects, use several different methods whenever possible to round out the picture. Combining the results of more than one research method can compensate for the weaknesses of each technique; this is called triangulation.

- *Using the wrong model.* Social marketing is not hard science. Although rigorous standards still apply to the research we do, the "A causes B" type of model that is found in the biomedical sciences is not as clear-cut in the behavioral sciences. Human behavior cannot be put into a vacuum to test the effects of various messages; external and internal factors always are at work, and controlling for them is not easy. For this reason, the experimental model so often used in clinical trials does not always yield accurate results for communications-based programs. The type of evaluation done by those in the advertising and marketing fields to assess the effectiveness of their communications is more appropriate for a social marketing program than that of the medical world. Scientists would be aghast at social marketers using preliminary evaluation data to adjust the program in midstream. Remember that you are not testing various hypotheses of behavior change theory. Your mission is not to produce pristine data but rather to implement the most effective campaign possible.

- *Asking the wrong questions.* Maybe it would be nice to know the height, weight, and nutritional habits of all the respondents to your survey, but if you are assessing the results of a breast cancer screening campaign, do you really need to know that? Avoid the temptation to learn as much about the participants as possible while you have their attention and cooperation; do not take advantage of the situation to ask 20 additional questions that are irrelevant to your evaluation. Questions should focus on whether you achieved the program objectives as laid out in the planning phase. Always ask yourself "What will I learn from this question, and how will I use the responses?"

- *Technical problems.* Even when you structure the evaluation research correctly, other issues can arise that make your results invalid. Statistics software, for example, can make data analysis much easier; however, when someone who does not fully understand the meanings and limitations of various statistical tests runs the analysis on that software, the results might be misinterpreted or meaningless. Other problems might affect the evaluation process outside of imperfect procedural techniques such as a small target audience making it difficult to find people to interview, a low response rate to your survey, and inexperienced interviewers. Seeking advice from an expert evaluator, or at least someone in your field who has conducted evaluation research previously, can help you to identify potential problems and to pose solutions.

- *Resistance from program staff or participants.* Staff often feel threatened by evaluations. Members of the target audience might not see any benefit to themselves in giving you information on their private lives. This can wreak havoc with collecting evaluation data. Your staff and others working on the program might need assurances that their jobs or reputations will not be put in jeopardy by negative evaluation results. Process evaluation examining project management can be done anonymously. Any data collection done by frontline staff should be as unobtrusive to their normal responsibilities as possible to avoid their balking at additional work. Target audience members might need incentives (monetary or otherwise), as well as a guarantee of confidentiality, to get them to participate.

■ *Waiting until the program is over to start evaluation.* Do not get all the way through implementation of your program before starting to think about evaluation. Ideally, you should collect baseline data at some point before implementation begins to be able to compare factors such as attitudes and behaviors before and after the campaign. Process, outcome, and impact evaluation need to be designed into the program to have meaningful results at the end. In addition, ongoing evaluation provides real-time feedback to help you adjust and improve the program while it still can make a difference.

■ *Failure to use evaluation results.* There is an epidemic among program managers (social marketing and otherwise) of the "put it on a shelf" syndrome. Every year, thousands of evaluation reports that were sweated over for months end up on bookshelves, never to be touched again. Do not let this happen to your evaluation. If designed well, your evaluation results should provide you with recommendations for how to improve the next phase of your campaign. The feedback also can assist you with designing and implementing social marketing programs on other issues, based on what you learned about the process and target audience. Make the evaluation report a living document rather than just a pile of dead tree pulp on the shelf.

chapter twenty

EVALUATION DESIGN

With any research method you choose, you first will decide how to structure your evaluation design. This will determine where you find your data, at what points you take measurements, and whether you will use comparison groups. The design you use to carry out the evaluation will depend in part on your resources and the length of time the program is implemented. An evaluation design can be either cross-sectional (i.e., administered to people randomly chosen at particular points in time) or prospective (i.e., following the same individuals over time). Prospective studies involve more intensive recruitment and follow-up but can yield more detailed data.

In your summative evaluation, the ultimate goal is to determine the effects of your program on the target audience. How accurately you do this relates to whether or not you use an experimental approach. A true experimental design allows you to state with relative certainty that it was your campaign, rather than other outside influences, that caused any differences you find. By randomly assigning people or communities either to participate in the social marketing program or to serve as a comparison group that is not exposed, you can eliminate much of the "noise" that obscures the program's effects. Because true experimental research can be very costly and requires a high level of expertise, it is not practical to expect from most small-scale social marketing programs. You can, however, structure your evaluation to increase your chances of obtaining valid results even if you do not use the most rigorous design.

Before you decide the actual method you will use, such as a survey, observations, or qualitative techniques, determine the points at which you will collect the data and how complex the

---

ELEMENTS OF AN EVALUATION DESIGN

An evaluation design consists of the following elements:

1. *Program goals and objectives.* The goals and objectives you set during the planning phase will be used to assess whether the program achieved what it set out to do.
2. *Data to be collected.* You must specify exactly what information will be collected in the evaluation to measure attainment of the goals and objectives.
3. *Methodology.* The research methods that you will use to collect the data should be laid out clearly. This includes how you will recruit research participants or find the data to be used, the sample size needed, when the research will take place, and exactly how the research will be conducted.
4. *Data collection instruments.* The survey questionnaire, focus group topic guide, or other research instrument should be developed and pretested before using it in the actual evaluation.
5. *Data processing and analysis.* Before collecting any data, determine how they will be converted into a usable format and analyzed. This will assist you in designing a data collection instrument that will facilitate these processes before it comes time to input the data.
6. *Evaluation report.* To be most useful, write up the resulting data analysis into an evaluation report that relays the key findings and recommendations for changes in the program.

EVALUATION RESEARCH TERMS TO KNOW

Although this book cannot teach you the technical aspects of evaluation research and statistical analysis, here are some terms you might need to understand as you design your program's evaluation:

Validity. This is the degree to which the research actually measures what it is supposed to measure. Improperly constructed questions or research methods, as well as other types of bias or error, can affect the validity of your research.

Reliability. This refers to consistency of measurement. Your data collection instruments and research methods should produce the same results if applied twice to the same people or if administered to similar people in similar situations.

Sampling. This is the process of selecting people to research from a particular population. Results from the sample are then used to generalize back to the entire population. For this reason, samples usually are chosen randomly to provide a representative group of people. Statistical methods are used to determine the sample size needed to ensure validity.

Descriptive statistics. These are techniques to organize and summarize data. They include numerical values that describe the characteristics of a sample such as frequencies, means, medians, and standard deviations (a measure of the variability of the data). Descriptive statistics are fairly simple to calculate and might be sufficient for your purposes.

Inferential statistics. These are techniques to test relationships between variables, changes within a population, or differences between groups. They include tests such as correlation, regression, chi-square, and analysis of variance. Inferential statistics generally require a good understanding of how each test works and are the best way for you to determine quantitatively whether your program made a difference.

Probability level. This is used with inferential statistical tests to determine the probability that any changes or differences in the results are due to chance alone. The most common probability (p) level used is .05, meaning that there is only a 5% chance that the results occurred randomly, and any p value less than that indicates that there is something nonrandom causing those differences. This might not necessarily mean that it was your program that created the changes, but if you design the research well, then it can be a good indication.

Correlation. This refers to the statistical association between two sets of numerical variables. You might, for example, find a high correlation between someone performing your target behavior and being exposed to elements of your campaign.

Confounding. This is when two variables are related because of an association of both with a third, perhaps unknown, variable. For example, the children of women who use more expensive strollers may score higher on an intelligence test, but is it because of the strollers or because of their mothers' higher socioeconomic status? The mothers' social class might be a confounding factor in the relationship. You may encounter similar confounding variables when evaluating the effects of your program.

---

evaluation design will be. The following four sections discuss the most commonly used approaches.

DATA FROM EXISTING RECORDS

You do not always need to create an elaborate questionnaire to find information that is useful for your evaluation. Use data that are already being collected, either by your organization or by secondary sources, to compare relevant measurements before and after the social marketing program. These measurements could be statistics your program collects routinely such as the monthly numbers of visits to your clinic, phone calls to your toll-free hotline, and mammograms done by your program. Or, you might be able to obtain data from other public or private organizations such as frequencies of diagnoses from a local disease or emergency room registry, condom sales from local drug stores, and state morbidity and mortality statistics. The Behavioral Risk Factor Surveillance System (BRFSS), a telephone survey conducted by all states, might be a useful source of data on knowledge and behaviors for your purposes.

The advantage of using existing data is clear: You do not have to start from scratch by conducting new research. If you can find data that answer your evaluation questions, then by all means, use them. In cases where the exact information you need is not available or easily measurable, consider using proxy measures, that is, variables that often occur along with or are caused by the phenomenon you wish to measure. For example, you can get an idea of changes in behaviors related to HIV risk by looking at trends in the rates of Hepatitis B, which is transmitted in a similar way and is reportable in all states.

Disadvantages of this design are common to all approaches that measure changes only in the population that is exposed to the campaign. There is no way in which to tell whether changes in your evaluation indicators were the result of your program. Other factors occurring simultaneously with your campaign, such as a major news story about your issue, a splashy new advertising blitz by another organization, and changing demographic trends, might be the impetus for the changes you see. The effects of an event such as basketball star Magic Johnson's announcement that he was HIV positive far overshadowed the efforts to raise awareness by most AIDS prevention programs. Your environmental analysis during the planning phase, as well as issue monitoring throughout implementation, will help you to identify any possible factors that might obscure the effects of your program in the evaluation.

SAME GROUP PRETEST-POSTTEST

For small-scale social marketing programs, the most common evaluation design is to take measurements of the target audience before and after implementation (and sometimes at additional midpoints for long-term programs). This generally is the least expensive method of collecting valid data if you are conducting primary research. For example, if you wish to test changes in knowledge, attitudes, and behaviors, you can conduct a survey during the planning phase and then administer the same survey with additional questions to assess exposure to the campaign after implementation. Because your media communications likely will be seen throughout your whole community or geographic area, it might be difficult to find a control group that has not been exposed to the campaign. As discussed earlier, the disadvantage of following only the exposed group is that you might not be able to attribute changes in outcomes specifically to the campaign.

COMPARISON TO A STANDARD

If you cannot use a control group in your design but wish to have an external standard with which to compare your results, you might be able to find state or national data for the same time period that will give an indication of overall trends. Look for a large-scale survey being conducted with a similar population, such as the BRFSS or the Youth Risk Behavior Surveillance System (which includes national, state, and local school-based surveys of adolescents), and use the same questions in your own questionnaire. If the survey you are using as the standard is done annually or more frequently, then you can compare the differences you find in your population to those of the larger population over the same time period. National surveys of this type, however, might not analyze their results quickly enough for your purposes, or you might not be able to find an analogous standard for the type of research you wish to do.

If your target audience is significantly different in key ways from the population used to determine the standard, then this design will not yield accurate results. For example, your community might have a better high school health curriculum than do most districts in your state, which would make adolescents in your target audience more knowledgeable about health issues from the start. Or, the death from steroid use of a well-known local athlete during the course of your campaign might increase awareness of the issue in your community but not within the larger population being used as a comparison. For this reason, this research design should be used only when the target audience is very similar to the standard's population.

USING CONTROL GROUPS

To be the most certain that your evaluation results truly reflect the effects of your social marketing program, use a control group that has not been exposed to the campaign for comparison. This more complex and costly evaluation design is not often used by community-based programs that have fewer fiscal and professional resources, but it is the most rigorous type of research. In an experimental design, you randomly assign

---

BEHAVIORAL RISK FACTOR SURVEILLANCE SYSTEM

The U.S. Centers for Disease Control and Prevention (CDC) sponsor several large-scale, health-related surveys that you can use to follow trends over time or as a comparison for your own survey results. One ongoing survey that you can use to analyze changes in your state is the Behavioral Risk Factor Surveillance System (BRFSS). You might be able to work with your state's behavior risk factor coordinator to add questions on your issue or to get a copy of the questionnaire for your own use.

The BRFSS is the primary source of state-based information on risk behaviors among adult populations. Questions elicit information from adults on their knowledge, attitudes, and behaviors related to issues such as health status and access to care, tobacco and alcohol use, dietary patterns, leisure time physical activities, injury control, women's health issues, use of preventive services (e.g., immunization; screening for breast, cervical, and colorectal cancer), and HIV/AIDS.

Every month, states select random samples of adults for telephone interviews. The questionnaires have three parts:

- ▓ Core questions used by all states
- ▓ Standard sets of questions on selected topics that states may choose to add
- ▓ Questions developed by individual states on issues of special interest (e.g., prostate cancer, bicycle helmet use)

(continued)

the research participants either to be exposed to the campaign or to serve in the control group. Because it can be difficult to do this when using mass media throughout the community, an experimental design works best when you are able to control exposure to the program's elements such as with one-on-one counseling or in a classroom setting.

A "quasi-experimental" design might be more appropriate for a program using mass media in one or more communities. Your control group could be a community or population that is similar demographically to the target audience but is not exposed to the campaign. The comparison might be, for example, with those who fit the target audience definition in another similar community outside of the range of the mass media channels you use in the target community. A college-based alcohol abuse prevention program could use another college with similar demographics and alcohol use rates as a control. A statewide immunization program could randomly select some of its clinics to participate in the campaign in their communities, with the rest serving as controls.

If both the exposed and control groups are similar to each other in key ways, then you can assume that any changes you detect between the beginning of the program and after implementation are a result of your campaign. This is the basis of the experimental design; any differences in the people selected for the exposed or control group will be taken care of through randomization. In the quasi-experimental design, however, you take a risk that the control group might differ from the exposed group in an important but unforeseen way. Administering both a pretest and a posttest will help to assess the similarity between the groups on key variables such as knowledge, attitudes, and behaviors. With an experimental design, however, you may assume a similar starting-off point for both groups and collect only postimplementation data (although a pretest still will be useful as a check).

EVALUATION INDICATORS

Changes in the evaluation indicators, or key outcomes to be measured, will tell you whether you have achieved your social marketing objectives. By carefully selecting the indicators you track, you will be able to identify where your program has been most successful or where it needs more work. Indicators should be linked to the program objectives you set at the beginning and must be measurable. You can use indicators occurring at either the individual or community level.

BEHAVIORAL RISK FACTOR SURVEILLANCE SYSTEM
(continued)

Information on age, gender, racial/ethnic background, education, and other demographic factors is gathered so that estimates can be made for specific population groups. The CDC edits and processes data from each state's monthly interviews and then returns prevalence information and selected reports to all states for their use.

For more information or to locate your state behavior risk factor coordinator, contact the agency at the following address:

Behavioral Surveillance Branch
National Center for Chronic Disease Prevention and Health Promotion
Centers for Disease Control and Prevention, Mail Stop K-30
4770 Buford Highway NE
Atlanta, GA 30341-3724
http://www.cdc.gov/nccdphp/brfss/
e-mail: ccdinfo@cdc.gov
phone: (770) 488-5303
fax: (770) 488-5974

Individual-level indicators consist of data for particular individuals, which are then aggregated and analyzed. Surveys are the most common method used to collect this type of information. Individual-level indicators encompass measures such as the following:

- Knowledge
- Attitudes
- Beliefs
- Behaviors
- Stage of change
- Demographics

The advantage of using individuals as the base of analysis is that you can directly measure changes in the factors your program seeks to influence. You also can examine the characteristics of those who adopted the behavior versus those who did not. Collecting the data you need from a large number of individuals, however, can be expensive and time-consuming and, therefore, is not always feasible.

For this reason, community-level indicators might be more appropriate to use when you have limited resources. Community-level data cannot provide firsthand information about items such as knowledge, attitudes, and behaviors linked to individual attributes; rather, they show trends occurring on a larger scale. Data come from organizations, public agencies, providers, and businesses rather than from the individuals who are your primary target audience. Unobtrusive observations of relevant factors in the community or of people's behavior are a key method of tracking community-based indicators. Instead of asking people directly whether they smoke, you could work with local stores to obtain sales data for cigarettes, observe the number of people smoking in a particular location, track enrollment in smoking cessation programs, or look at surveillance data for smoking rates in your community.

Community-based indicators can be related to the following[2]:

- *Environmental change* (e.g., number of cigarette vending machines in local restaurants, availability of fresh fruit at convenience stores)
- *Policy and regulation* (e.g., number of companies with no-smoking policies, whether local school districts have an effective AIDS education curriculum)
- *Information accessibility* (e.g., percentage of health care providers that routinely counsel their patients to quit smoking, extent of local media coverage about your issue)
- *Behavioral outcomes* (e.g., tobacco sales to minors, proportion of shelf space devoted to low-fat foods in grocery stores)

EXAMPLES OF COMMUNITY-LEVEL INDICATORS

The following community-level indicators are among those generated by participants in a project to evaluate community-based cardiovascular disease programs sponsored and organized by the U.S. Centers for Disease Control and Prevention (CDC).[a]

Tobacco Use

Policy and regulation:

- Clean air laws for public buildings, restaurants, worksites, and so on
- Vending machine regulations in communities
- Enforcement of "no sales to minors" ordinances throughout the community

Information accessibility:

- Materials for screening and cessation in use by health professionals
- Signs telling of environmental tobacco smoke

Environmental change:

- Percentage of restaurant seats in no-smoking sections
- Percentage of worksites with no-smoking areas
- Presence of vending machines in restaurants

Behavioral outcomes:

- Surveillance data on tobacco sales to minors
- Disappearance of tobacco products (store inventory)
- Observations of behavior in no-smoking areas

Physical Activity

Policy and regulation:

- Presence of local policy to include physical education in K-12 curriculum
- Amount/percentage of local budget per capita devoted to physical activity or recreation
- Presence of policies promoting inclusion of recreation facilities with new construction

Information accessibility:

- Percentage of health care providers that routinely advise patients to exercise more
- Availability of materials at worksites linking physical activity to cardiovascular disease

Environmental change:

- Miles of walking trails per capita
- Number of physical activity facilities per capita in schools
- Availability of exercise facilities to community members

Behavioral outcomes:

- Observations of use (e.g., in malls, on trails)
- Membership in physical activity organizations (e.g., YMCAs, YWCAs, health clubs)
- Sales of selected physical activity items (e.g., sports equipment, exercise videos)

Diet and Nutrition

Policy and regulation:

- Percentage of schools with lunch options congruent with dietary guidelines
- Presence of low-fat foods in commodity food programs
- Policy to monitor nutrition claims made by local food retailers

Information accessibility:

- "Point of purchase" information provided (e.g., cafeterias)
- Presence of food pyramid charts in learning environments

Environmental change:

- Presence of healthy food in vending machines in schools
- Healthy menus in schools, at worksites, and other locations
- Number of low-fat items in restaurants (menu analysis)

Behavioral outcomes:

- Bar code sales data
- Inventory control data for food use (e.g., school and worksite cafeterias)
- Proportion of low-fat items in stores (via use of marker items such as low-fat milk)

a. Terrie Sterling, Allen Cheadle, and Thomas Schmid, "Report from a CDC-Sponsored Project to Develop Community-Level Indicators for Evaluating Cardiovascular Health Promotion Programs" (unpublished manuscript, Centers for Disease Control and Prevention, Division of Chronic Disease Control and Community Intervention, 1997).

Because you are collecting data from a relatively small number of organizations rather than from many individuals, community-based indicators can be less expensive and time-consuming to track. It might be difficult, however, to identify indicators of this type that are relevant to your program. Also, if you did not actively work to address the indicators you choose to assess, then you would be hard-pressed to link any changes back to your program.

twenty one

EVALUATION
METHODS

Collect the evaluation data using a variety of research methods, both quantitative and qualitative, for the broadest view of the effects of your social marketing program and areas that need improvement. The methods you use will be determined in part by the evaluation design and indicators you select. For example, focus groups will not yield data on the rate of adoption of the target behavior but can provide important feedback on how the campaign was received among target audience members and how they used the information and materials. The most common research methods used in evaluation are discussed in this chapter.

SURVEYS

Surveys are by far the most widely used method to assess the success of a social marketing program. Quantitative data, preferably those that can be compared to the same measurements before the campaign was implemented, are the only way in which to really demonstrate behavior change and other effects to funders or critics of your program. If you conducted a knowledge, attitudes, and behaviors survey in the planning phase of your program, then use the same questions in the evaluation questionnaire and the same methodology to assess overall changes in responses. You also can add questions to assess whether the respondents were exposed to the campaign and what actions they might have taken as a result.

Many methods of collecting survey data exist, each with its own advantages and disadvantages, including the following:

■ *Mailed questionnaires.* The survey questionnaires are sent by mail to randomly selected respondents along with cover letters and stamped return envelopes. This is a low-cost, low-effort way of distributing and collecting the questionnaires. The problem is that the response rate generally is low as well. Providing an incentive to return the questionnaires, such as a chance for winning a prize in a drawing of all the respondents or a gift certificate in exchange for participation, will help to increase the number of responses you get back. Mailed questionnaires also offer the respondents anonymity and more time to consider their answers.

- *Telephone interviews.* Trained interviewers call potential respondents, either by randomly dialing or by using a prescreened list of numbers, and ask the survey questions by telephone. This method is more labor intensive, but having a live person to persuade the individual to participate can increase the response rate dramatically. With the rise of telemarketers, people are more wary of phone calls from strangers asking them questions, but a good interviewer or an introductory letter telling them they will be receiving a phone call can dispel those concerns. Telephone interviews might not be appropriate for asking questions on sensitive or very personal topics because respondents might not be comfortable or truthful. Although this method excludes anyone who does not have a telephone, you might be able to reach more people over the phone than in person.

- *In-person interviews.* Trained interviewers meet with the survey respondents, whether chosen randomly or through a preselection process, in person to administer the questionnaire. This type of survey can take up a significant amount of the interviewers' time, especially if the interviews take place at different locations, and the interviews often run longer than telephone interviews. Interviewing someone in person means that you can ask questions that involve audiovisual components or can conduct observations during the same session. You also can establish rapport with participants to enlist their cooperation more readily and to be able to ask sensitive questions. This method, unlike the previously described designs, requires interviewers who are geographically near the people participating in the survey.

- *Computerized surveys.* A fairly recent development is the advent of surveys administered by computer in which participants read each question on the computer screen and directly input their responses using a touchscreen, keyboard, or mouse. Portable computers make it easy to collect data quickly anywhere and have them immediately available for data analysis, skipping the data input step. Wording of questions can be personalized based on previous responses, and the users need not worry about skipping inapplicable questions. Respondents might be more comfortable providing answers to sensitive questions directly into the computer, particularly if they are familiar with the technology. For certain populations that are not used to working with computers, however, this technique might be intimidating.

OBSERVATION

As Yogi Berra once said, "You can observe a lot just by watchin'." Observation is a technique you can use to measure people's actual behavior in a given situation or to assess whether they have the skills needed to perform

SAMPLE OBSERVATION CHECKLIST

This is a sample of an observation checklist used to track bicycle helmet use in one community.

Date: _____   Time: From _____ a.m./p.m. to _____ a.m./p.m.

Location: _____

Weather: _____

Observer: _____

For each person observed riding a bicycle, circle the appropriate mark:

Observation	Sex		Age (years)			Group/Alone		Helmeted?		Child on Board?		Child Helmeted?	
1	M	F	<12	12-18	>18	G	A	Y	N	Y	N	Y	N
2	M	F	<12	12-18	>18	G	A	Y	N	Y	N	Y	N
3	M	F	<12	12-18	>18	G	A	Y	N	Y	N	Y	N
4	M	F	<12	12-18	>18	G	A	Y	N	Y	N	Y	N
5	M	F	<12	12-18	>18	G	A	Y	N	Y	N	Y	N
6	M	F	<12	12-18	>18	G	A	Y	N	Y	N	Y	N
7	M	F	<12	12-18	>18	G	A	Y	N	Y	N	Y	N
8	M	F	<12	12-18	>18	G	A	Y	N	Y	N	Y	N
9	M	F	<12	12-18	>18	G	A	Y	N	Y	N	Y	N
10	M	F	<12	12-18	>18	G	A	Y	N	Y	N	Y	N
11	M	F	<12	12-18	>18	G	A	Y	N	Y	N	Y	N
12	M	F	<12	12-18	>18	G	A	Y	N	Y	N	Y	N
13	M	F	<12	12-18	>18	G	A	Y	N	Y	N	Y	N
14	M	F	<12	12-18	>18	G	A	Y	N	Y	N	Y	N
15	M	F	<12	12-18	>18	G	A	Y	N	Y	N	Y	N
16	M	F	<12	12-18	>18	G	A	Y	N	Y	N	Y	N
17	M	F	<12	12-18	>18	G	A	Y	N	Y	N	Y	N
18	M	F	<12	12-18	>18	G	A	Y	N	Y	N	Y	N
19	M	F	<12	12-18	>18	G	A	Y	N	Y	N	Y	N
20	M	F	<12	12-18	>18	G	A	Y	N	Y	N	Y	N

NOTE: M = male; F = female; G = group; A = alone; Y = yes; N = no.

a particular task. Research that relies on self-reports of behavior runs the risk of obtaining answers that the respondents think reflect best on themselves, whether accurate or not. Observing people in a natural setting without their awareness of you watching them can provide a better indication of what they actually do. Of course, this technique might not always be appropriate, but for behaviors such as wearing a bicycle helmet or looking at nutrition labels in the supermarket, observation is very effective. Observation also can assess whether a particular skill promoted by the campaign, such as mixing an oral rehydration solution in the proper proportions or lifting heavy boxes with the knees rather than with the back, is being done correctly (with or without the individual's knowledge of participation in the research). In some situations, researchers have ethical concerns related to observing people without their consent, so consider whether you need to address privacy or informed consent issues in your research plan.

Although it sounds very simple, observation requires a systematic approach to ensure valid research results. You create a protocol for the observers to follow that tells them where and when to conduct the research, what behaviors to look for, and how to code their observations. The categories must be clearly delineated and often are coded by the observer using a checklist or tally sheet. To verify the reliability of the research, you might wish to have two people code the same situations and compare their results. Making observations on different days of the week and times of day also can help to increase the validity of the results. Every Tuesday at noon, the bicycle safety club might take its weekly ride through the neighborhood; multiple observations will help you identify the unusual number of helmet wearers at that time and take it into account in your pre- and postcampaign research design. Another source of bias may come from the influence of the observer on the research participants. People often will behave differently when they know that they are being watched, so observations should be carried out as unobtrusively as possible.

In addition to conducting observations of people's behavior directly, you can measure the evidence of their actions. Percentage of supermarket shelf space, for example, is a good indicator of the types of food that neighborhood shoppers buy; the proportions of low-fat and skim milk compared to all milk on the shelf will be similar to the proportions of people who purchase them. The number of fitness center memberships in a community can give an indication of the extent of awareness about the benefits of exercise (if not how frequently people use the facilities). The quantity of cigarette butts in and around the ashtray outside an office building can provide evidence of the number of smokers working there. Make sure, however, that the things you are observing truly do reflect the behaviors you wish to measure.

QUALITATIVE METHODS

Just as you used qualitative methods to flesh out your exploratory research while planning your program, so too can these methods help you to better understand the effects of your campaign from another perspective. Although you generally cannot validly compare the results of qualitative research before and after the campaign, the data gathered using these methods will give a good indication of which elements were effective from the target audience's perspective and how the campaign could be improved for the next phase. For qualitative evaluation research, the most useful type of person to recruit as a participant is someone who has been at least moderately exposed to the campaign messages or materials. If you talk to people who do not have any knowledge of the campaign, then the results might be very similar to those of your exploratory research.

The questions you ask using qualitative methods will be somewhat different from those in a survey because you can draw out more detail and context. Although you still will be looking for evidence of changes made as a result of your social marketing program, you will find it couched in the experience and viewpoint of individuals rather than as general trends in a population. Questions you might wish to explore include the following:

- What elements of the campaign have you seen or heard?
- Where have you seen or heard the campaign?
- Do you think that many of your peers saw or heard the campaign? If so, how do you know?
- What do you think about the campaign?
- What do you particularly like about the campaign?
- What do you dislike about the campaign? What would you change?
- Why do you think the campaign was successful or unsuccessful?
- How could we reach more people like you with the campaign?
- Do you have any questions that the campaign materials left unanswered?
- What changes have you made as a result of the campaign?

Qualitative methods for gathering evaluative data include the following:

- *In-depth interviews.* A trained interviewer meets one-on-one with individuals who have been exposed to the campaign. Through these interviews, the researcher can learn about the context in which the program's messages and materials were received and how they were interpreted by the participants. This method might be appropriate when the subject of the campaign is sensitive or when you wish to delve more deeply into individuals' experiences.

- *Focus groups.* You can bring together either formal or informal groups of people to discuss the campaign and its effects. As discussed in Chapter 13, the groups should be composed of people similar to each other in key ways related to the campaign (e.g., separate men/women or adopter/nonadopter groups). The group setting is ideal for eliciting information on the campaign's influences in peer groups and for generating ideas on how to improve the program.

- *Anecdotal feedback mechanisms.* The stories of individual people can be quite powerful as a way of demonstrating the program's effects at a personal level. By themselves, anecdotes do not prove anything about the program, but they can be used to bring to life the people behind the statistics. In addition to collecting stories and comments through in-depth interviews and focus groups, you can use other mechanisms to accumulate feedback from your target audience members. For example, blank journals with a message on the front cover inviting comments on particular issues can be placed in waiting rooms. Postage-paid comment forms can be provided to people who participated in your program. You can personally invite people to submit testimonials describing what the social marketing program did for them. These types of stories are effective to use when seeking additional funding, media attention, or volunteers to assist with your program.

USING FEEDBACK TO IMPROVE YOUR PROGRAM

The ultimate purpose of each of your evaluation activities should be to learn how to improve your current and subsequent social marketing programs. The results will do no good to anyone if they are not acted on or are immediately retired to a shelf.

REAL-TIME FEEDBACK

Ideally, the feedback function should not wait until the end of the program when summative evaluation activities are complete. Responding to relevant information in real time—as events actually occur—allows you to improve your program when it counts rather than retrospectively realizing what you should have done. Effectively using feedback is an interactive, as well as iterative, process in which the elements of your program constantly are adjusted in relation to other components based on new information.

You can make your evaluation results more practical and actionable by considering the following strategies[3]:

- Involve key decision makers and stakeholders in the design of program objectives and evaluation planning.

- Keep in mind the technique of backward research to ensure that all the data you collect drive your programmatic decisions rather than sitting around unused.

- Focus on strategic, rather than exploratory, formative research to answer questions about the target audience and development of the program.

- Use pretesting results to build a strong communication strategy and to explain and justify the executions to stakeholders who are not part of the target audience.

<table>
<tr><td>

WRITING AN EVALUATION REPORT

The following information should be included in your evaluation report.

Program background:
- History of the program
- Description of the program
- Goals and objectives

Evaluation methodology:
- Evaluation design
- Research participants
- Research protocols
- Research instruments

Evaluation findings:
- Research results
- Strengths and weaknesses of the program

Recommendations:
- Elements of the program that should be kept or enhanced
- Elements of the program that should be changed or eliminated
- Future opportunities

</td></tr>
</table>

- Use your process evaluation to go beyond bean counting and toward more diagnostic qualitative research that can uncover problems or opportunities for your program during implementation.

- Conduct preliminary evaluations before the program's completion to identify potential improvements and highlight program successes.

- Stay flexible enough to make changes in the program or evaluation based on the feedback you receive in the evaluation process.

- Use summative research to make future program decisions as part of a process rather than as just an end point.

IMPROVEMENTS FOR THE FUTURE

Whether you will continue with additional phases of implementation of the same campaign or design future social marketing programs on other topics, you can learn and apply the lessons gleaned from the outcomes of this program. These lessons might include the following:

- How to make the social marketing process run more smoothly

- Which elements of the campaign worked and which did not

- Which objectives require additional effort or a new approach

- Which distribution channels were most effective

- How to realistically budget your time and funds for the next phase

- What types of challenges to anticipate and how to overcome them

In addition to considering the elements you would change or eliminate from your program, think about what you might add. Are there any new developments in the issue you addressed that should be included in future campaigns? Or, has anything changed about the target audience, the community, or your organization that necessitates creating new goals and objectives?

Summarize these guidelines in a written evaluation report so that a record exists for others to read in the future, in case you leave your position or for those in other organizations who might wish to replicate your program. This report should be

"DON'T KID YOURSELF" CAMPAIGN EVALUATION

The evaluation of the "Don't Kid Yourself" campaign included a pilot testing phase and both process and outcome measures for the regionwide campaign.

PILOT TEST

The campaign was pilot tested in Butte and Salt Lake City to determine how best to implement it in all six states (Colorado, Montana, North Dakota, South Dakota, Utah, and Wyoming).

Process Evaluation

The process evaluation in the pilot testing phase provided information on whether the campaign was reaching the target audience and how callers had found out about each clinic. Clinic surveys were filled out by clients when they came in for their appointments to assess their exposure to the campaign. In the Butte clinic, 61% of the target audience members had seen or heard campaign materials. In Salt Lake City, 51% of target audience members coming into the clinics had been exposed. The surveys also revealed that younger teens, outside of the target audience, also were seeing and hearing the campaign. Caller surveys, which asked "How did you find out about us?," revealed that the campaign represented the third most common method of learning about the clinics in both cities.

Based on the process evaluation results, campaign planners felt that they had chosen the right media to reach the target audience. However, the campaign had to be delayed from its original start date because the printing and distribution of the materials took longer than anticipated. In addition, campaign monitoring revealed that clinics received very few community complaints, although an official in the Butte health department had one of the newspaper ads pulled because he felt that it was too explicit. Clinic directors found that several community organizations were less enthusiastic about using two of the four posters; they also felt that the size of the posters was too large for the locations where they wanted to hang them up such as bulletin boards and restroom stall doors.

Outcome Evaluation

The outcome evaluation methods varied in each of the two cities, depending on the resources available to each community. Pre- and postcampaign knowledge, attitudes, and behaviors (KAB) surveys were planned for both cities using random telephone sampling of the target audience (see Appendix B for an example of the survey used in the posttest). In Butte, the state health department was able to provide access to a professional research firm, which conducted the surveys. In Salt Lake City, the campaign had to rely on volunteers to serve as interviewers; despite some training, it soon became apparent that respondents were not willing to answer the sensitive questions they were being asked. This might have been because of the more conservative nature of Salt Lake City residents or because of the inexperience of the interviewers. The surveys were completed in Butte but were deemed too inefficient to pursue in Salt Lake City.

The significant differences between the pre- and postcampaign surveys in Butte included a doubling of awareness of the Butte family planning clinic as a place to go to for information, from 21% in the pretest to 40% in the posttest. Attitudes about responsibility for birth control also changed between the pre- and posttest surveys in a statistically significant way. More people agreed or agreed more strongly with the statements "Men should take responsibility for birth control during sex" and "Women should take responsibility for birth control during sex." Because one of the radio ads discusses the benefits of the birth control pill, the surveys also tested knowledge about "the pill." Although respondents were not better able to name benefits of the pill in the posttest, fewer people stated that the pill had no good effects (pretest = 11%, posttest = 1%).

(continued)

"DON'T KID YOURSELF" CAMPAIGN EVALUATION
(continued)

The posttest survey also asked respondents about their exposure to the social marketing campaign. Overall, 51% of the respondents reported that they had seen or heard at least one element of the campaign. Of those who reported exposure to campaign materials in the postcampaign survey, 79% said it made them think about the message, 29% said they talked about the ads with friends or family, 18% said they discussed the ads with their partners, and 11% said they used birth control more often because of the campaign. On the less encouraging side, nobody reported calling the phone number featured in the materials, and the clinic's records did not show a noticeable change in the number of clinic visits during the period in which the campaign was implemented.

Planned Parenthood has a toll-free number that automatically routes callers to the affiliate clinic nearest them; this was the phone number the campaign promoted in Salt Lake City. The Salt Lake City clinics provided phone records showing the numbers of incoming calls to them each month. During the 2 months of the campaign, the clinics experienced a 72% increase in the number of calls received to the toll-free number. The number of calls declined after the campaign ended. When compared to the same months in previous years, the increase did not appear to be related to seasonal patterns. There was not, however, a noticeable change in the number of clinic visits during the period in which the campaign was implemented. Although the campaign appears to have spurred the adoption of desirable behaviors in Butte, as well as an increase in phone calls to the Salt Lake City clinics, the decision to visit a family planning clinic might not be immediate or even necessary for behavior change to occur.

REGIONWIDE IMPLEMENTATION

To expand the successful pilot campaign to the entire six-state region, several changes and new procedures had to be put in place. Each state's campaign was directed at the state level, with an on-site campaign coordinator at each participating clinic. The materials were customized for each state with its own toll-free phone number. Based on the pilot testing, the contractor knew to leave extra time for printing and disseminating the materials to make sure that they were out in the community at the same time as the radio spots were airing. In addition, the posters were made smaller, and only two of the four designs were reprinted. Different sets of the radio spots were used in each state, based on the results of the pilot test and the decision of the state-level coordinator as to which spots were most appropriate for her state.

The campaign was implemented in 55 cities throughout the six states for a 3-month period. An independent evaluator was hired to assess the effectiveness of the regionwide campaign. The process evaluation consisted of (a) qualitative questionnaires completed by the state grant directors, clinic managers in targeted cities, and the project director; and (b) focus groups with clinic staff at three sites. The outcome evaluation provided qualitative and quantitative data from 19 evaluation sites regionwide through (a) pre- and postcampaign KAB surveys, (b) qualitative in-depth interviews with target audience members, and (c) caller tracking sheets from the clinic evaluation sites.

Process Evaluation

The process evaluation identified some areas that required improvement. Despite having begun production of the print materials well in advance, one state delayed printing because it took much longer than expected to receive approval through its bureaucratic channels for a toll-free phone number. In addition, a mix-up by the printer resulted in boxes of coasters being sent to the wrong states. This cut the time available for the state-level coordinators to get the materials out to the local clinics and delayed the start date of the campaign.

(continued)

"DON'T KID YOURSELF" CAMPAIGN EVALUATION
(continued)

Although a comprehensive implementation guide was provided to each state-level coordinator to assist clinics in their dissemination efforts, some clinic managers did not always read it or required additional guidance. This resulted in several local clinics not distributing the print materials (e.g., posters, brochures, coasters) in their communities. There were clear differences in the visibility of the campaign in cities with active clinic outreach efforts versus those that relied solely on the radio spots and newspaper ads.

The focus groups with clinic staff revealed that some of the clinics actually taped over the toll-free phone numbers on the posters and wrote in their own local numbers. Several participants noted that their clients would feel more secure knowing exactly who they were calling. In addition, staff at participating clinics preferred to use the publicity from the campaign to increase clients at their own clinics as opposed to other competing providers. The low use of the toll-free numbers also suggested that use of local phone numbers might be preferable.

When buying newspaper space, a small number of the media outlets declined to run the ads because their staff felt that the ads were too explicit. This occurred in some of the college newspapers, particularly the religiously affiliated schools, and in community newspapers primarily in South Dakota and Utah. Two major newspapers in South Dakota refused to run the ads, but then both wrote substantial articles about the campaign that included the main messages and toll-free number, with one even including a picture of one of the posters.

Outcome Evaluation

The outcome evaluation produced both good news and bad news. The bad news was that the campaign media had not saturated the markets to the desired extent. Based on the postcampaign KAB survey, only 15% of the target audience reported being exposed to the "Don't Kid Yourself" campaign. The good news was that those target audience members who were exposed to the campaign responded quite positively.

The survey revealed that 92% of those exposed to the campaign materials reported that they "liked the message." Nearly 70% saw posters, more than double the exposure of any other campaign medium. Significant attitude changes about the use of birth control also were correlated to the number of campaign media to which the respondents were exposed.

Survey respondents who were exposed to the campaign also overwhelmingly took some desirable actions. More than three quarters of those exposed indicated that they "talked with friends, boy/girlfriend, or parents about family planning" as a result of the campaign. More than 55% reported that they called for information or appointments at doctor's offices or family planning clinics as a result of the campaign, but less than 5% of the respondents called the toll-free phone number advertised in the materials. Despite not calling the toll-free number, about one quarter of the respondents said that they called for appointments at family planning clinics as a result of the campaign, most likely on the clinic's local phone number.

The campaign started its third phase of implementation in the spring of 1998. Based on results of the first year of regionwide implementation, the next iteration of the campaign focused on a smaller number of cities in each state to maximize the media exposure that was possible with available resources. The use of toll-free numbers was discontinued in most states, and materials were created for each community using local clinic names and phone numbers. Greater outreach and accountability from local clinics was required as a condition of the inclusion of their communities in the campaign.

user-friendly—no longer than necessary, easy to read, and providing clear action items. Compile all the documentation from the development and evaluation of the campaign as an appendix for easy reference. Share your results with all those involved in the development of the program including staff, partners, and funders.

If you feel that others could learn from your efforts, then take the time to write up a synopsis of your project for publication as either a journal article or a brief program note. You also could submit your program's results as a conference presentation or poster session to get the word out further. Use what you learned from the experience to continually improve your program. That is what social marketing is all about.

SECTION VI NOTES

1. George Balch and Sharyn Sutton, "Keep Me Posted: A Plea for Practical Evaluation," in *Social Marketing: Theoretical and Practical Perspectives,* eds. Marvin Goldberg, Martin Fishbein, and Susan Middlestadt (Mahwah, NJ: Lawrence Erlbaum, 1997), 62.

2. Terrie Sterling, Allen Cheadle, and Thomas Schmid, "Report from a CDC-Sponsored Project to Develop Community-Level Indicators for Evaluating Cardiovascular Health Promotion Programs" (unpublished manuscript, Centers for Disease Control and Prevention, Division of Chronic Disease Control and Community Intervention, 1997).

3. Balch and Sutton (1997), 70-72.

WORKSHEET 15: Evaluation Planning Worksheet

1. At what points in the program will you collect evaluation data?

☐ Pre- and postcampaign

☐ Postcampaign only

☐ Periodic monitoring at specified intervals

☐ Other

2. From where will you collect your evaluation data?

☐ Existing records:

_____

_____

☐ One group exposed to the campaign

☐ Comparison to a standard: _____

☐ Comparison to a control group: _____

3. Which evaluation indicators will you use to assess the effectiveness of the program?

Individual-level indicators:

☐ Knowledge:

_____

_____

☐ Attitudes:

_____

_____

☐ Behaviors:

_____

_____

☐ Other _____

Community-level indicators:

☐ Environmental change:

_____

_____

☐ Policy and regulation:

_____

_____

(continued)

WORKSHEET 15: Evaluation Planning Worksheet *(continued)*

☐ Information accessibility:

_____

_____

☐ Behavioral outcomes:

_____

_____

☐ Other _____

4. **Which evaluation methods will you use?**

    ☐ Knowledge, attitudes, and behaviors survey:

        ☐ Mail

        ☐ Telephone

        ☐ In-person interviews

        ☐ Computerized

        ☐ Other _____

    ☐ Observation

    ☐ In-depth interviews

    ☐ Focus groups

    ☐ Anecdotal feedback mechanisms

    ☐ Other _____

5. **Do you or your staff members have the necessary skills to conduct and analyze the evaluation?**

    ☐ Yes. We have the expertise on staff.

    ☐ Possibly. We need some additional training.

    ☐ No. We need to hire outside assistance.

    If more training or outside assistance is needed:

        a. What is your available budget? $_____

        b. What aspects of the evaluation do you need assistance with?

            _____

            _____

            _____

        c. From which companies or consultants will you solicit bids?

            _____

            _____

            _____

(continued)

WORKSHEET 15: Evaluation Planning Worksheet *(continued)*

If evaluation will be done in-house:

6. What is your available budget? $_____

7. Who will be responsible for coordinating the evaluation activities?

_____

8. Who will assist in the evaluation activities?

Name	*Role*
_____	_____
_____	_____
_____	_____
_____	_____

9. Evaluation timeline:

Activity	*Date to Be Completed*
Put evaluation team in place	_____
Design evaluation plan	_____
Develop questionnaires or other research instruments	_____
Test and finalize evaluation instruments	_____
Train people who will be conducting the research	_____
Recruit research participants	_____
Conduct research	_____
Input or organize data	_____
Analyze data	_____
Create evaluation report	_____

10. How will you use the results of your evaluation?

_____

_____

_____

_____

_____

_____

(continued)

SOCIAL MARKETING RESOURCE LIST

The online resources in the following list are up-to-date as of the printing of this book. Because Web site addresses change frequently, you can find updated links to all the addresses listed here, as well as new resources that become available, at the author's Web site, http://www.social-marketing.com.

SOCIAL MARKETING (GENERAL)

Print

Andreasen, Alan. 1995. *Marketing Social Change: Changing Behavior to Promote Health, Social Development, and the Environment.* San Francisco: Jossey-Bass.

Backer, Thomas, Everett Rogers, and Pradeep Sopory. 1992. *Designing Health Communication Campaigns: What Works?* Newbury Park, CA: Sage.

Center for Substance Abuse Prevention. 1994. *Technical Assistance Bulletins: Guides for Planning and Developing Your ATOD Prevention Materials.* Rockville, MD: U.S. Department of Health and Human Services, Public Health Service, Substance Abuse and Mental Health Services Administration. (Free from the National Clearinghouse for Alcohol and Drug Information, [800] 729-6686)

Frederiksen, Lee, Laura Solomon, and Kathleen Brehony, eds. 1984. *Marketing Health Behavior: Principles, Techniques, and Applications.* New York: Plenum.

Goldberg, Marvin, Martin Fishbein, and Susan Middlestadt, eds. 1997. *Social Marketing: Theoretical and Practical Perspectives.* Mahwah, NJ: Lawrence Erlbaum.

Kotler, Philip, and Eduardo Roberto. 1989. *Social Marketing: Strategies for Changing Public Behavior.* New York: Free Press.

National Cancer Institute. 1992. *Making Health Communication Programs Work: A Planner's Guide*. Washington, DC: U.S. Department of Health and Human Services. (Free from the Cancer Information Service, [800] 4-CANCER, or online at `http://rex.nci.nih.gov/NCI_Pub_Interface/HCPW/HOME.html`)

National Center on Child Abuse and Neglect. 1996. *Marketing Matters: Building an Effective Communications Program*. Washington, DC: U.S. Department of Health and Human Services. (Free from the National Clearinghouse on Child Abuse and Neglect Information, [800] 394-3366)

Ogden, Lydia, Melissa Shepherd, and William A. Smith. 1996. *Applying Prevention Marketing*. Atlanta, GA: Centers for Disease Control and Prevention, Public Health Service. (Free from the National AIDS Clearinghouse, [800] 458-5231)

Online

Academy for Educational Development, *The ABCs of Human Behavior for Disease Prevention*
`http://www.aed.org/publications/news/fall95/disease_prev.html`

AIDSCAP Project of Family Health International, *Behavior Change Communication Handbooks*
`http://www.fhi.org/en/aids/aidscap/aidspubs/behres/bhcomhb.html`
(Handbooks on how to create an effective communication project and behavior change through mass communication)

Centre for Health Promotion, University of Toronto, *Health Communications Unit Online*
`http://www.utoronto.ca/chp/hcu/hcu-publications.html`
(Health communication workbooks and other resources)

Health Canada, *The Social Marketing Network*
`http://www.hc-sc.gc.ca/hppb/socialmarketing/`
(Introductory information, presentations, case studies, tutorials, and links to other sites)

Johns Hopkins University, *Center for Communication Programs Website*
`http://www.jhuccp.org`
(Publications and resources on population, health communications, and development)

Novartis Foundation for Sustainable Development, *A Short Course in Social Marketing*
`http://foundation.novartis.com/social_marketing.htm`
(Discussion of the elements of social marketing)

Ohio University, *Social Marketing Manual*
`http://oak.cats.ohiou.edu/~cm130791/social/social.htm`
(Definitions, references, and links)

Weinreich Communications, *Social-Marketing.com*
`http://www.social-marketing.com`
(Social marketing-related articles, resources, conference calendar, and extensive links to other sources of information)

SOCIAL MARKETING RESEARCH

Print

Agency for Health Care Policy and Research. 1996. *A Compendium of Selected Public Health Data Sources.* Publication No. AHCPR97-0004. Washington, DC: U.S. Department of Health and Human Services, Public Health Service. (Free from the AHCPR Clearinghouse, [800] 358-9295)

Andreasen, Alan. 1988. *Cheap but Good Marketing Research.* Homewood, IL: Business One Irwin.

Debus, Mary. 1986. *Handbook for Excellence in Focus Group Research.* Washington, DC: Academy for Educational Development.

Fowler, Floyd, Jr. 1993. *Survey Research Methods.* 2nd ed. Newbury Park, CA: Sage.

Krueger, Richard A. 1994. *Focus Groups: A Practical Guide for Applied Research.* Newbury Park, CA: Sage.

Online

AIDSCAP, *Evaluation Tools: An Introduction to AIDSCAP Evaluation*

http://www.fhi.org/en/aids/aidscap/aidspubs/evaluation/evmodule.html

(A useful guide to developing an evaluation plan, particularly for AIDS prevention programs)

American Marketing Association, New York Chapter, *The Green Book*

http://www.greenbook.org

(International directory of marketing research companies and services including focus group services)

Center for Substance Abuse Prevention, *Identifying the Target Audience*

http://www.health.org/pubs/makepub/tab13.htm

(Online publication in CSAP's Technical Assistance Bulletin series)

Cornell University, *The Knowledge Base*

http://trochim.human.cornell.edu/kb/index.htm

(Online textbook by William Trochim on applied social research methods including sections on research, sampling, measurement, design, and data analysis)

ERIC Clearinghouse on Assessment and Evaluation, *ERIC/AE How-to Series*

http://ericae.net/ft/tamu/

(A set of online, full-text books and booklets addressing practical evaluation, research, measurement, and statistical issues)

Hospital Council of Western Pennsylvania, *Evaluation Resources*

http://hcwp.org/step.htm

(Step-by-step guide to program evaluations)

Indiana State University, *Community Health Research Methods*

http://isu.indstate.edu/gabanys/course341/341home.htm

(Information on research methods and how to conduct a research project)

National Science Foundation, *User-Friendly Handbook for Mixed Method Evaluations*
   http://www.ehr.nsf.gov/EHR/REC/pubs/NSF97-153/start.htm
   (Guide to integrating quantitative and qualitative research techniques)

Quirks Marketing Research Review
   http://www.quirks.com
   (A one-stop source of information on marketing research including articles, a glossary of marketing terms, and a sourcebook of research providers)

Tilburg University, *Marketing and Marketing Research Homepage*
   http://cwis.kub.nl/~few/few/be/marketin/links.htm
   (Links to journals, professional associations, academic marketing departments, etc.)

University of Alberta, *Qual Page*
   http://www.ualberta.ca/~jrnorris/qual.html
   (Qualitative research resources)

University of Kansas, *Community Tool Box*
   http://ctb.lsi.ukans.edu/ctb/tb-toc.html
   (Information on promoting health issues and community resources, strategic planning, etc.; useful section on conducting needs assessments and focus groups)

University of Houston, *Marketing Research Index*
   http://www.reinartz.com/index.htm
   (Data resources, publications, methodology, and glossary of marketing research terms)

University of Newcastle, Australia, *SurfStat*
   http://surfstat.newcastle.edu.au/surfstat/
   (Online statistics textbook)

University of Washington, *Community-Level Indicators for Evaluation*
   http://weber.u.washington.edu/cheadle/cli/
   (General information about community-level indicators, references to academic literature, and descriptions of projects using community-level indicators)

AUDIENCE SEGMENTATION

Print

Albrecht, Terrance L., and Carol Bryant. 1996. "Advances in Segmentation Modeling for Health Communication and Social Marketing Campaigns." *Journal of Health Communication* 1:65-80.
Maibach, Edward W., Andrew Maxfield, Kelly Ladin, and Michael Slater. 1996. "Translating Health Psychology into Effective Health Communication: The American Healthstyles Audience Segmentation Project." *Journal of Health Psychology* 1:261-77.
Myers, James H. 1996. *Segmenting and Positioning for Strategic Marketing Decisions*. New York: American Marketing Association.
Slater, Michael D. 1995. "Choosing Audience Segmentation Strategies and Methods for Health Communication. In *Designing Health Messages: Approaches from Communication*

Theory and Public Health Practice, edited by Edward Maibach and Roxanne Parrott. Thousand Oaks, CA: Sage.
Slater, Michael D., and June Flora. 1991. "Health Lifestyles: Audience Segmentation Analysis for Public Health Interventions." *Health Education Quarterly* 18:221-32.
Weinstein, Art. 1987. *Market Segmentation.* Chicago: Probus.

Online

American Demographics, *Marketing Tools for Audience Segmentation and Market Analysis*
http://www.marketingtools.com
(Links to market research data)

Indiana Prevention Resource Center, *Demographics Market Research*
http://www.drugs.indiana.edu/publications/iprc/misc/demogrph.html
(Article on using demographic software for segmentation)

SRI International, *The Values and Lifestyles (VALS) Program*
http://future.sri.com/vals/valshome.html
(A model for segmenting your audience members based on their attitudes and values)

MESSAGE DEVELOPMENT

Print

Glanz, Karen, Frances M. Lewis, and Barbara K. Rimer, eds. 1997. *Health Behavior and Health Education: Theory, Research, and Practice.* 2nd ed. San Francisco: Jossey-Bass.
Maibach, Edward, and Roxanne Parrott, eds. 1995. *Designing Health Messages: Approaches from Communication Theory and Public Health Practice.* Newbury Park, CA: Sage.

Online

Agency for Toxic Substances and Disease Registry, *Health Risk Communication Primer*
http://atsdr1.atsdr.cdc.gov:8080/HEC/primer.html
(Health risk communication principles and practice)

Cancer Prevention Research Center, University of Rhode Island, *Transtheoretical Model of Behavior Change*
http://www.uri.edu/research/cprc/cprc.htm
(Explanation of the model and psychological measures of stages of change for various behaviors)

National Cancer Institute, *Theory at a Glance: A Guide for Health Promotion Practice*
http://rex.nci.nih.gov/NCI_Pub_Interface/Theory_at_glance/HOME.html
(Introduction to various theories used to develop health promotion programs)

MEDIA/ADVERTISING/PUBLIC RELATIONS

Print

Keding, Ann, and Thomas Bivins. 1996. *How to Produce Creative Advertising*. Lincolnwood, IL: NTC Business Books.

Kirkman, Larry, and Karen Menichelli, eds. 1991. *Strategic Communications for Nonprofits*. Series of 10 publications. New York: Center for Strategic Communications and the Benton Foundation.

Levine, Michael. 1994. *Guerrilla P.R.: How You Can Wage an Effective Publicity Campaign . . . without Going Broke*. New York: HarperBusiness.

Prevention Marketing Initiative. 1996. *Media Relations* and *Managing Issues*. Atlanta, GA: Centers for Disease Control and Prevention, Public Health Service. (Free from the National AIDS Clearinghouse, [800] 458-5231)

Ryan, Bernard, Jr. 1996. *Advertising for a Small Business*. New York: Doubleday.

Smith, Jeanette. 1995. *The New Publicity Kit*. New York: John Wiley.

Wallack, Lawrence, Lori Dorfman, David Jernigan, and Makani Themba. 1993. *Media Advocacy and Public Health: Power for Prevention*. Newbury Park, CA: Sage.

Online

The Ad Council

http://www.adcouncil.org

(Information on social marketing campaigns produced by the Ad Council and information on how they may be able to assist you)

Direct Contact Publishing, *U.S. All Media Jumpstation*

http://www.owt.com/dircon/mediajum.htm

(A launchpad to more than 3,000 magazines, journals, and trade publications)

Editorial Media and Marketing International, *PR Central*

http://www.prcentral.com

(Articles, directories, case histories, and newsgroups on public relations)

Gebbie Press

http://www.gebbieinc.com/index1.htm

(A directory of television, radio, and print outlets, as well as public relations and marketing firms, on the Web)

Mediapost, *Contact Directory*

http://www.mediapost.com

(An advertising and media interactive directory with more than 15,000 industry contacts)

Oxbridge Communications, *MediaFinder*

http://www.mediafinder.com

(A searchable database of more than 90,000 print publications, from newsletters to catalogs, that you can use to reach your target audience)

Population Reports, *Helping the News Media Cover Family Planning*

http://www.jhuccp.org/pr/j42edsum.stm

(Tips on working with the news media)

Public Relations Society of America, *Practitioner's Workshop*
    http://www.tech.prsa.org/nfindex.html
    (Public relations and marketing resources)

Radio Advertising Bureau, *Radio Marketing Guide and Fact Book for Advertisers*
    http://www.rab.com/station/mgfb98/radfact.html
    (Information on advertising on radio)

Standard Rate and Data Service, *Media Resource Center*
    http://www.srds.com/media_resource/index.html
    (Useful links to advertising-related tools and organizations)

University of Texas at Austin Department of Advertising, *Advertising World*
    http://advweb.cocomm.utexas.edu/world/
    (Extensive collection of advertising-related links)

SOCIAL MARKETING-RELATED
JOURNALS AND ORGANIZATIONS

American Journal of Health Behavior
    PNG Publications
    P.O. Box 4593
    Star City, WV 26504
    phone: (304) 293-4699
    fax: (304) 293-4693
    http://131.230.221.136/ajhb/

Centre for Social Marketing
    University of Strathclyde
    173 Cathedral Street
    Glasgow, Scotland, United Kingdom G4 0RQ
    phone: (0141) 552-4400, ext. 3192
    fax: (0141) 552-2802
    http://www.strath.ac.uk/Other/csm/

Health Education & Behavior
    Society for Public Health Education
    1015 Fifteenth Street, NW, Suite 410
    Washington, DC 20005
    phone: (202) 408-9804
    http://www.sph.umich.edu/hbhe/heb

Journal of Health Communication
    Academy for Educational Development
    1255 23rd Street, NW, Fourth Floor
    Washington, DC 20037
    phone: (202) 884-8145
    fax: (202) 884-8844
    http://www.aed.org/JHealthCom/

Social Marketing Quarterly
Society for Social Marketing
National Training Center for Social Marketing in Public Health

c/o Best Start Inc.
3500 E. Fletcher Avenue, Suite 519
Tampa, FL 33613
phone: (800) 277-4975
fax: (813) 971-2280

beststart@mindspring.com

Appendix
B

SAMPLE KNOWLEDGE, ATTITUDES, AND BEHAVIORS SURVEY

Phone: _____ Date: _____ Time: _____ Initials: _____

Call disposition: _____ Residence, person answered

_____ No answer/answering machine/busy signal

Callback 1 date/time/initials: _____

Callback 2 date/time/initials: _____

A. WHEN SOMEONE ANSWERS "HELLO" (RESIDENCE)

Hello, I'm calling with a research firm called Weinreich Communications. We are doing a survey on health issues to help us develop a health education program. We have selected your phone number from a random sample. We are not selling anything, and the survey will take only about 5 minutes. All responses are completely confidential.

A1. May I ask how many people between 18 and 24 years of age live in your household? _____

    IF NONE: Thank you for your time.

                [TERMINATE INTERVIEW.]

    IF 1:   May I speak with [him or her]?

                _____ Yes   [GO TO SECTION B.]

                _____ Not available   [GO TO QUESTION A2.]

                _____ Refuses interview [GO TO QUESTION A3.]

IF 2 OR MORE: May I speak with one of them?

_____ Yes   [GO TO SECTION B.]

_____ Not available   [GO TO QUESTION A2.]

_____ Refuses interview   [GO TO QUESTION A3.]

A2. IF NOT HOME OR CANNOT COME TO PHONE:
When would be a good time to call back? _____
Who should we ask for? _____

A3. IF PERSON ANSWERING PHONE REFUSES INTERVIEW:
The interview will take only about 5 minutes and is completely confidential. Our research results will be more accurate if we can speak with everyone who we have randomly selected. Can I ask you to reconsider?

_____ Yes   [GO TO SECTION B.]

_____ No   SAY: Thank you for your time.

               [TERMINATE INTERVIEW.]

B. WHEN YOU HAVE THE PERSON
18 TO 24 YEARS OF AGE ON THE PHONE

[IF DIFFERENT PERSON FROM WHO ANSWERED PHONE:]
I'm working with a research firm called Weinreich Communications. We are conducting a random survey with men and women between 18 and 24 years of age. The information will help us to develop a health education program. The survey will take only about 5 minutes, and your responses are completely confidential.

B1. Would you mind taking 5 minutes to answer some questions for us?

IF YES: Thank you. [GO TO QUESTION C1.]

IF NO: Are there any concerns you have that I can answer for you? This will take only a short time, and your answers will not be able to be traced back to you. Our research results will be more accurate if we can interview everyone who we have randomly selected. Can I ask you to reconsider, or can we call you back at another time?

            IF NO: Thank you for your time.

                    [TERMINATE INTERVIEW.]

            _____ Check if interview terminated at this point.

C. INITIAL DEMOGRAPHICS

C1. How old are you as of your last birthday? _____

C2. Just for the record, I need to ask you if you are male or female?

    1. Male

    2. Female

C3. Are you:

    1. Single [GO TO QUESTION C4.]

    2. Married [GO TO QUESTION C5.]

    3. Separated or divorced [GO TO QUESTION C5.]

    IF SINGLE:

        C4. Would you describe yourself as:

            1. Not dating anyone right now

            2. Dating, but with no steady [boyfriend/girlfriend]

            3. Dating a steady [boyfriend/girlfriend] or engaged

C5. Do you have any children?

    1. Yes   [GO TO QUESTION C6.]

    2. No   [GO TO QUESTION D1.]

    IF YES:

        C6. How many? _____

D. INFORMATION SEEKING

D1. If you had questions about sexual health or birth control issues, how would you get the answers? [DO NOT READ ANSWERS. CODE FIRST TWO RESPONSES.]

    1. Friends

    2. Parents

    3. Brother or sister

    4. Doctor

    5. Other   _____

    6. Butte Family Planning [GO TO QUESTION E1.]

    IF DOES NOT LIST BUTTE FAMILY PLANNING:

        D2. Are there any organizations you would call?

            1. Butte Family Planning

            2. Other _____

            3. No

        IF DOES NOT ANSWER BUTTE FAMILY PLANNING:

        D3. Have you ever heard of an organization called Butte Family Planning?

            1. Yes

            2. No

            3. Not sure

E. ATTITUDES

I'm going to make some statements, and I want you to tell me for each whether you agree or disagree with it. The possible answers are *strongly agree, agree, no opinion, disagree,* and *strongly disagree.* [CIRCLE NUMBER CORRESPONDING TO RESPONSE.]

	Strongly Agree	Agree	No Opinion	Disagree	Strongly Disagree
E1. Caring for a baby at my age would be difficult.	1	2	3	4	5
E2. I will not have a baby until I am financially secure.	1	2	3	4	5
E3. Using condoms is a way to show you care about the other person.	1	2	3	4	5
E4. A parent should talk to his or her child about sex and birth control.	1	2	3	4	5
E5. Using condoms is a way to take care of yourself.	1	2	3	4	5
E6. You cannot get pregnant the first time you have sex.	1	2	3	4	5
E7. If no birth control is available, then you should not have sex.	1	2	3	4	5
E8. Men should take responsibility for birth control during sex.	1	2	3	4	5
E9. Sexual encounters should happen the way they are shown on television.	1	2	3	4	5
E10. It is hard to talk about birth control with a partner.	1	2	3	4	5
E11. People should wait until they are married to have sex.	1	2	3	4	5
E12. Women should take responsibility for birth control during sex.	1	2	3	4	5

F. KNOWLEDGE ABOUT BIRTH CONTROL PILL AND UNINTENDED PREGNANCIES

F1. Now I would like to ask you what good things you have heard the birth control pill can do besides preventing pregnancy. Please name as many as you can.

[DO NOT READ ANSWERS. CODE ALL RESPONSES.]

1. Prevents cancer of the ovaries
2. Prevents cancer of the uterus
3. Prevents some types of cancer
4. Relieves premenstrual syndrome (PMS)
5. Relieves menstrual cramps
6. Strengthens bones
7. Protects against some forms of arthritis
8. Helps clear up skin
9. Other _____
10. No good effects
11. Do not know

F2. What are the bad things you have heard that the birth control pill causes? Please name as many as you can.

[DO NOT READ ANSWERS. CODE ALL RESPONSES.]

1. Acne
2. Blood clots
3. Breast tenderness and/or enlargement
4. Cancer
5. Emotional swings or depression
6. Headaches
7. Heart attack
8. High blood pressure
9. Nausea
10. Stroke
11. Weight gain
12. Other _____
13. No bad effects
14. Do not know

F3. What percentage of all pregnancies do you think happen by accident? _____%

F4. If 10 young women have sex without birth control a few times a month, how many of them do you think will become pregnant within a year? _____

G. CAMPAIGN EXPOSURE

G1. In the past 2 months, have you heard any radio commercials about birth control, condoms, or other sexual issues on KAAR-FM or Y-95?

1. Yes
2. No
3. Not sure

G2. In the past 2 months, have you seen any newspaper advertisements in the *Montana Standard* about birth control, condoms, or other sexual issues?

1. Yes
2. No
3. Not sure

G3. In the past 2 months, have you seen any posters or drink coasters with the slogan "Don't Kid Yourself" in locations around Butte?

1. Yes
2. No
3. Not sure

[IF ANSWERED YES TO ANY OF G1, G2, OR G3:]

G4. After you [heard/saw] the [radio ads/newspaper ads/posters/drink coasters], did you do any of the following? Please answer yes or no.

[READ EACH ANSWER AND CIRCLE IF ANSWER IS YES.]

1. Think about the message?

2. Talk about the ads with your friends or family?

3. Talk about the ads with your partner?

4. Call the phone number?

5. Make an appointment with a health professional to discuss sexual issues or to get birth control?

6. Use birth control more often?

7. Use condoms more often?

H. SEXUAL BEHAVIOR

Now I'm just going to ask you for some information we need for our statistics.

H1. Have you had sex in the last 6 months?
1. Yes   [GO TO QUESTION H2.]
2. No   [GO TO QUESTION H4.]
IF YES:

H2.   I would like you to think back to the last time you had sex. Did you use birth control?

1.   Yes [GO TO QUESTION H3.]

2.   No [GO TO QUESTION H4.]

IF YES:

H3. What type of birth control did you or your partner use?

[DO NOT READ ANSWERS. CODE ALL RESPONSES.]

a. Birth control pill
b. Norplant
c. Depo-Provera (the shot)
d. Condom
e. Spermicide
f. Diaphragm/cervical cap
g. Intrauterine device
h. Withdrawal/pulling out/coitus interruptus
i. Rhythm method/natural family planning
j. Other _____

H4. Have you ever [become pregnant/gotten someone else pregnant] when you did not intend for that to happen?

    1. Yes

    2. No

I. INCOME LEVEL

I1. My last questions are about your annual income. I am going to list ranges of incomes, and I want you to stop me when I reach the range that includes your income:

    1. $0 to $20,000

    2. $20,001 to $30,000

    3. More than $30,000

I2. Do you live with your parents or receive financial support from them?

    1. Yes

    2. No

Thank you very much for your time. We appreciate your participation.

Sample Focus Group Recruitment Questionnaire

WHEN SOMEONE CALLS IN RESPONSE TO FOCUS GROUP RECRUITMENT ADVERTISEMENTS, DETERMINE WHETHER THEY ARE ELIGIBLE THROUGH THE FOLLOWING QUESTIONS.

To determine whether you fit the particular characteristics of the women we need for our focus groups, I need to ask you some quick questions.

Screening Questions

1. How old are you? _____ [IF NOT 18 TO 24 YEARS, THEN THANK CALLER AND TERMINATE CALL.]

2. Do you have any children? ☐ Yes   ☐ No

    IF YES: Is your yearly income more than or less than $20,000?

    ☐ More   ☐ Less

    IF NO: Is your yearly income more than or less than $15,000?

    ☐ More   ☐ Less

    [IF ANSWER IS "MORE," THEN THANK CALLER AND TERMINATE CALL.]

3. Are you currently sexually active?   ☐ Yes   ☐ No

    [IF ANSWER IS "NO," THEN THANK CALLER AND TERMINATE CALL.]

Focus Group Assignment Questions

4. When you have sex, how often do you use a method of birth control (either prescription or from the drug store)?
   ☐ Always
   ☐ Most of the time
   ☐ Half of the time
   ☐ Rarely or never

5. Have you ever become pregnant when you did not want to be?   ☐ Yes   ☐ No

Assigned to the following focus group:
   ☐ Group 1: Contraception always or most of the time
   ☐ Group 2: Contraception half the time, rarely, or never
   ☐ Group 3: Had unintended pregnancy

Group 1	*Group 2*	*Group 3*
☐ Thursday 10-12	☐ Thursday 2-4	☐ Thursday 6-8
☐ Friday 6-8	☐ Friday 10-12	☐ Friday 2-4

(Mark "1" for first choice, "2" if can attend other time also.)

Tell the person that we will call to confirm which time and date he or she is assigned to. If the person cannot attend the time and date for his or her group, then put the person on the list for future focus groups.

Name _____   Phone _____

SAMPLE FOCUS GROUP TOPIC GUIDE

I. INTRODUCTION

Welcome and thank you for coming to our session today. My name is Nedra Weinreich, and I am an independent consultant working with Planned Parenthood of Utah. Assisting me is Jane Smith from Planned Parenthood of Utah.

We are developing a statewide campaign to prevent unintended pregnancies, and we have chosen Salt Lake City as one of the locations we are developing the campaign in first. These focus groups are a research method that will help us to develop the campaign. They are like an opinion survey, but rather than asking questions of one person at a time, we bring a group of people together to discuss a particular topic.

We have invited you to this focus group to find out what you think about birth control and family planning services. There are no right or wrong answers, just differing points of view. Please feel free to disagree with one another; we would like to have many points of view. Keep in mind that we are just as interested in negative comments as in positive comments; sometimes, the negative comments are the most helpful. Also, I want you to know that I do not work for Planned Parenthood, so you will not hurt my feelings if you make any negative comments about the organization.

Before we begin, let me explain the ground rules. We are tape-recording the discussion because I do not want to miss any of your comments. All of your comments are confidential and will be used for research purposes only. We will be on a first-name basis today, and in our later reports, there will not be any names attached to comments. I want this to be a group discussion, so you do not need to wait for me to call on you. But please speak one at a time so that the tape recorder can pick up everything.

We have a lot of ground to cover, so I might change the subject or move ahead. Please stop me if you want to add something. Our discussion will last about 1 hour and 45 minutes, and then we have a short questionnaire we would like you to fill out. When you turn in your questionnaire, you will receive your $25 honorarium.

First of all, let's just go around the room and introduce ourselves. Please give us your first name; what you do; and whether you are single, are married, or have any children. Also, how about telling us your favorite thing to do on a Saturday night? I will start. . .

II. GENERAL CONTRACEPTIVE KNOWLEDGE/INFORMATION SEEKING

1. Where do you get your information about birth control? Who do you trust to give you that information? What about information about sex?

2. Do you have any worries or concerns about using birth control pills, condoms, or other contraceptives? Are these worries or concerns based on things you have heard or on your own experience? Are there things you need more information about?

III. ATTITUDES/MOTIVATIONS

1. When I mention the words "birth control," what is the first thing that comes to your mind? What type of person uses birth control?

2. I am going to name some birth control methods. I want you to tell me what you think of each—what you like and what you do not like about it. [NAME: THE PILL, CONDOMS, DIAPHRAGM, NORPLANT, SPERMICIDE, DEPO PROVERA, THE MORNING-AFTER PILL]

3. What affects your decision to use birth control or not? [PROBE: PARTNER, SITUATION, FRIENDS, TIME OF MONTH, CONCERN ABOUT PREGNANCY, MEDIA]

4. Do your friends use birth control? Pretend that I am a friend of yours considering whether or not to start using birth control. What advice would you give me?

IV. ATTITUDES TOWARD PREGNANCY

1. I would like you to think back to the last time you had sex. Did you plan for it to happen, or did it just happen? In general, which way do you think it should be? Why?

2. What about having a baby? Do you think that it should be planned, or should it just happen when it happens? What is the ideal time or situation to have a baby?

3. What do you think your odds are of becoming pregnant in the next year or so? What are you basing that on?

4. What do you think would happen if you became pregnant? Do you ever think about that as a possibility when you do not use birth control? Are there good things about becoming pregnant?

V. MEDIA AND LEISURE HABITS

Now I am going to shift gears a little bit and ask you some questions to help us plan how to get our message out.

1. Where do you and your friends tend to hang out?

2. What types of entertainment do you and your friends prefer? Television? Radio? Where and when do you listen to the radio? Which stations/shows? Do you read a newspaper? Magazines?

3. If we wanted to reach a lot of people similar to you in our campaign, where should we place our ads or messages? Do not worry about whether it is feasible. Where and when do you think you would be most receptive to messages promoting the use of birth control?

READABILITY
TESTING FORMULA

The SMOG Readability Formula is one of the most common and easiest to use readability tests. Use it to check the reading level needed to understand your printed materials. In general, the sixth- to eighth-grade level will be appropriate for most general audiences, but consider the educational attainment of your target audience to determine the correct readability level.

To determine the approximate reading level of a publication, use the following steps[a]:

1. Mark off 10 consecutive sentences each at the beginning, middle, and end of the piece.

   ■ A sentence is a string of words that ends with a period (.), a question mark (?), or an exclamation point (!).

2. Count the total number of words containing three or more syllables (polysyllabic), including repetitions, in those 30 sentences.

   ■ Hyphenated words count as one word.

   ■ Numbers and abbreviations should be pronounced to count the number of syllables.

   ■ Proper nouns should be counted as well if they are polysyllabic.

3. Use the conversion chart below to determine the approximate reading level.

   ■ Keep in mind that some polysyllabic words (e.g., exercise) are the simplest and clearest way in which to say something. In other cases, a one- or two-syllable word (e.g., larynx) might be more difficult. Use your judgment, and try to write as simply as possible.

SMOG Conversion Chart

Polysyllabic Word Count	Grade Level
0-2	4
3-6	5
7-12	6
13-20	7
21-30	8
31-42	9
43-56	10
57-72	11
73-90	12
91-110	13
111-132	14
133-156	15
157-182	16
183-210	17
211-240	18

SOURCE: a. Center for Substance Abuse Prevention, *You Can Prepare Easy-to-Read Materials* (Rockville, MD: U.S. Department of Health and Human Services, 1994).
NOTE: Grade level predicts the grade-level difficulty ± 1.5 grades.

INDEX

ABOUT THE AUTHOR

Nedra Kline Weinreich is President of Weinreich Communications, a social marketing firm based in Los Angeles. She has worked in the fields of social marketing and health communications for many years for clients such as the U.S. Public Health Service Family Planning Grantees, Virginia Department of Health, U.S. Department of Energy, National Institute of Mental Health, and National Center on Child Abuse and Neglect Clearinghouse. She earned her master's degree in health and social behavior from the Harvard School of Public Health and is a certified health education specialist. In addition to conducting trainings and providing consultation on developing social marketing programs, she has written several articles on social marketing. She publishes a Web site, http://www.social-marketing.com. You can reach her via e-mail at weinreich@ social-marketing.com. She lives in West Hills, California, with her husband, Gil, and son, Ariel.